BEFORE
THE EYES OF
THE WORLD

Before the
Eyes World
of the
Mexico
and the 1968
Olympic
Games

KEVIN B. WITHERSPOON

Northern Illinois

University

Press

DeKalb

© 2014 by Northern Illinois University Press

Published by the Northern Illinois University Press, DeKalb, Illinois   60115

1st printing in paperback, 2014

ISBN 978-0-87580-696-9 (paperback : alk. paper)

Design by Julia Fauci

Library of Congress Cataloging-in-Publication Data

Witherspoon, Kevin B.

Before the eyes of the world : Mexico and the 1968 Olympic Games /

Kevin B. Witherspoon.

p.   cm.

Includes bibliographical references and index.

ISBN 978-0-87580-388-3 (clothbound : alk. paper)

1. Olympic Games (19th : 1968 : Mexico City, Mexico). 2. Olympics—Social aspects.

3. Olympics—Political aspects. I. Title. II. Title: Mexico and the 1968 Olympic Games.

GV7221968 .W58 2008

796.48—dc22

2008012902

To Jacky, Alexis, and Andrew

Contents

Preface

As a child of the Cold War, memories of my youth are flecked with images of great American Olympic heroes. Bruce Jenner was the first, appearing on my cereal box even before I was aware of his significance or what he had done. Among the first sporting events I watched televised live, after a handful of Super Bowls, was the "Miracle on Ice," in which the U.S. hockey team pulled the most shocking of upsets over the seemingly unbeatable Soviets at the 1980 Winter Olympics. From then on, I was hooked. I collected scrapbooks and articles in the months leading up to the 1984 Los Angeles Games—Soviet boycott be damned—and Edwin Moses, Carl Lewis, and Mary Lou Retton were my favorite athletes for a time.

As a student of history and an avid reader of all manner of sports literature, I soon became acquainted with the raised fists of Tommie Smith and John Carlos, the most indelible image from the 1968 Mexico City Games. They, too, were heroes in my eyes. Their act of protest, though controversial, was the ultimate representation of what it meant to be an American. Let a Russian try such a thing and see what happens, I thought. While some thought their protest disgraceful, I viewed it as an act of tremendous courage—one that all Americans should be proud of.

It was Smith and Carlos who drew me to 1968, and the struggling Mexican nation and haunting memories of the slaughter at Tlatelolco kept me there. The '68 Olympics were a complex tapestry of national and international politics, racial tensions, intriguing personalities, and athletic achievement. In conversations about my research, when I mentioned the 1968 Olympics, Americans would immediately recall the protest of the black athletes; Mexicans just as quickly recalled the student massacre—and with powerful emotions. These seemingly contradictory recollections of these Games fueled my interest in an already rich topic.

What follows is the result of that exploration: an examination of the 1968 Mexico City Games and its many scandals and controversies, political and diplomatic elements. In examining the 1968 Olympics, I find it impossible not to reflect on the current state of the Games. The Mexico City Olympics were the first to confront several of the issues that have challenged the most recent Games, including drug testing and the threat of terrorism. In other areas, those Olympics were a pivotal turning point: the intrusion of politics into the athletic contests, notably Cold War tensions; the enormous expense and complexity of staging the Games; the evolution of the "professional"—as opposed to amateur—athlete; corruption of the bidding process; and protest carried out on the fields of sport. Such links to 1968 form one of the themes of this book, and it is examined more closely in the last chapter.

This project has not been without challenges. Mexico has struggled with the mixed memories of an Olympics almost universally praised by the global media, coupled with the tragic massacre of over 200 students only ten days before the Opening Ceremonies. Documents of the period are filled with contradictions and fabrications; interviews vary widely depending on the political and economic position of the interviewee, and many potential sources have either been destroyed or remain hidden by the Mexican government. I have attempted as carefully as possible to assemble a thorough and objective version of the story, corroborating as many details as possible, and accepting vagaries and inconsistencies when necessary. The facts have become clearer in the past several years. A government investigation of the massacre has been ongoing as I researched this project, and with each revision new developments have come to light. As I write this work in summer 2006, recent news releases have again declared that Luis Echeverría will not be prosecuted for his alleged orchestration of the massacre, and Mexico has just held a presidential election, the results of which are contested. The true extent of the political changes that followed 1968 still remains in doubt. It is nonetheless exciting to be researching an event of nearly forty years ago, the ramifications of which continue to be so clearly felt today.

This project could not have been completed without the help of many individuals. Thanks go first to my mentor and friend Jim Jones, who has reviewed my work every step of the way and whose interest and enthusiasm kept me on task. Other readers of the work whose suggestions and constructive criticism have been central to producing the final product include V.J. Conner, Robinson Herrera, Patrick O'Sullivan, Joe Richardson, Joel Cleland, Elwood Watson, William H. Beezley, and the editorial staff at Northern Illinois University Press, especially Melody Herr. Thanks as well to Bill Baker, who continues to inspire me from afar and whose example as a sports historian I can only hope to imitate.

I also extend thanks to those who offered interviews, without which this project would have surely failed: Juan Martinez, Manuel Billa, Pedro Aguilar Cabrera, Carlos Hernandez Schafler, Florenzio and Magda Acosta, Anatoly Isaenko, Ray Hegstrom, and Dr. Eduardo Hay. Thanks go, too, to architect Pedro Ramírez Vázquez, who kindly offered access to a sampling of his private papers. Thanks to those who made my research in Mexico

City possible, especially Ana Mary Ugalde, whose guidance and knowledge was indispensable. Thanks as well to Ellis Leagans, Carroll and Mitzi Golden, and Lorna Daniell.

Thanks to the staffs of the various libraries and archives I mined in researching this project: the staff at the National Archives and Records Administration; at the Mexican Olympic Committee, especially Samantha Rangel B.; and the microfilm staff at Strozier Library, Florida State University; at Lander University, especially Adam Haigh. Thanks also to F.S.U. for a University Fellowship and to the F.S.U. History Department for a Dissertation Grant in support of this project.

Thanks to the "breakfast club," whose assistance in translation of various documents was invaluable: Monica, Paul, Tam, Sara, and Vinnie. Thanks to all my family and friends whose support never wavered and whose nagging questions served as motivation to finish this project. And there are not words enough to thank my wife, Jacky. When others doubted, she believed.

BEFORE
THE EYES OF
THE WORLD

Introduction

In a crowded banquet hall in the lavish resort town of Baden-Baden, Germany, a cluster of well-dressed, middle-aged Mexicans danced a conga line. Observers of the scene looked on with emotions ranging from happiness and amusement to bitterness and disappointment. On that cool evening in October 1963, the offending dancers could not have cared less about decorum, manners, and the emotions of the spectators. They danced like no one was watching—shuffling, kicking, and waving with unbridled joy. Just a few moments before, Mexico had been awarded the Olympic Games.

If, for a few moments, the Mexican delegation was able to ignore the stares of the crowd, it was not long before the reality set in that they had won a prize that carried with it unparalleled international scrutiny. Winning the Olympic bid was perhaps the signal achievement in an image building project in Mexico that had been decades in the making. Government officials and Olympic organizers had convinced the world that Mexico was stable enough, prosperous enough, and sufficiently prepared to host the Olympics. Now the task fell upon Mexico to prove to the world that this image was not a mirage.

No one actually knew whether Mexico was capable of successfully staging an Olympics. Even those within Mexico were perplexed by its paradoxes. On the one hand, Mexico presented itself to the world as a "miracle," a third-world nation with first-world stability and economic growth. A paragon of stability when compared with most other Latin American nations, Mexico passed the torch of leadership from one president to the next peacefully for the better part of the twentieth century. Yet the stability of the political succession came at the price of true democracy. While six-year "elections" gave the appearance of democracy, in actuality they scarcely obscured a ruling party accepting only the barest contributions from the masses. The vast majority of Mexicans simmered in discontent. Only a thin sliver of the population reaped the benefits of the economic miracle while the rest saw their condition decline even from meager beginnings. As the century approached its final quarter, the dissatisfaction of the Mexican people, both in material terms and in frustration at lack of participation in the government, threatened to boil over.

Despite such internal strife, the Mexican government endorsed a bid to host the 1968 Summer Olympics. According to historian Roger D. Hansen, even as it confronted malaise and student rioting, "paradoxically, the Mexican government had enthusiastically agreed to host the Olympic Games."[1] Faced with a populace growing ever more dissatisfied, it decided to undertake an expensive process of construction and beautification, absorbing great financial costs while most Mexicans clamored for assistance. The benefits of hosting the Olympics are more readily apparent now than they were in the early 1960s, still several decades away from the financial windfall of the 1984 Los Angeles Games. Even now, in the words of historian Alan Tomlinson, "the clear and tangible gains of hosting the Olympics are difficult to identify."[2] The Mexican presidents who oversaw the project, Adolfo López Mateos and Gustavo Díaz Ordaz, were both obsessed with their own reputations and that of their nation, and they were convinced that staging the greatest Olympics to date would solidify both. At the same time, both were focused so much on their legacies that they turned a deaf ear to the complaints of their citizens, and by the summer of 1968 many of those citizens simply refused to be ignored. Hopes for a peaceful Olympics were shaken by a swelling student movement, strengthened as the year wore on by similar movements around the world.

The students in Mexico were well aware of developments in France, Cuba, the United States, and elsewhere. It was a time for rebellion and a time for change, and Mexican students did not want to be left behind. The Mexican student movement began over a spontaneous street fight and police brutality in suppressing it, but it quickly evolved into a challenge to authoritarian government and lack of democracy. Their methods, too, borrowed from other student movements as they engaged in ever-growing peaceful marches, handed out fliers, held meetings, and fought back against the authorities with rocks, sticks, and Molotov cocktails "touched by the same fever that . . . gripped students everywhere."[3] To the tragic misfortune of the students—and Mexico's national image— Díaz Ordaz was similarly swept along by the global tumult. Observing the repression of youth movements in France and Chicago earlier in the year, Díaz Ordaz, with the opening of the Olympics only days away, elected to crush the student movement with violence. The resulting massacre of students at Tlatelolco on 2 October was one of the transformative events in recent Mexican history.

Like many students in Mexico, black athletes in the United States were gripped by the global wave of protest. These athletes started a movement to protest an athletic system that was stacked against black athletes, but they quickly embraced the broader methods and aims of the Black Power movement and protest against apartheid in South Africa. The movement of black athletes was about much more than hiring more black coaches and the restoration of Muhammad Ali's title; it was about equality, democracy, and independence for all black Americans. The athletes represented a small portion of the Civil Rights Movement as a whole, a continuation of the efforts of Martin Luther King, Jr., Malcolm X, and all those who had come before. By 1968, as the movement turned away from nonviolence and pacifism, so too did black athletes.[4]

These Olympics were not simply a contest among athletes. As historian Richard Espy has noted, "The Olympic Games system is both actor and stage . . . a stage upon which world political forces are displayed in competition."[5] The Olympics were a forum for protest among students demanding change in Mexico. They were the scene of demonstrations of black athletes demanding respect and change in the United States. They were an opportunity for the superpowers to challenge one another without the destruction of the world at stake. These Games united politics, culture, diplomacy, and athletics as no Olympics before or since.

And yet, with so much at stake, the Mexicans staged a grand athletic festival. In the hyperbolic words of one Olympic chronicler, "They pulled off a coup of enormous magnitude and produced so magnificent a show that even their severest critics were forced to admit the stunning success of their unexpectedly superb fiesta."[6] Records fell as at no other Olympics, and several records set in Mexico City survived for decades. While there were epic clashes between athletic teams, none of them carried over into clashes off the field, as competitors from all parts of the globe seemed genuinely interested in meeting peacefully with their opponents.[7] For all its controversy and protest, the Mexico City Olympics largely succeeded in its mission of bringing the world together in peace.

At the conclusion of the 1968 Summer Olympic Games, Deputy Luis Farias read a letter of thanks to Mexican President Gustavo Díaz Ordaz, which read in part, "The eyes of the world were watching in anticipation from October twelfth through twenty-seventh. What those eyes witnessed was a grand athletic competition, extraordinary sporting facilities, and a feeling that our organization is not inferior to any other nation in the world."[8] Congratulations like the one cited above flowed freely in the immediate aftermath of the Games. Indeed, the Olympics had attracted the attention of the international community as few events in Mexican history. For the first time, the Olympics were hosted by a "developing" nation, by a Spanish-speaking nation, and by a nation in the Americas other than the United States. The athletic competition had indeed been grand and the sporting facilities extraordinary. But upon further reflection, one has to wonder whether the rest of the world would have agreed with the last bit, that Mexico's organization was "not inferior to any other nation in the world." The Mexico City Olympics had been fraught with controversy from the start. Some were concerned that athletes would suffer harm in the high elevation and thin air. There were divisive debates over the nature of amateurism, especially the differences between Western athletes and those of the Soviet bloc. There was a bitter clash over the admission of South Africa to the Olympics, which sparked a worldwide boycott movement. There was the student movement in Mexico, which escalated as the Opening Ceremonies approached, and which ended in a bloody massacre of hundreds of students at the hands of Mexican military and police. And there were two gloved fists thrust skyward from the medal podium.

Mexico was a nation unaccustomed to such intense international scrutiny. It pursued the Olympic endeavor with a self-conscious determination, and organizers paid attention to the smallest details, wary of the message they might send, the image they might depict. There were many slogans associated with these Olympics, but the most telling is *"ante los ojos del mundo,"* "before the eyes of the world." The phrase captures not only Mexican self-awareness of the magnitude of the undertaking but also the attention paid to the Games by the rest of the world.

At its core, this book is about Mexico's quest to join the ranks of the world's "modern" nations by successfully staging the world's largest athletic competition. More precisely, it is about Mexico's quest to portray itself as "modern" by fashioning a particular image during the Olympics. This process of image building was initiated in the late nineteenth century through increasingly elaborate exhibitions at world's fairs and continued in the twentieth century in tourist publications, film, and a variety of other venues, including participation in international sporting festivals. Through such efforts, Mexican policy makers crafted a specific image of a nation that was modern and cosmopolitan as well as steeped in culture and tradition. The Olympic Games offered a unique opportunity to hone this image, as the Games themselves are so multi-faceted, and in this rich landscape of cultural expression, the Mexicans found an ideal forum for displaying the many layers of their national image.[9]

On another level, it is a book about cultural diplomacy. As explained by Lincoln Allison and Terry Monnington, nations have used sports in two ways: to enhance their own image through success; and "to penalize international behavior of which they disapprove."[10] In Mexico City, both methods were at work. Not only Mexicans were concerned about the image they presented in these Olympics: Americans, Russians, and everyone in attendance hoped to advance national prestige by performing well. Also, the Mexican student movement, the black protest, and especially the boycott movement against the inclusion of South Africa in the Olympics are all linked to the concept of using sport as a means of penalizing unpopular behavior.

The chapters in this book are arranged topically, though as much as possible they flow chronologically as well. Chapter 1 answers the question, "How did the Olympic Games come to Mexico?" Part of the answer lies in Mexico's ability to market itself successfully as a nation capable of staging such a huge event; another part lies in a genuine evolution in Mexico's economy, government, and athletic infrastructure. Mexico's successful Olympic bid was not all about image; the nation had in fact made great advances in the half century preceding its bid. Its successful application also depended on the expansion of the Olympic vision to include nations outside of the traditional European/American sphere. Finally, even with the necessary conditions in place, Mexico City had to out-do some formidable opponents in the final competition to host the 1968 Olympics, waged at the German resort town of Baden-Baden in 1963. The Mexicans faced stiff competition from the French city of Lyon, and especially the American nominee, Detroit. Only after an intense and inventive publicity campaign, and a skillfully crafted final presentation, did the Mexicans prevail.

Mexico's quest to stage the Olympics, and thus enhance its national image, faced a number of serious threats even before the Games began. The 1968 Olympics were awash in controversy from the start, and Mexico's efforts to negotiate such issues is discussed in Chapter 2. Most pressing was the question of elevation. No one knew how the thin air would affect athletes of the highest caliber, and several incidents from the 1955 Pan-American Games, also held in Mexico City, led many experts to believe that athletes risked suffering great harm by competing at such altitudes. This controversy also took on a political element, as both the Soviet Union and the United States offered high-altitude training facilities to visiting athletes in an effort to fortify diplomatic relations. The Olympic community also wrestled with issues of amateurism. Some wondered in 1968 if the whole order of amateur athletics was crumbling. Meetings at both the Winter and Summer Olympics of 1968 failed to produce a definitive resolution to this issue, but it was clear that some relaxation of the Olympic amateur requirements was in order. The most threatening issue of all was the admission of South African athletes, who would be allowed to attend the 1968 Olympics according to the decision of the International Olympic Committee at its February meeting in Grenoble, France. That decision immediately inspired a massive boycott movement, including all other African nations, many other nations from around the world, the Soviet bloc, and black American athletes. Any doubts about the ability of the Mexico City Olympics to survive such controversies were ultimately put to rest, in part due to the Cultural Olympics, which was ongoing for the entire year before the Olympics. This celebration of international culture not only advanced Mexico's image as a "harmonizing nation" but also became still another mechanism for the superpowers to engage in cultural warfare.[11]

The most enduring image of the Olympics was the raised fists of Tommie Smith and John Carlos. The "Revolt of the Black Athletes" is the subject of Chapter 3. What were the ties between the Black Power movement and the athletes? Why did the boycott movement ultimately fail? Building on the efforts of several black athletes from the early- to mid-1960s, in the fall of 1967 a group of athletes from San Jose State, led by their imposing coach, Harry Edwards, launched a movement for greater equality and better treatment. Borrowing ideology and methodology from the broader Black Power movement, the athletes made their greatest statement in threatening to boycott the 1968 Olympics. In the months before the Olympics, the boycott movement crumbled but ended with the understanding that individual athletes could protest however they wished in Mexico City, an understanding that sprinters Tommie Smith and John Carlos determined to uphold.

Even as the black athletes waged their campaign to boycott the Olympics, within Mexico a burgeoning student movement gained momentum, discussed in Chapter 4. The student movement was closely linked to the Olympics, though it began as a wholly independent protest against police brutality. As the summer wore on, students came to see the Olympics as representative of all that was wrong with the Mexican government, and the Olympics came to be a common target of their chants and slogans. Though they pledged not to interfere with the Games, the students were crushed by a brutal attack from the Mexican military and police only a few days before the Opening Ceremonies. This attack had a profound impact on the Mexican psyche, and 2 October remains a date of somber remembrance in the Mexican calendar.

Having weathered the protest movements of both the black athletes and the Mexican students, the Olympic Games carried on in October. The athletic competition is the subject of Chapter 5. What was the significance of an international contest at the height of the Cold War? Who prevailed between the United States and the Soviet Union? The scintillating athletic competition was interrupted by a variety of controversies. Smith and Carlos' black power protest interrupted an otherwise spectacular performance by the American team and brought the issue of racism in the United States to a global stage. Also entering the athletic arena were issues of doping and drug use, gender testing, and the Cold War. Particularly stirring was a volleyball match between the Soviet and Czechoslovakian teams early in the week. In spite of such controversies, the athletic contests were roundly declared a great success, and the Olympics concluded to Mexican jubilation.

What did the 1968 Olympics mean for Mexico? For the black American athletes? For the student movement? For the Olympics in general? Such questions, and the aftermath of the Games, are the subject of Chapter 6. In this chapter are analyzed the complex economics of the Games, the successes and failures of the Cold War superpowers, and the aftermath of the protest movements of Mexican students and black American athletes. Also explored is the politicization of the Olympic Games that continued throughout the Cold War, which continues in some ways today. Finally, Mexico's self-image in the years since 1968 and the lasting impact of the student massacre and the Olympics are examined.

That Mexico City finds itself at the crux of Olympic history is remarkable. The Olympics, born from the lofty ideals of a French physical educator and for years perched on the shoulders of the amateur ideal of only European and American athletes, by the early 1960s had only just begun to expand its vision to include representatives from the rest of the globe. And Mexico itself, for much of the twentieth century, suffered through revolution, violence, chaos, and economic and social malaise. Even once it had achieved political and economic stability, it was only after World War II that Mexico began to assemble even a respectable international sporting movement, let alone one ready to welcome the largest sports festival in the world. How did this unlikeliest of nations come to host the Olympics? The story begins in 1926, in the dark of night, at a train depot in Mexico City.

How the Olympics
Came to Mexico

one

At three a.m. on 11 October 1926, a dark and drizzly morning at the Mexico City train depot, a train pulled into the station. It chugged to a halt, and through the blasts of steam a handful of bleary-eyed passengers stepped to the loading dock. The trumpet players and mariachis had left hours before, and scant evidence remained of the welcoming party that had long since drifted into the night. A few streamers clung to the sidewalk, and bits of paper blew in the breeze. Not a soul remained to greet the disembarking passengers, and they exchanged pensive glances as they gathered their bags.[1]

The Cuban athletic group had traveled to international sporting events before and might have expected more from their hosts. But for Mexico City, the 1926 Central American Games were a first attempt at staging such an event, and the inexperience showed. In the weeks leading up to the tournament, the anticipated number of participating nations had dwindled from seven to three, the minimum allowable to hold an official contest, as Honduras, Costa Rica, Nicaragua, and El Salvador accepted the invitation only to withdraw. The Cuban group rolled into the train station almost twelve hours late, after a long boat trip and a slight derailment of their train. Still, their corps of fifty-six athletes was eager to launch the new festival. Guatemala, the only other visiting team, also nearly missed the event. The Guatemalan President, José María Orellana Pinto, died the month before, and it seemed unlikely that the Games would go on. At length, the new president, Lázaro Chacón González, decided to honor his predecessor's vision and send a squad of fifty athletes, enough to compete in scarcely more than half the planned events. They arrived a few hours after the Cubans, after a harrowing train ride of their own.[2]

Some must have wondered if it was worth the trip. The Mexican team of over 200 athletes dwarfed those of both visiting nations, and many events did not go smoothly.[3] The Guatemalans struggled to field athletes in some events, and in one of the shooting contests a visiting delegate competed even with no training or prior notice. Not only did he fail to win, but he initiated one of the Games' many scandals when he refused to draw his gun against a Cuban opponent, conceding valuable points that helped give Cuba a victory. It was but one of many problems. A mob of angry Mexican fans stormed the field in the eighth inning of a baseball game in which Mexico trailed Cuba 10–0, so disgusted were they at their team's play.[4] The Cuban athletes struggled mightily with the high elevation and thin air, as several of their top players managed to play only a few minutes of the basketball game, and their long-distance runners gasped and wheezed in poor finishes.[5]

Even with these wrinkles, though, both the Cubans and Guatemalans enjoyed the hospitality of their hosts, attending parties and dinners when they were not competing. The visiting teams were greeted warmly by fans, and the festival was a significant news story in Mexico City for several weeks.[6] For two weeks, the teams competed vigorously in baseball, basketball, track and field events, tennis, swimming, and shooting events, the latter of which were the most popular. While performances fell short of the world's elite athletes, and there were numerous glitches, Mexico's era of hosting international sporting events had begun.[7]

Less than forty years after this humble beginning, Mexico secured the bid to host the largest sporting festival in the world, the Olympic Games. That any nation might achieve such an evolution is remarkable, and that it might be done so quickly is even more so. In order to achieve such a startling transformation, enormous change and development had to occur along three broad fronts: 1) Mexico's political and economic stability; 2) Mexico's sporting interests and infrastructure; 3) and the attitudes of the international sporting community toward Mexico. Even after significant change in each of these areas, Mexico still confronted the difficult challenge of securing the bid to host the Olympic Games.

From Revolution to Stability

In the early 1960s, when the International Olympic Committee awarded the Olympic Games to Mexico City, the international community viewed Mexico as remarkable among its Latin American peers, a "developing" nation worthy of the honor of hosting the Games. This image of Mexico had been decades in the making and incorporated a complex blend of celebrating Mexico's rich history and indigenous culture along with its growing promise as a modern, urban, cosmopolitan nation. Much of that image was exaggerated or fabricated, and it certainly shrouded a much darker reality, as will be examined in later chapters. Under consideration for the moment is the question, Can we fault the international community for awarding Mexico the Olympic Games?

Mexico's earliest efforts at creating a national image for international consumption came during the Porfirian Era (1877–1910), largely through the increasingly grandiose and elaborate Mexican exhibits at various world's fairs. Ably described by Mauricio Tenorio-Trillo, these displays were carefully designed by an elite group of Mexican leaders and experts he calls the "wizards of progress" and reflected the deep desire of these elites to "fit in" with the developed Euro-American nations, especially France, as well as to "attract immigrants and investment."[8] To that end, the exhibits emphasized "form, style, and façade," rather than an attempt to convey deep truths about Mexican society.[9] At first, Mexico was introduced as part of an exotic sideshow along with other peripheral nations and colonies. Complying with this image, Mexican displays incorporated a full complement of indigenous culture and images, food, clothing, and characters. Gradually the "wizards" fashioned a more "modern" image of Mexico and included exhibits of Moorish architecture, Mexican art, women's exhibits, education statistics, public works, and Mexico's economic staples of mining and agriculture.[10]

The possibility of staging a world's fair in Mexico was discussed during this period but was ultimately dismissed—principally because such an event would mean having to display the *real* Mexico to a world of visitors rather than a carefully staged and limited picture as was presented abroad. Exhibits of modern architecture and structures belied a largely rural population who toiled in poverty; celebrations of newspapers and communications obscured the reality of a nation in which freedoms of expression were repressed. Already Mexican elites were aware that the image they promoted abroad did not reflect the harsher realities endured by most Mexicans. Nonetheless these exhibits contributed to the construction of a national image and mythology that ultimately permeated much of the society. With the Revolution, the specific goals of Mexico's leaders would change, but the pattern of elites creating a romanticized national image that obscured the suffering of the masses was established.[11]

Image building, and nation building for that matter, were wholly disrupted by the Mexican Revolution that followed the Porfirian Era. Emerging from the chaos and destruction was a political system that provided some measure of peace and stability and created the most enduring political party in all of Latin America. The political chaos of the revolution was finally settled during the presidency of Plutarcho Elías Calles, who ruled as president from 1924–1928 and continued to rule behind a series of puppet presidents from 1929–1934. Calles laid the foundations of Mexico's modern political system with the creation of the Party of the Mexican Revolution (PRM), which would evolve into the Institutional Revolutionary Party (PRI), and the precedent of a six-year presidential term with no reelection. Beginning with the succession of the last of Calles' puppet presidents, Abelardo L. Rodríguez, to Lázaro Cárdenas in 1934, every president since has come to power peacefully.[12]

Cárdenas, who ruled from 1934–1940, is still remembered as a hero in Mexico. Among presidents during this period, he was the most deeply committed to social reform. He redistributed more land to the rural masses than all of his predecessors combined, launched an extensive program of rural education, and expropriated the oil industry in 1938, which galvanized Cárdenas' reputation as a Mexican hero.[13] By the end of Cárdenas' term, Mexico showed signs of the growth and progress that would help it win the bid for the Olympics. His commitment to land reform drove the distribution of some fifty million acres of land to the peasants. Paved roads began to replace dusty and rutted dirt roads, tractors replaced oxen, motorized vehicles replaced horses and mules, more peasants were able to buy shoes and adequate clothing, and electricity began to creep into the countryside. Rural schools, too, multiplied in this era, challenging the church for control of the practical, and cultural, education of the peasantry. Illiteracy declined. Improvements in medical facilities led to a decrease in infant mortality and an increase in life expectancy. Life in the cities improved as well. As labor organized and campaigned for change, salaries increased and working conditions improved, if only in tiny steps. Technology increased, and the mechanization creeping into the countryside was even more evident in the cities.[14]

Perhaps the most important development of this time was a change in the national psyche. Mexicans took pride in the improvements going on around them, and they took pride in their own abilities to read and work better. And not least important, they rejoiced in a president who won the oil industry from the Americans. The patriotism of this era surged during the "Mexican miracle" to follow and contributed to the growing sense of nationalism necessary for making a successful bid for the Olympics.

But even the extensive accomplishments of the Cárdenas era have been viewed as fleeting by a growing number of historians. Alan Knight has called the regime more "Jalopy" than "Juggernaut," arguing that Cárdenas was never able in practice to live up to his radical goals. Even as he addressed the desires of the populace more closely than other presidents, Cárdenas advanced the development of a strong centralized government. Most notably, close government supervision of the labor unions stifled the freedoms and limited the gains of workers. And political realities forced him to clip the wings of many of his programs before they took flight. Conservative protest from the Catholic Church, businesses, the universities, foreign interests, and others ultimately led Cárdenas to pull back his reform movements between 1938 and 1940. The conservatism of the presidency was cemented when Cárdenas named Manuel Ávila Camacho as his successor. Some historians claim that the revolution itself ended with this succession.[15]

Under the presidencies of Ávila Camacho and Miguel Alemán Valdés, the social measures of Cárdenas were discontinued in favor of government investment in industries such as the railroads and other transportation, construction, communications, and energy. Alemán shifted the focus of the economy to urban, high-technology production, which left a large body of workers either unemployed or forced to the fringes of the industrial process, working as janitors, street sweepers, prostitutes, or criminals. Many others lived in abject poverty. It is during this period that Mexico achieved the economic and industrial growth that came to be known as the "Mexican miracle."[16]

Driving the miracle, too, were the riches that lay beneath the harsh, scraggly Mexican landscape: oil and minerals. Beginning with the expropriation of the oil industry in 1938, the Mexican economy came to depend more and more on oil as its chief export. The transportation boom sparked by World War II and the explosion of the American automotive industry in the 1950s and '60s were fueled in part by Mexican oil, and the economy flourished as a result. The nation achieved remarkable growth: the gross national product increased at an annual rate of over 6 percent from 1940 through 1970, among the highest rates in the world over that period.[17]

It was this image that was sold to voters on the International Olympic Committee who judged the Mexican application in 1963. Historians today, working with the benefit of hindsight, understand that with the end of the 1960s came dramatic changes to Mexico and its national image. Some historians still refer to the era from 1940 to 1970 as the "Golden Age" in Mexico, a time of peace and prosperity. And while most historians now recognize that even the idea of a "Golden Age" is largely mythologized, in the early 1960s, international observers would likely have been impressed with what they were hearing about Mexico and would have had little reason to question the future of what had become one of the fastest-growing economies in the world.[18]

In short, international observers would likely agree with what Arthur Schmidt has called the "Revolution to evolution" narrative. Such a view celebrated the "ongoing" revolution that, after a decade of horrific violence and destruction, had ultimately resulted in the creation of a stable government and peaceful nation. It especially praised Mexico's phenomenal economic growth in the post–World War II era, the growth of its media and communications systems, and its thriving modern popular culture.[19]

This was the "Golden Age" of Mexican cinema, producing some of the most highly regarded films in Latin America. Sparked by an infusion of U.S. money and technology to support the production of propaganda films during World War II, Mexican cinema enjoyed its period of greatest success in the post-war era. Many of its top-grossing films mimicked American methods and emphasized the infusion of Euro-American culture in Mexico. During this period, Mexico also updated its image, marketing itself in tourism guides as a nation offering sleek, new hotels with all the modern amenities in addition to a land of the "exotic," featuring rustic getaways, indigenous culture, and folklore. Tourists could visit ancient pyramids and historic cathedrals one day and enjoy elite golf courses, fine dining, and luxurious hotels the next.[20]

Improvements to roads, hotels, tourist agencies, and ticket policies made Mexico a favorite destination of American and international tourists. As historian Eric Zolov has noted, Mexican efforts to preserve and market traditional or indigenous culture struck some visitors as forced and staged. "Hippies" and beatniks preferred to seek out more authentic and obscure samples of Mexican culture in the countryside. Still, most visitors were impressed with the blend of traditional and modern offered in mainstream culture, and this image of Mexico was successfully marketed in the 1960s in the slogan, "So foreign . . . yet so near." In total, the impressive economic gains, the political stability and sustained era of peace, and the appealing image of Mexico as both a modern and an "exotic" land all made Mexico an attractive choice for Olympic voters.[21]

The realities of Mexico were not as rosy as this image suggests. Stability did not translate into prosperity and happiness for all Mexicans. As historian Jorge Castañeda has pointed out, the system was plagued by contradictions that resulted, in part, in a gross disparity of wealth. For example, the Mexican electoral system could not be considered a democracy, and yet the proper term for it is elusive. The people came to the polls, and even before the recent defeat of the PRI, candidates were advanced by other parties, but corruption of the electoral system was so complete that challenging the ruling party was impossible. The chosen successor "campaigned" before the people, but his election was secure.[22]

Deepening this corruption of the system was the ability of the presidential party to control virtually every group of any import in Mexico. Opposition was either co-opted into the PRI political machine, destroyed by propaganda campaigns, or allowed to exist at some permissible level of agitation. The Communist Party, for example, has endured all three types of treatment during its eighty-plus years of existence. The Congress, the judicial system, the Catholic Church, labor unions, the media, and others were either directly chosen and controlled by the president or were forced to cooperate by pressures either subtle or overt. Finally, Mexican stability was not achieved entirely without violence or repression, though it remained far more peaceful than other Latin American nations. Sporadically over the more than sixty years of PRI rule, the government squashed strikes or movements, often with startling brutality. But such instances are limited in number, and Mexico has always allowed at least some presence of opposition, including internationally renowned intellectuals such as Octavio Paz and Carlos Fuentes. If democracy was not the right word to describe the Mexican system, neither was autocracy or dictatorship.[23]

The problems did not end there. Increased production with little attention to environmental concerns, especially in Mexico City, led to severe pollution problems. One has only to drive to the pyramids at Teotihuacán, some forty miles north of the city, to see the extent of this pollution today, as Mexico City is visible from vast distances as an ominous black cloud on the horizon. The noxious air is almost intolerable for visitors who are unaccustomed to it, and it has had detrimental effects on the health of residents of the city. Another problem exacerbated by the new industrial society was corruption. The sheer volume of construction contracts offered ample opportunity for corruption at all levels of government, and many politicians took full advantage of those opportunities. Inflating costs of various projects, skimming from the enormous construction budgets, kickbacks, and bribery enabled a small minority of Mexicans to amass huge fortunes. Others benefited from legal, if unethical, practices such as capitalizing on knowledge of future building projects or partnering with well-positioned companies.[24]

Such practices did allow for the creation of a small class of the spectacularly wealthy but also encouraged dissatisfaction among the millions of underemployed, whose slums often rested in the shadows of the palatial estates of these new rich. Even at the height of the "miracle," as Mexico was hailed as a model of economic growth for other Latin American nations, the majority of the population suffered. The poorest half of the population in 1950 only earned 19 percent of the national economy, a number that continued to decline throughout the 1960s. By contrast, the wealthiest 20 percent held 60 percent of the national income in 1950, which climbed to 64 percent by 1969.[25]

International observers, though, saw little of the downside of this new economic focus. Mexico was a bustling nation, and Mexico City was a bustling city. Construction was ubiquitous: during the Alemán presidency, the government sponsored innumerable projects to improve roads, the water system, and the university. U.S. State Department commentary preferred to accentuate these positives while playing down the troubles of the lower classes. Memoranda within the department praised the high growth rates of the Mexican GNP. Its economy was "growing rapidly," with the future showing nothing but "sustained economic growth." Most important for U.S. business interests, this growth meant "favorable prospects for U.S. traders to build on the billion-dollar market which Mexico has become for them and for U.S. interests to make further productive investment [there]."[26]

On the eve of the 1968 Olympics, the State Department made its most expansive commentary on the Mexican economy, in response to an article published in a Latin American issue of *The Economist* that criticized the economy and pointed out a host of problems and concerns for the future. In retrospect, these concerns were legitimate, in some cases even prophetic. The article criticized the lack of diversity in the economy, dependence on foreign investment, high inflation, huge disparity in wealth, and reliance on oil—all of which contributed to the collapse of the Mexican economy in the 1970s. Experts in the State Department found the article to be "overly sombre [*sic*]," its predictions "not justified by recent performance and present policies."[27] Mexico was, in the words of another State Department memo, "in the vanguard of progressive Latin American nations."[28] Mexico had successfully polished its image enough to impress the international community, despite its combustible internal problems. Still, more extensive changes were needed to secure the Olympic Games.

The Evolution of Mexican Sport

Mexican sporting interests and infrastructure, too, underwent an impressive evolution before the nation secured the bid for the Olympics. Even before those first hesitant steps in hosting the 1926 Central American Games, sport in Mexico had begun to change. The beginnings of modern sport began to percolate in the Porfirian Era, from 1880–1911. As historian William Beezley has described, the peace and stability of the Porfiriato allowed the populace, previously too consumed with revolution and mayhem to care much about sport, to take an interest in it. The substantial economic growth during the period was reflected in sport as well. The rising upper class adopted the sports of elites from other successful nations, especially the United States. Bicycles, imported from France and the United States, were a major fad in the 1890s. Cycling clubs flourished, and for a time the cycling lobby wielded enough clout among civic leaders to arrange for the paving of many roads and improvements in safety on the streets. Cycling, though, was not for everyone; while the wealthy rode, the lower classes jeered and threw rocks.[29]

Horse racing came to be a favorite pastime among the wealthy, whose men owned and raced the horses and whose women dressed up and properly supported their men. The middling classes also enjoyed the horse races, where their ceaseless gambling further allowed them to mimic Americans and other successful Westerners. Díaz influenced the bullfights, too, which were banned for a time as too gruesome and bloody for a "sophisticated" nation. As Mexico's stock improved, though,

Díaz not only brought back the bullfights, but he brought them back with all the pomp and circumstance of a national holiday. Bullfights were not to be a source of national shame but rather a source of national pride.

Baseball, too, found its way to Mexico during this period. Carried south by American railroad workers in the 1880s, the sport quickly replaced cricket, just as Americans replaced Britons as the Westerners to be most admired. The railroad workers promoted the game as they traveled through Mexico, and especially Mexico City. It grew in popularity throughout the 1890s, becoming a staple at athletic clubs in the city and the countryside. By the early 1900s the first Mexican leagues were established, and in 1906 Charlie Comiskey brought the world champion Chicago White Sox south for a week of exhibition games. Although the games were one-sided in favor of the champs, and the high price of tickets made for small crowds, the visit legitimized baseball in Mexico, and it has remained the nation's second most popular sport (next to Mexicans' favorite sport, soccer) ever since.[30]

Despite these developments, prior to the 1920s the Mexican government and other Mexican institutions had shown little interest in organized sport. There was no political pressure on Mexicans to choose one sport over another, and there was little political or financial support for any sports at all. Activities were largely spontaneous and disorganized and were the domain of a small upper class, as with basketball, soccer, baseball or tennis, or for an even more elite group participating in polo, fencing, horsemanship, or gymnastics. The masses, when not embroiled in revolutionary activities, might practice ranching sports such as riding, bullfighting, or shooting, or entertain each other with cockfights. Traditional Mexican sports intermingled with another popular leisure activity, drinking, and thus many Mexican politicians discouraged sports as being associated with laziness and immorality. If the "support of governments" was necessary for the Olympic movement to succeed, as the founding Congress of Sorbonne determined in 1894, then Mexico had a long way to go before it might be suitable for Olympic consideration.[31]

But governmental support of international cultural activities was not unprecedented, as Mexican attendance at world's fairs in the Porfirian Era demonstrates. In time, government officials came to recognize a similar value in promoting national sporting interests. During the revolution, competing factions were too consumed with destroying each other to pay any attention to organizing sport, and even as the fiercest violence receded, few politicians saw the value in sport. The first school for training physical education instructors was founded in 1908, but it closed in 1914 in the midst of the revolution. From the beginning, the goal of the public sports system was to replicate similar programs from Europe. Early in the 1920s, José Vasconcelos, an administrator of the Mexican National University and later Minister of Education, brought a new perspective on sport to Mexican leadership. His assertions mirror those of socialist sporting groups that were particularly popular in Europe during this period. He argued that physical activity and organized sports would encourage not only fitness of the mind and body but also cooperation and satisfaction within Mexican society. At his urging, Mexico constructed a new National Stadium, completed in May 1924. Still, his ideas had only a minimal impact on the national scene, as few new programs in Mexican sport surfaced during the period.[32]

The inspiration to join the international sporting community came not from anyone within Mexico but rather from a representative of the International Olympic Committee, Count Henri de Baillet-Latour. The IOC was interested in reaching new regions of the globe, and Baillet-Latour launched a tour in the early 1920s to encourage developing nations to participate in the Olympic movement. His tour brought him to Mexico in 1923, where he met with Carlos Rincon-Gallardo y Romero de Terreros, a leading Mexican sportsman. Rincon-Gallardo arranged a meeting with Mexico's president, General Álvaro Obregón, making an important link between the sporting community and political leadership. After a series of meetings, Baillet-Latour concluded his visit with an encouraging speech, in which he advised: "(1) the formation of Mexican federations for each sport and their affiliation with international federations; (2) the formation of a National Olympic Committee; (3) participation of Mexican athletes, which would be for the first time, in the 1924 Olympic Games in Paris; and (4) the hosting by Mexico of a regional sport festival, to be called the Central American Games, in 1926."[33]

In the wake of these announcements, Mexican sport began to grow more organized, with more of an eye toward participation in international contests. The Mexicans sent their first contingent to the 1924 Olympics in Paris. Alfredo B. Cuéllar, a track and field coach, drove the early Mexican Olympic movement, lobbying the government for funds to support a national team. He met with little success from politicians, but by 1924 he had raised enough money from private donations to send a team of nineteen athletes to Paris. The largest contributions came from the two largest newspapers in Mexico City, *El Universal* and *Excelsior*.[34]

Results for the young team were not spectacular, as the Mexicans dropped out of several events and failed to make the finals in most of them. One Mexican hurdler finished last in the field, injuring his foot while tripping over a hurdle. While their performance had not been world-class, the very presence of Mexican athletes at the Olympics made an important statement to global observers that the nation sought to leave behind the violence and chaos of its recent past. If politicians had not yet grasped the value of such public relations, Mexican newspapers had. They, along with a few determined individuals, remained the strongest supporters of the international sport movement in Mexico throughout the 1920s.[35]

Equally important was the decision to host the Central American Games in 1926. Mexican athletes had traveled to meets within Latin America on a limited basis beginning in 1923, when a Mexican team participated in a series of soccer, basketball, and tennis matches in Guatemala City. At the Paris Olympics, plans for the 1926 Central American Games began to take shape. In meeting with international officials in Paris, and in several other meetings before 1926, Mexican sporting leaders began to lay the foundation of the modern sport movement in Mexico. To fill various committees, they selected prominent coaches, athletes, and even political figures, including President Plutarco Elías Calles. They established the National Sport Confederation and several regional organizations and planned for the Central American Games. Those Games were something of a disappointment when measured against early expectations. At the peak of enthusiasm for the Games, organizers expressed hopes for a festival that would rival the Olympics in scope and importance. As Mexican newspapers noted, the event failed to meet even more reasonable expectations for a significant athletic festival among Latin American nations. But even with only three nations participating, the Central American Games were an important landmark in Mexican sport history. Mexico had successfully hosted an international festival, however modest.[36]

Still, hosting the Central American Games was a far cry from hosting the Olympics, and the 1926 Games had demonstrated the weakness of Mexican sport federations. They had drawn little interest, even from Mexico's neighbors, and had attracted little attention within Mexico itself. A small group of men, at great personal expense and effort, arranged the event, with no support from the government. The masses, too, had not supported the event, as sports were still virtually the exclusive domain of the upper classes. The bulk of the sports contested at the Games, including basketball, fencing, shooting, swimming, and tennis were unavailable to the average Mexican. The other sports, baseball and track and field, were played by the lower classes only in primitive and disorganized forms. Before the Olympic Games would come to Mexico, both the government and the populace needed to support this still budding national sport movement.[37]

Mexican participation in international sporting events continued to increase after the Central American Games, and interest in sports within Mexico also grew. It was a slow process, yet one that fueled itself. As more Mexican athletes traveled abroad, representing the nation in international contests, more Mexican sporting officials and politicians began to encourage sports programs within Mexico. Mexico also followed the sporting trends of Europe, where the workers' sport movement was at its height. Sport improved physical fitness, encouraged cooperation, and allowed workers an avenue for recreation and enjoyment and thus was to be encouraged. While national pride and recognition certainly motivated the growing interest in sport, it was this latter reason that the PRI empha-sized when it announced the formation of the Mexican Sports Confedera-tion in 1932. One of the stated goals of the new organization was to form "an integrated nation [composed] of healthy, virile, and dynamic men."[38]

Educational programs began to include more athletics during the 1930s as well, reflecting a similar interest in raising healthy and produc-tive children. Sport not only developed the physical abilities and senses but also encouraged social skills and cooperation among students. As an added benefit, it offered a productive alternative to such habits as drink-ing, loafing, and fighting. National organizations continued to develop, especially through participation in the Olympics of 1932 and 1936. At the 1932 Los Angeles Games, Mexico won its first medals. And at those Games Mexico joined other Latin American nations in planning what would grow into one of the world's most important competitions, the Pan-American Games. Participation in the Pan-Am Games continued Mexico's rise in international sport, and its hosting of those Games in 1955 strengthened its bid for the Olympics.[39]

Throughout the Cárdenas years, the recognition and sponsorship of sport in Mexico increased. In 1935, the government founded the Depart-ment of Physical Education whose leader, General Tirso Hernández García, helped establish a school of physical education. These organizations gen-erally promoted sports among all social classes, lobbied for additional fa-cilities and supplies, published a monthly magazine, and educated the public through classes and lectures. Rationale for these efforts continued to echo the workers' sport movement, as sport strengthened workers and promoted order and discipline. Cárdenas also emphasized patriotic week-end fiestas, which typically included athletic competitions between vil-lages or communities and included basketball, baseball, and footraces. These events were designed not only to promote health and positive habits but also local and national pride. Even if Mexican athletes still rarely triumphed in international competitions, government sponsorship of athletic programs was a significant step, and sport in the 1930s grew quickly. By one account, during the Cárdenas era "the number of physical education teachers increased from 58 to 300."[40] But things had not im-proved so much that Mexican athletes did not occasionally complain of a lack of government support, and one study of the athletes concluded that they were not competitive internationally due to insufficient training.[41]

As in most nations, Mexican sport during World War II focused on meeting wartime needs, and sporting facilities were co-opted by the mili-tary. In the post-war era, though, sport achieved heights of popularity un-approached before the war. In 1945 the first magazine devoted to sports hit Mexican newsstands, appealing to the public's demand for updates, gossip, and merchandise. Mexicans seemed to be as interested in American sports as their own and as interested in the latest fashions and equipment as in the news. Rather than building a unique sporting tradition, Mexico attempted to mimic the great Western nations, especially the United States. This theme was best exemplified by Mexican efforts, led by Jorge Pascuel Casanueva, to found a professional baseball league. The occasional exhibitions and barnstorming tours from one side of the Rio Grande to the other had continued throughout the first half of the century, and American ballplayers were familiar with the Mexicans. Pascuel Casanueva hoped to lure some star players across the border to solidify his upstart league. Major League Baseball understandably balked at such a prospect and used its considerable influence to ensure that the Mexican League failed. Still, the attempt attracted the attention of international journalists and may have improved the self-esteem of some Mexican sportsmen.[42]

The 1950s only enhanced the growing reputation of Mexican sports. Mexico was host to a number of meetings of international sporting commissions, most notably the 1953 Congress of the International Olympic Committee. The crowning event of the decade was the 1955 Pan-American Games, held in Mexico City. That March, 2,583 athletes from 22 countries came to Mexico City, demonstrating that the 1926 Central American Games were a distant memory. In preparation for the Pan-Am Games, the Mexicans built a number of sporting facilities as well as an athletic village. Over one and a half million tickets were distributed free to the Mexican public, and virtually every venue was packed with enthusiastic fans. A Pan-American Sport Congress was held in conjunction with the Games, in which IOC members and Latin American sport leaders discussed the present and future of Olympic sports in the region. Avery Brundage, president of the IOC, attended the Congress and announced that he looked forward to further expansion of the Olympic movement in Latin America. Brundage had long advocated the development of major international sporting contests in Latin America, and it is clear in several of his speeches that Brundage believed hosting the Pan-Am Games advanced the Mexican cause. As early as 1950 Brundage noted after a trip to Mexico City that, "the [second] Pan-American Games will be held in Mexico City in 1955 and new facilities of Olympic caliber are already under construction."[43]

The Pan-Am Games were a great success, and athletes, spectators, media, and organizers praised the facilities and organization of the events. A host of records fell in the track and field competition, including the world record in the long jump, and a few athletes obviously struggled with the thin air; both such features would be repeated in 1968. The 1955 Pan-Am Games were not only a preview of things to come in 1968 but also offered a powerful precedent as the Mexican Committee prepared to make its bid for the 1968 Olympics.[44]

By the late 1950s, Mexico's sporting interest was sufficient to support a serious bid for the Olympic Games. In fact, Mexico had begun exploring the process as early as 1949, making a preliminary application for the

1956 Olympics (Melbourne). Building on that experience, in 1955 Mexico made a more serious bid to host the 1960 Olympics (Rome). These early efforts were merely exploratory, familiarizing sporting leaders with the process and preparing them for the ordeal of an all-out bid. After the success of the Pan-American Games, huge numbers of fans were eager to attend a great sporting event. Additionally, a well-developed sporting hierarchy had the ear of high-ranking government officials. By the time of their successful bid in 1963, their strongest supporter was the president of Mexico, Adolfo López Mateos. Indeed, this combination of popular interest and government support was vital to a successful bid. As one historian has noted, "the nations of the world have interpreted participation in the Games as an opportunity to express national identification."[45] It was not until the late 1950s that Mexico truly fit this description—just in time to make a bid for the 1968 Games.

The Evolution of the Olympic Community

Even with its own impressive development, for Mexico to be considered as a host for the Olympics, the will of the International Olympic Committee needed to evolve as well. Despite its message of global unity through sport and universal participation, evidenced in its idealistic five-ringed logo, it was not until after World War II that the Olympic Games became a truly global event. All of the Olympics from their revival in 1896 to the 1952 Games in Helsinki were held in either Europe or the United States. Indeed, only one city from outside these regions even made a bid, when the Egyptian city of Alexandria applied for the 1916 Games. The bid was not seriously considered against the competition of Budapest, Cleveland, and Berlin, which ultimately won the contest— although the Games were cancelled due to the First World War, making the point moot. Mexico would not host the Games until the Olympics themselves had overcome their Western bias.[46]

The limited scope of the Olympics might be traced to the beginnings of their revival in the late nineteenth century and to the man whose vision drove that revival, the French educator Pierre Frédy, Baron de Coubertin. While Coubertin deserves the praise he has garnered for his efforts in reviving the Olympics and promoting world peace, his vision of the Games was quite different from what they have become. He promoted sport principally to improve the health and vigor of the youth of his own country, France. Based on the Greek and English examples, Coubertin developed his own vision of a complete education, which would incorporate training in academics, morals and ethics, and athletics. From this vision grew the Olympic ideal.[47]

While his vision was certainly admirable, it was understandably rooted in upper-class, Western ways that were reflected in the Olympic Games of the early twentieth century. Coubertin himself was wealthy, as were the other men who met in Sorbonne, France, in 1894 to establish the new Olympics. They looked to upper-class English prep students as their model of athletic achievement and took much from their own athletic experiences in sports such as tennis, rowing, cycling, cricket, and yachting —all these activities almost exclusively the preserve of the wealthy. Clearly missing in the early manifestations of Olympism was any sign of color and any sign of the inclusion of the common sporting man. Those things would come later, after changes in five important areas: the growth of the Olympic Games themselves; advances in technology; the devastation of World War II, and the political changes wrought by it; the end of colonialism and the development of new, free and independent nations; and the selection of Avery Brundage as IOC president in 1952.[48]

Prior to World War I, the Olympics could scarcely be considered a truly global sporting event. The Games were small—infinitesimal by modern standards—and the range of participating nations was limited. Only thirteen nations and twelve reporters attended the first Olympics, held in Athens in 1896. Virtually everyone in attendance, and all participants, were from either Europe or the United States. The best athletes in the world either did not attend or were disappointed in their performance, as no world records were broken. Hoping to encourage even greater attendance in the future, Coubertin sought to spark the growth of the festival by having a different host every four years. In an era before radio and television, this method of relocating the Games did bring sport to new audiences, but Paris in 1900 and St. Louis in 1904 failed to draw sizable crowds.[49]

The disappointments of these early Games led Coubertin to experiment with an idea that has surfaced periodically throughout Olympic history: a permanent site. In 1906, the Olympics returned to Athens for what would be the first and also last in an anticipated series of Olympics held at their original site. While not part of the traditional four-year Olympiad, this contest marked the beginning of a transition to the modern Games as more nations attended than ever before (20), and those nations submitted their athletes to a more rigorous entrance process than in earlier Games. This transition continued in London in 1908, when numerous controversies inspired the installation of international, "neutral" teams of officials, since the hometown British judges made several questionable rulings in favor of British athletes. By the 1912 Olympics in Stockholm, Sweden, the Games were well established as a major sporting event and had begun to take on the modern implications of nationalism. Everyone—athletes, organizers, and spectators—was beginning to take the Olympics more seriously. With such innovations as electric clocks, photo-finish equipment, and brand-new athletic and housing facilities, Stockholm launched the Olympics on their way to becoming the mega-event that the Games are today.[50]

The Olympics enjoyed their period of greatest growth and innovation during the interwar years, as the host cities fell into a pattern of one-upmanship that made each festival more grandiose than the last. After a hiatus during World War I, the IOC, determined to resume the tradition in spite of the devastation of the war, hurried to hold the Olympics at Antwerp, Belgium, in 1920. A poorer choice could hardly be imagined, as Belgium was perhaps the most ravaged of all European nations, and the destitute populace could not support the Olympics. Even a meager gate fee of about 10 cents was too much for the average Belgian to bear, and the stands were more empty than full for these gloomy, rain-filled Olympics.[51]

The expansion of the Games accelerated four years later when the Olympics returned to Paris. They were a celebration of excess, a not-so-subtle symbol to the world that the war was over, and all was well. The splendor and decoration, the pomp and circumstance of the modern Games began to appear, as national flags and national anthems were ubiquitous. The excitement surrounding the Paris Games was almost matched by the Amsterdam Games of 1928. Returning to a smaller country lent an international flair to the '28 Games, as more nations won medals than ever before, and the traditionally dominant teams from the United States, Britain, and France all saw their medal totals drop. Forty-six nations sent teams, and athletes from faraway places such as Algeria and Japan claimed victories. The Anglo-American proclivity of the Games was weakening.[52]

The interwar blossoming of the Games is best exemplified by the 1932 Los Angeles and 1936 Berlin Games. Each nation expanded the importance of the Olympics far beyond what had been attempted before. In 1932, not only did the Olympics make a celebrated return to the United States, but they also provided an opportunity to show the world that the Depression was not so bad, that Americans could put on a great show in spite of the hard times. It was the biggest, brassiest Olympics to date, as Los Angelinos outdid all previous hosts in construction of new facilities and excitement. The Americans awed the world with a brand-new, massive 105,000 capacity stadium, as well as many other smaller venues, such as an indoor auditorium, swimming pool, and arenas for cycling and shooting, and the largest Olympic Village yet constructed.[53]

Four years later, the Germans took every innovation from the Los Angeles Games and made them even bigger and more elaborate. The 1936 Games are probably the most famous, as Adolf Hitler and the Nazis publicized their regime and organizational abilities by staging the largest Olympics to date. The entire city of Berlin underwent a face-lift, as Nazi regalia adorned seemingly every building, and the streets were pristine. The Opening Ceremonies in Berlin dwarfed even those of Los Angeles, as the Olympic torch paraded before thousands of rod-stiff German soldiers and a row of massive German flags before lighting the flame. These

Olympics were infused with political tensions, as the draconian measures and racist policies of the Nazi regime led to many protests. The Berlin Games, the last held before 1948, set a standard for spectacle, as well as for politicization, that would remain unmatched, perhaps until 1968.[54]

Even as the Games had increased in size and importance, it was not until after World War II that circumstances allowed for a nation such as Mexico to host. The Olympics had not yet been hosted by a city outside of Europe or the United States, and membership in the IOC was restricted to those regions, reflective of the elitist views of the IOC leadership, which was rooted in the imperialist age. As described later in this chapter, the massive political changes wrought by World War II led the Olympics to new lands, including Melbourne in 1956 and Tokyo in 1964. The postwar period is best characterized by its continued expansion, not only in sheer numbers of participants, but more importantly its extension to all corners of the globe.

After an understandably tepid resumption of the Olympics in war-torn London in 1948, the Games resumed their prosperity in Helsinki in 1952. More nations and more athletes participated than ever before, a trend speeded by the entry of the Soviet Union for the first time. The Cold War was palpable in Helsinki, as every match-up pitting a prominent American against a prominent Soviet was highlighted, and newspapers on both sides of the Iron Curtain updated medal counts daily.[55]

The Melbourne Games in 1956 were the last held before Mexico City began making a serious push to bring the Olympics to Mexico, and these Games brought to light many of the problems of the ever-expanding Olympics. One disturbing trend on the mind of IOC members was the possibility that the Olympics were expanding to a point at which it was not feasible for most nations to stage them. An effort to bring the Games to new locales almost ruined Australia as the Australians struggled to raise money for improvements that were barely completed by the Opening Ceremonies. Then, too, there was the overwhelming weight of outside diplomatic events lingering over the Games. Clashes between the Soviet Union and Hungary, and Israel and Egypt, led to boycotts and protests, as did a number of other events. Politics and the Olympics, contrary to the hopes of IOC founders and visionaries, such as new president Avery Brundage, were inextricably tied. By the mid-1950s, the Olympic Games approached the size and scope of those in 1968, and they had expanded enough to make a Mexican bid credible.

Other changes in the Olympic movement encouraged the Mexicans even more.[56] One such development was the advance of technology. One of the problems plaguing the early Games was the prohibitive expense of travel. Only eleven nations could afford the time or money of sending a team to the St. Louis Games of 1904; many of the best athletes even from within the United States failed to make the trip. With improvements in automobiles, ships, and airplanes, more teams could realistically travel to the Olympics. One reason for the monopoly of Western cities in the early Olympics was their centrality; other locations were simply too remote. By the World War II era, this hurdle, while not entirely removed, was more easily cleared by many nations.

Technology also encouraged the publicity of the Games and hence encouraged interest even in faraway lands. The explosion in print media during the late nineteenth and early twentieth centuries allowed many individuals to read of the exploits of their favorite athletes. While in America this led to the creation of athletic heroes such as Red Grange and Babe Ruth, other nations also took pride in the achievements of their athletes. Nations not involved in the Olympics could at least learn about them and aspire to them. As the spread of media introduced sporting events and stars to new regions, previously uninformed or disinterested youths began to play. Within only a generation or two, athletes, coaches, and organizers from all over the world clamored for broader inclusion by Olympic governing bodies.

The development of radio and, later, television only hastened such growth. Sport was a central component of much early programming for both of these technologies. Radio, which blossomed in the 1920s and '30s, allowed listeners to hear the action at their favorite sporting events live, getting some sense of the thrill of actually being there. While baseball games and boxing matches were standard radio events, the Olympics offered different fare for the sports aficionado by featuring events that had attracted only limited interest on-air by the early 1930s. With the 1932 Los Angeles Olympics, that began to change. The Olympics were on the radio for the first time, and many Americans tuning in to support their homegrown Games became lifelong fans. By the mid-1930s, radio was universal enough to strengthen the Nazi movement, and Hitler capitalized on it to publicize the 1936 Berlin Olympics. Those Games were the first to be broadcast internationally, and individuals in distant nations learned of Hitler and of the Olympics at the same time. They grew even more famous through the production of Leni Riefenstahl's massive documentary film *Olympia*. Finally, newsreels shown before feature films brought Olympic highlights to millions of viewers throughout the middle of the twentieth century.[57]

Television provided still another forum for publicity in the post–World War II era. Viewers were able to watch the athletes in real time and therefore study their techniques and improve their own. They could finally "see" their heroes, and this attachment launched the popularity of sports in general to new heights. Television also offered new financial opportunities that irrevocably changed the way sports operated. While the Games were first televised in 1936, the first television exposure delivering the Olympics to a larger audience came after World War II.

With television came dramatic increases in revenue. Squabbling over television rights for the 1956 Melbourne Olympics led international broadcasters to refuse to pay any rights, and thus there was a virtual blackout. Avery Brundage recognized the damage such lack of exposure could mean to the Olympic movement, but at the same time he dreaded the prospect that escalating rights fees might turn the leaders of the Olympic movement into a bunch of greedy money-grubbers instead of ambassadors for amateur sport. As Brundage said in 1965, "One should be suspicious of any amateur organization that has money. The minute this occurs its complexion changes and not for the better."[58]

In spite of the ominous rumblings inspired by increased revenue, the late 1950s and early 1960s saw the Olympics and television grow up together. Television brought the Olympics to nations too remote for actual travel and too small to host a large sporting festival, and the Olympics brought a guaranteed huge viewing audience every four years. Beginning in Rome in 1960, the Olympics became one of the most sought-after athletic events for viewers and advertisers alike. The cost for rights to televise the Olympics ran well into the millions, and it continues growing today. The advent of satellite transmissions in 1962 sparked even more growth, as now audiences could watch the Games live around the world, regardless of where they were being held. With increased money and exposure came more interest from aspiring athletes around the world. This increased exposure contributed to the prestige and visibility associated with hosting the event, a fact that drove Mexican interest in making a bid.[59]

Certainly the growth of the Games and increased exposure through improved technologies helped create an environment in which Mexico City might be considered as a host city, but there were other factors at work as well. It is impossible to envision Mexico City winning the bid for the Games in a world that was not deep in the throes of the Cold War. World War II hastened the global expansion of the Games. Upon the end of the war in 1945, the IOC was determined to resume the regular staging of the Games at four-year intervals; however, Europe was decimated by the war, and few countries could even conceive of hosting the Olympics, let alone the huge costs in time, money, and labor that such an undertaking would entail.

There was only one city on the traditional Olympic circuit with the facilities to hold the Games on relatively short notice: London. It had suffered through years of bombing and the terrors of war and, in 1945, was more a wasteland than one of the greatest cities in the world. Still, its facilities were the best available and could be restored in time for the 1948 Games. The Games did go on that year but were cause for great controversy and calls for change from IOC members. The world in general could mount but little enthusiasm to attend the Games as it recovered from the war, and witnessing the shell-pocked buildings and streets of London, even after three years of recovery, revived tragic memories more than it buried them. The IOC recognized that a change of scenery, away from the war-torn nations, might help and at the same time would spread to new regions the "amity and understanding the Games would promote."[60] With that in mind, the selection of host cities in the years after World War II abandoned the pattern of the pre-war years. New European cities were chosen: Helsinki in 1952 and Rome in 1960. But the IOC also sent the Games far afield during this period: to Melbourne in 1956, Tokyo in 1964, and Mexico City in 1968.

The war changed the world in more profound ways than the ruins of bombing and the scars of battle. Politically and ideologically, the postwar era delivered radical changes that took the Olympic movement in new directions. Seizing on the weakened state of virtually every colonial power, colonial territories launched revolutions around the world in the late 1940s. As Germany, France, Britain, and Japan lost control of their former territories, the 1940s and '50s saw the creation of a spate of new nations, most important of which for the IOC were those in Africa. Not only did these nations create their own governments, but many also created their own national Olympic committees. No longer willing to be held down, they demanded a fundamental restructuring of the IOC. Previously, the IOC had been an entirely independent body, designed to rise above the shifting plates of the geopolitical world. The Committee, its original members chosen by Pierre de Coubertin himself, chose its own members based on criteria related only to one's sporting experience and expertise. National or political allegiance was theoretically of no significance. In the post–World War II world, however, this system proved unmanageable, for a committee that chose its own members was under no obligation to select representatives from the newly created countries. Under literally a world of pressure, the IOC changed its format to allow each national Olympic committee to nominate representatives to the IOC, which then voted on the membership. With this change came a dramatic shift in the direction of Olympic policy away from its early roots in America and Europe and toward other regions. This new direction was a key component in the selection of Mexico City for the 1968 Olympics, as its support derived mainly from nations in Africa, Latin America, and Asia, rather than the United States and Europe.[61]

Another influence on the evolving Olympic community was the Cold War. Sport was but one of many cultural arenas in which competition between the superpowers took on heightened significance. Both sides devoted extensive time, money, and man power to "achieving prestige through victory in competition"—and competition in this period ranged from artistic endeavors to scholarship and scientific advance, to the "space race," to the fields of sport. Such competition reached the Olympic stage in 1948, when Soviet sporting leadership committed itself to competing in the Olympics. The Soviets, dispelling the Western belief in the separation of sport and politics, drew direct connections between success in athletics and political strength. As such, they sought to defeat other nations, most importantly the United States, in sport, to symbolize the superiority of their political system as well. While there was considerable resistance to this effort, by 1948 the IOC, true to its apolitical doctrine, allowed the Soviets to send a team of observers to the London Games in preparation for full participation in 1952. The entry of the Soviet Union into the Olympic fold had a profound impact on many aspects of international sport, among them Mexico's bid for the Olympic Games. Without the support of the Soviets and the bloc of nations that came with them, Mexico had no chance.[62]

A final factor that helped ripen conditions for Mexico City's selection was the ascent of Avery Brundage to the presidency of the International Olympic Committee. Brundage, an American, spent his entire life involved in the Olympic movement. He had participated in the 1912 Stockholm Olympics, bested by Jim Thorpe while finishing sixth in the pentathlon. He was a lifelong supporter of the Olympic movement who held in highest order the mandate to separate sport from politics.[63]

In his role as president of the IOC, Brundage attempted to elevate its workings above the inevitable political differences among nations. In fact, it was impossible to keep the two completely separated, and the 1968 Olympics themselves were embroiled in political controversies. Still, Brundage's neutrality in decision making trickled down throughout the IOC and encouraged many members to consider the candidacy of a city like Mexico City, which would have been unthinkable before. It was with Brundage's blessing and support that Mexico City ultimately won the bid for the 1968 Games.[64]

In 1926, the world was no more ready for Mexico to host the Olympics than Mexico itself was ready to assume such a monumental task. Only after nearly a half-century of political and economic development was the nation capable of bearing the organizational and structural demands of staging the Games. Only after many years of improving sporting facilities and groups were Mexicans even interested in hosting them. And only with monumental changes within the organization of the International Olympic Committee and its guiding vision was the international sporting community ready to consider a site such as Mexico City. Even as this remarkable evolution along so many fronts did take place, Mexico City was by no means the favorite to win the bid. Facing stiff competition from cities representing the traditional Olympic powers of the United States and France, it took a dramatic showdown in the German resort town of Baden-Baden to swing the IOC vote in Mexico's favor.

Organizing the Olympic Bid

The driving force behind the Mexican Olympic bid in the early 1960s was President Adolfo López Mateos. An exquisite orator, a poet, and a romantic, López Mateos ruled Mexico through a combination of skillful delegation of authority to capable men and passionate zeal for reviving the "glory days" of the Mexican Revolution. His admiration for Lázero Cárdenas, the most beloved of Mexican presidents, led him to emulate the great reformer, matching or exceeding his achievements whenever possible. He strived to make historic changes, which led him to expropriate the electric power companies, as Cárdenas had done with oil; to launch an "eleven-year plan" of educational reforms, including free textbooks; to open a series of museums, most notably the world-renowned Museum of Anthropology in Mexico City; and to launch the most extensive agrarian and health reforms since the Cárdenas era. In keeping with this trend of history-making acts, López Mateos enthusiastically embraced the idea of winning the Olympic bid as an important achievement in advancing Mexico's respectability. He supported the effort both financially and rhetorically. Mexico already had most of the required facilities and infrastructure to host the Games, and with an extensive building plan, it had the potential to truly dazzle foreign visitors. López Mateos made it his mission to gain such attention for Mexico.[65]

With the full backing of the president, the Mexican Olympic Committee launched an aggressive campaign in 1962 in order to win the bid for the 1968 Summer Olympics. This campaign concluded with the successful selection of Mexico City by the International Olympic Committee, a choice that shocked many observers, most of whom had anticipated that Detroit would win the bid. The explanation of the Mexican victory is both mundane and complex. The Mexican organizing committee spent many painstaking hours assembling a thoughtful and attractive campaign, which outlined the many merits of Mexico City as an Olympic host. In short, Mexico City deserved to win, as it was the best candidate. But the bidding process was much more complicated than that, and international politics played a central role. Mexican representatives exploited their position as an alternative to the United States and skillfully deflected any criticisms of their campaign. It was not only a solid presentation that won them the bid but also deft diplomacy in the hallways and back rooms of the convention that secured their nomination.

Mexico City, along with all other interested cities, was required by the IOC to answer a detailed questionnaire and assemble many supporting documents. The Mexican Olympic Committee responded to these petitions with vigor. They assembled a 180-page book that not only answered those questions posed by the IOC but volunteered additional information about Mexican culture and history, sporting traditions and facilities, and the omnipresent elevation issue.[66]

From the beginning, the Mexican campaign revolved around marketing a unique Mexican identity, in keeping with the "modern and exotic" theme of tourism advertisements of the day. More than that, though, Mexican organizers sought to distance themselves from the United States and to strengthen ties with Europe and the rest of the world, a strategy that paid dividends in the final vote. From the first application to the final presentation, the Mexicans projected an "everyman" image that was designed to appeal to IOC members outside of the traditional U.S./European sphere. It accentuated contrasts with the Americans: simplicity versus grandeur; public versus corporate; genuine versus fake; humble versus arrogant. The organizers of the Mexican campaign may have been every bit as wealthy and out-of-touch with the masses as Olympic leaders elsewhere—indeed, distribution of wealth was a huge problem in Mexico—but by projecting an image of a "nation of the people," they won over the support of many non-Western nations, most notably the Communist bloc.[67]

In that first application, the Mexicans seemingly promised everything. They would stage all the expected athletic competitions and also a "Cultural Olympics" to include exhibitions of fine arts, such as "painting, engraving, architecture, photography, pre-Columbian art and popular handicrafts," and an extensive program of events such as "concerts of symphonic and chamber music, modern dance recitals, native dances by Indian groups, theater, . . . rodeos, and fireworks displays."[68] They would build stadiums, pools, ball courts, a new canal for rowing events, and extensive housing facilities for athletes and spectators alike. Problems of financing such facilities could be dealt with later; for the time being, the important thing was to make the right promises to win the vote.[69]

Another key element of these early documents, which ultimately would be a major factor in the successful bid, was an extensive list of sporting events that had been held in Mexico as well as a list of existing sporting facilities. While other prospective cities could provide virtually no résumé of major events, Mexico City had established a tradition of bringing international festivals to the country, including the "Central American and Caribbean Games of 1926 and 1954; the Pan American Games of 1955; the Modern Pentathlon World Championship of 1962, and the National Children and Junior Sports Games of 1961 and 1962."[70] Mexico City's sports facilities were so extensive that, in reply to a question asking for a list of them, the MOC simply wrote, "Mexico City enjoys sufficient installations for competitions and practice."[71] In other documents, they would provide a more detailed list of such installations, including over 7,500 civic ball courts, fields, and arenas that could be used in hosting the Games. Few, if any, cities in the world could match those numbers.[72]

This initial application served as a blueprint for the detailed presentations the Mexican group would give the following year before the official vote. It anticipated much of their argument, including explaining the plans to construct the Olympic Village to house athletes, financial plans, demographic information, hotel accommodations, and legal and public programs in place to secure the safety of visitors. It began to construct an identity as an alternative to the United States in the selection process, incorporating subtle jabs against the U.S. and its Cold War conflicts. It also included an appeal to the diverse nature of IOC members, emphasizing Mexico's promotion of "harmony" between human beings, encouragement of "independence and justice" and "the ideals of brotherhood and equal rights for all men."[73]

Based on similar submissions from several nations, in December 1962 the International Olympic Committee narrowed down the competition to four cities: Mexico City, Detroit, Lyon, and Buenos Aires. Even after providing a wealth of information, all four committees were required to answer more questions, most of which revolved around the elevation issue for Mexico City. To meet such demands, López Mateos established the Organizing Committee for the Games of the XIX Olympiad, made up of members of the Mexico City government, the federal ministries, and the Mexican Olympic Committee. The creation of this body not only facilitated the bidding process but also provided the foundation upon which the organization of the Games themselves would rest.

The central figure in the preliminary stages of the application was General José de Jesús Clark Flores, whose life had been dedicated to two passions: the military and sport. Not only was he the highest-ranking military official in Mexico, but he could also claim legitimate title as the highest-ranking sporting official as well. Skilled in fencing and basketball, Clark presided over the Mexican Basketball Association, the Mexican Sports Confederation, and had been on the organizing committees of both the 1954 Central American and Caribbean Games and the 1955 Pan-American Games. As the vice president of the IOC, Clark had reached the highest post ever achieved by a representative from a Latin American country. López Mateos appointed General Clark to chair an executive commission that supervised the completion of various tests and reports, most of which refuted altitude as a problem or a danger to the athletes. In one of these reports, the Mexican representatives "offered to defray the costs incurred in making physical adaptation" by hosting practice "Olympics" and allowing athletes to acclimate to the thin air for a sufficient amount of time.[74] The IOC ultimately shelved its questions until the final meeting, but the international press never quieted on the issue, and most writers seemed to give Mexico only a slim chance of winning the bid, proclaiming that the altitude was an insurmountable problem. As the time for a decision approached in late 1963, a Mexican victory seemed unlikely.[75]

If Mexico City seemed a long shot, there was no sure winner among the other candidates. The stiffest competition, Detroit, in some minds was not even the first choice in the United States. Los Angeles, which had hosted the Games as recently as 1932, contested Detroit's bid only six months prior to the vote in Baden-Baden. The Los Angeles group noted weaknesses in Detroit's bid, such as lack of hotel space, lack of experience in hosting major sporting events, and lack of funding. Just as important, since October 1962, when it was awarded the United States Olympic Committee (USOC) nomination, the city of Detroit had shown only modest interest in making a serious bid for the Games. Civic rallies and promotional efforts had failed to stir much excitement. The Detroit committee flooded the city with billboards and television commercials, editorials and print advertisements; but while several thousand Detroiters had sent letters to local papers in support of the bid, more important groups such as hotel owners and tourist agencies were slow to come around. One hotel owner summed up his feelings for Detroit Olympic Committee member Frank Hedge, saying simply, "Detroit really isn't a good place to hold the Olympics."[76]

While advertisements and billboards failed to arouse much enthusiasm from Detroit's business community, a challenge from the powerful Los Angeles committee did. Between February and March of 1963, Los Angeles relaunched a bid for the Games that had been considered dead after the October USOC meeting. While the bid received a tepid welcome from business interests in Detroit, the city of Los Angeles was firmly behind efforts to regain the Games. Not only had Los Angeles hosted the Olympics before, but it also had facilities ready to do so again: a 102,000-seat coliseum, a 17,000-seat indoor arena, and dozens of Olympic-sized swimming pools. While Detroit struggled to win support for a bill to rush production of a $20-million stadium, Los Angeles was ready and waiting to usurp the bid.[77]

On 12 February 1963, the USOC finally yielded to growing pressure from the Los Angeles team and agreed to reconsider their selection at their next meeting, March 18–19, in New York. The most damning grievance they presented was that only a handful (later shown to be seven) out of the 34 voting members of the USOC had witnessed the presentation of the Los Angeles group, and many of them did not see any of the presentations. Equally troubling was the fact that only four of those voting were official members; the others were assistants to members, who technically were not allowed to cast a vote. The loud grumblings of the Los Angeles contingent parlayed these oversights into renewed consideration of the candidates.[78]

Over the next month, Detroit and Los Angeles waged intense campaigns in which politicians, media members, celebrities, and former athletes flung barbs at each other and their cities. Detroit Mayor Jerome P. Cavanagh complained that the action was "shocking" and "totally inconsistent with the tradition of the Olympic Games," and Michigan Governor George Romney griped that Los Angeles was trying to "rob" Detroit.[79] Sent reeling for the moment, the Detroit team struggled to right itself over the next few weeks, which it spent dodging the attacks of a ferocious publicity campaign out of Los Angeles. The arguments from Los Angeles were more than just idle challenges; they raised serious questions about the legitimacy of Detroit's bid. Detroit lacked sufficient housing to support the athletes and coaches who attended the Olympics, let alone the huge crowds of spectators. It had little experience in staging large sports festivals. It had no Olympic stadium, an issue that the *Los Angeles Times* mentioned almost daily between 12 February and 18 March, and one that would be raised again in Baden-Baden. What plans Detroit did have for a stadium hinged on a massive bond issue, an increased tax on pari-mutuel horse track betting, and federal assistance, all of which combined might still fall short of footing the estimated $100 million bill to pay for the Games. Additionally, Detroit had received the nomination of the USOC for the last four Olympiads but failed to win the international vote each time.[80]

Los Angeles countered each of these weaknesses with a strength. It boasted some 30,000 hotel rooms, compared with less than 10,000 in Detroit. It had hosted many athletic festivals, including the Olympics in 1932, and had a stadium at the ready, which with minor improvement would be "the best of its kind in America."[81] Los Angeles' supporters also advanced other arguments, some of which could open questions about the integrity of the Olympic bidding process. One such argument, mentioned repeatedly in the press, was that the Los Angeles Olympics would profit between $2 and $5 million, which would be "divided among the United States Olympic Committee, the International Olympic Committee and various sports federations."[82] Paul Zimmerman, sports editor of the *Los Angeles Times* and the most vocal supporter of the Los Angeles bid, also noted that Southern California had contributed more money to the United States' Olympic effort than any other region, over $1 million from 1948–1960. Over the same period, Detroit had raised only a few hundred thousand dollars. He asked, "Would you, as a director of the United States Olympic Committee . . . kiss off that kind of money? Or forsake your friends who have raised a million dollars compared to peanuts from another city?" He concluded the column by wondering whether the USOC would be motivated more by "politics and bias" or by "a genuine interest in the betterment of the national Olympic effort."[83] Or, one might add, were they motivated by financial gain? The exchange of votes for financial support amounts to little more than bribery, and in light of more recent scandals associated with the Olympic bidding prospects, it is unlikely that the media would approach these issues so lightly today.

The Los Angeles team was not above making deals publicly, as they attempted to do with the organizers of San Francisco's bid attempt. When the USOC reopened consideration for the bid in February, San Francisco rejoined the contest with vigor. Still, it was lightly regarded, a dark horse at best, who might sneak in if Detroit and Los Angeles somehow cancelled each other out. In early March, county supervisors in Los Angeles approached those in San Francisco with a "trade" offer: if San Francisco dropped out of the race for the 1968 Olympic bid, Los Angeles would support San Francisco for the 1964 Democratic National Convention. San Francisco county supervisors accepted the offer and attempted to send the city's Olympic bid to a committee, where it would die. USOC member Tom Hamilton, a supporter of the San Francisco bid, got wind of the plan and attended the committee meeting. His impassioned pleas kept alive San Francisco's efforts, and the plot was foiled. Still, the episode demonstrates the seriousness, some would say deviousness, of Los Angeles' efforts to win the Olympics.[84]

In March 1963, the USOC reconvened to hear the presentations of each of the cities again. If star power alone had determined the winner, Los Angeles would have won in a landslide. During its presentation before the USOC on March 18, the committee rolled out celebrities such as Jackie Robinson, Bob Hope, Jack Benny, Peggy Lee, Zsa Zsa Gabor, John Carradine, and Rudy Vallee to support its bid. The group was further backed by a power-packed "Committee of 100" including other celebrities, radio and media personalities, businessmen, politicians, and sports officials. Several members of this group appeared on a local television program to publicize their case. In addition, the president of the USOC, Kenneth L. Wilson, was flooded with letters from Los Angelinos, the result of a letter-writing campaign engineered by Mayor Sam Yorty. Detroit countered with a powerful lobby of its own, including Governor Romney and Mayor Cavanagh. It also hired a "high powered public relations firm" that, a week before the final vote, issued false press releases that Wilson and Avery Brundage had conceded the race to Detroit.[85]

Two late revelations made the final vote even more compelling. The Detroit team was boosted by last-minute news that the Michigan legislature had approved a plan to finance the Olympic stadium, thus clearing a major hurdle for their bid. The Los Angeles group, after lobbying fiercely for the re-vote, was stung by the announcement that the neighboring city of Long Beach was planning to host the World's Fair in 1967 and '68. While this coincidence did not officially break the IOC rule against awarding the Olympics to a city holding the World's Fair at the same time, Long Beach was near enough that it made a Los Angeles victory unlikely. Even a hasty letter from Nelson McCook, the president of the Long Beach World's Fair board, promising to reschedule the event should Los Angeles win the Olympic bid, could not shake the pall from the Los Angeles team.[86]

After a month of bitter politicking, Detroit was reelected in resounding fashion, receiving 36 of the 44 votes, to Los Angeles' four, San Francisco's two, and one each for Portland and Philadelphia. Governor Romney, while perhaps excited at the outcome, could not resist the opportunity to throw a few final barbs at California Governor Pat Brown, who had challenged Detroit's financial stability and worthiness to host such an enormous festival. Romney said, "I told the committee . . . if you are interested in a stadium and you want a 1932 model, you can go to Los Angeles. But if you want a 1963 model, you come to Detroit."[87] Some in Los Angeles responded with bitter words of their own and suggested that they might undermine Detroit's international campaign. Bill Henry, president of the Southern California Committee for the Olympic Games, criticized the decision of the Olympic Committee and suggested that Detroit would be unable to fulfill its promises should it win the Olympic bid. If Detroit could not live up to its commitment, he said, "We might finally have to step forth and save the honor of the country." These jabs aside, the Los Angeles "Committee of 100" and others took their defeat graciously and promised to support Detroit's bid for the Olympics.[88]

Attacks from Los Angeles and the other challengers did weaken Detroit's bid for the Olympics and offered a clue about what was to come in Baden-Baden. Many of Detroit's flaws had been aired in the press for several months, and the Detroit organizing committee had been forced to waffle, waiver, whine, and change its stadium plans several times. None of these actions were becoming of a committee theoretically slated to put together the largest athletic festival in the world.[89]

The Showdown at Baden-Baden

When the contending delegations went to Germany that fall, Detroit was considered the heavy favorite to win the bid. Between March and October, numerous reports surfaced supporting the impression that the U.S. nominee would win the international vote as well. The press emphasized this point repeatedly, quoting members of the USOC such as Doug Roby, saying, "It looks more and more as if the United States is going to get the Games," and IOC President Avery Brundage, who later denied saying, "none of the other countries bidding for the Games is as serious as the United States." Neither the Mexicans nor the French were willing to concede without a struggle, and all three nations had reason to believe that the vote that October would swing their way.[90]

The Mexican group was the first to arrive, reaching Baden-Baden on 12 October after an exhausting two-day journey from Mexico City. Baden-Baden, an oasis on the edge of the Black Forest comprised of a dreamlike collection of gardens, spas, and palatial casinos framed in Greek colonnades, is, under normal circumstances, a vacationer's paradise.

For the Mexican delegation, though, it was the scene of constant effort, and the stress only heightened as the day of the vote neared.

The Mexicans hoped to capitalize on whatever advantages might be derived from being the "underdog," not least of which was a humility that brought with it a sense of purpose. They knew that a win was unlikely, so they paid attention to every detail, and they politicked with anyone and everyone. Two days before the presentations, before the other groups even arrived, the Mexicans ventured to the casino where the meetings would be held. Hotel staff showed them the meeting hall, and one of the Mexican architects, on hand to help assemble their display, asked what space they could have. The reply was exactly what they hope to hear, "Take whatever space you want. Just divide it into three and pick your space." The hallway leading into the room led up a ramp and into the left side of the room. The Mexicans astutely chose the far left portion for their display, so that all who entered the room would see the Mexican display first.[91]

They made good use of this advantage. The Mexican exhibit, much like those at earlier world's fairs, was a physical representation of the "modern and exotic" image that Mexican elites had constructed. Their presentation focused on the Mexican people, on their history and heritage. They imported hundreds of items from the Mexico City Archaeological Museum. One of these was a huge statue of the Aztec god Quetzlcoatl, which they propped in prime position at the end of the ramp leading into the room. As the foreign delegates arrived, the statue was there to welcome them, with one arm up pointing the way into the convention hall. They followed the way straight to the Mexican display, and throughout the convention the delegates were greeted by the Mexican display on their way into the meeting hall.[92]

Their persistence occasionally drew the ire of the other candidates, as in one instance when the Mexicans displayed one of their national symbols, an Aztec calendar imposed on an image of the sun known as *la piedra del sol* (the rock of the sun). The giant model overhung the display of the French, who protested. In this case the Mexicans relented, but their aggressiveness was noted by the other delegates and contributed to a growing buzz about the Mexican candidacy as the meeting wore on. Considered a long shot before their arrival in Baden-Baden, the Mexicans were the talk of the convention. While purely anecdotal and perhaps not a genuine factor in their ultimate victory, it was written that the Mexican display had become the favorite of many wives of delegates, who encouraged their husbands to support their candidacy.[93]

While the Mexicans did everything they could to gain some advantage prior to the final presentations, they still faced formidable competition from the other delegations. After struggling to hold off the challenge from Los Angeles, Detroit found its support strengthened within the city and throughout the nation. Its backers included many high-profile Americans. Governor Romney lobbied fiercely for the Games and flew to Germany as part of Detroit's delegation. He brought a 37-minute movie that included a greeting from President Kennedy. Former President Dwight D. Eisenhower had mailed personal letters to each of the 60 members of the IOC, bearing a special July 4 postmark from the Gettysburg post office, no great surprise considering Eisenhower's intense interest in sports and attention to the details of cultural diplomacy during his presidency. Such extravagances were a small part of the massive $250,000 publicity campaign launched by Detroit once it had secured the American nomination. Another was the celebrated running of the Olympic flame from Los Angeles to Detroit, which was intended to symbolize the passing of the torch from the 1932 Olympic hosts to the anticipated 1968 hosts. Skeptics noted that such antics were appropriate for the Detroit bid—all flash and no substance.[94]

But Detroit's bid was not to be taken lightly. If such things as the running of the torch provided flash, the substance of the bid came from a more profound source. Detroit was a true global economic hub, the nexus of the automobile industry. Also, with the burgeoning success of Berry Gordy's Motown, it was both a cultural center and a prime example of the growing black representation in the United States. More to the point, Detroit was the chosen nominee of the United States, the most powerful nation in the world. What the United States wanted, it usually got, and where the United States led, many others followed. The United States had not hosted the Summer Olympics since 1932, the longest such drought in U.S. Olympic history. A bid that brought with it the full support of some of the most important and visible men in the world, including Presidents Eisenhower and Kennedy, a huge publicity campaign, and all the muscle associated with being a superpower was difficult to deny.

The French were confident, too, as evidenced by French representative Tony Bertrand's comments the day before the final vote, when he laughed and said, "We're going to win, hands down. There is no question of that. We have all that Detroit lists—and much more besides."[95] He did have reason to be confident. As the site of the Olympic revival in the 1890s, France had a strong tradition of hosting the Olympics. Additionally, the Olympics hadn't been held in France since 1924, so like the United States, France was "due." Lyon also had the advantage of being centrally located in a region that nations from Africa and the Middle East could easily reach. A number of African delegations mentioned that they supported Lyon primarily for this reason. The Lyon delegation had promised to enlarge the local airport to satisfy the needs of such a large gathering, to expand the stadium from a capacity of 60,000 to 95,000, and had assurances from the French government that money would be provided to improve roads and lower hotel rates. Finally, Lyon offered a small-town charm that could not be matched by the other candidates and would be welcome after the gala affairs in Rome and Tokyo. Could any of the other cities match the appeal of walking from the Olympic stadium to some of the greatest restaurants in the world, enjoying a glass of fine local wine, and concluding the evening with a stroll along the Rhone River? As if to drive this point home, the French imported a special feast by train, distributing it as part of their display.[96]

To counter the impressive credentials of the traditional Olympic powers from the United States and France, Mexico launched an aggressive campaign to appeal to Olympic voters from outside of that sphere, many representing recently liberated colonial nations. The successful bid ultimately hinged on five factors, each of which the Mexican committee employed skillfully: 1) image building, emphasizing Mexico's position as an alternative to the other powers; 2) global politics, specifically utilizing Cold War tensions to its advantage; 3) bribery, flattery, and other forms of coercion; 4) defusing concerns about Mexico's elevation; 5) constructing an impressive exhibit and campaign.

The presentation committee consisted of five men whose task it was to overcome what many believed were the impossible odds against defeating both the Americans and the French. The chairman of the committee was Pedro Ramírez Vázquez. An architect by trade, Ramírez Vázquez was renowned for his design of the National Museum of Anthropology in Mexico City, the 100,000-seat Aztec football stadium, and dozens of other buildings. He had been drawn into the world of international events by his work on the Mexican pavilions at several world's fairs and found himself at the forefront of Mexico's efforts to win the Olympics. Marte Rodolfo Gomez was formerly secretary of agriculture in Mexico. His efforts in solving nutrition and health problems had led him naturally to the study of sport. Now 67 years old, Gomez had been an IOC member since 1934, and bringing the Olympics to Mexico had become his obsession. Dr. Josué Sáenz had been involved in the Mexican sporting movement as long as any of the others. While his background was in economics, he had a passion for organizing major sporting events, most recently Mexico's Pan-American Games of 1955. Dr. Eduardo Hay played a key role in defusing the altitude issue. An experienced athlete and former Central American champion in fencing, Hay knew well the dangers of the thin air, both real and perceived. The final member was General Clark.[97]

The Mexicans observed the presentations of the other groups with careful scrutiny, noting opportunities to gain approval for themselves. They noticed several weaknesses in the behavior and strategy of the American team; however small, they provided chinks in what had once seemed invincible armor. The American delegation routinely arrived at convention sites in stretch limousines with all the trappings, laughing and chatting amongst themselves with little attention to other delegates.

Their display celebrated corporate success and wealth. The film they presented was filled with corporate logos and business interests rather than social or cultural events. Even their titles, listed during introductions prior to the final presentation, read like an ostentatious laundry list, filled with higher degrees and honors. Finally, they spoke English, a weakness they perhaps could not help but which nonetheless connected them with a limited group of nations.[98]

Hay recalled several instances in which such flaws were on display, one involving a dinner outing on the night before the final presentations. Word got around that a world-class restaurant was not too far from Baden-Baden, hidden in the Black Forest. The Mexicans headed out, crammed into two simple cars. In mid-drive, they were startled as a massive limousine zoomed past, followed by several more. When they trickled in to the restaurant a few minutes later, the American and French teams had already ensconced themselves at most of the tables, while others waited near the door. There was no space. The Mexicans glanced around the restaurant, but seeing no open tables they resigned themselves to returning to Baden-Baden. In the parking lot, they were stopped by one of the restaurant staff, obviously unhappy with the crowd of Americans. "Are you the Mexicans?" he asked. "Wait a moment. We have a space for you." He led the delegation through a side door, where they were given a private room to enjoy a marvelous dinner.[99]

Impressing the staff at a local restaurant is hardly the same thing as winning over Olympic voters, but the incident does illustrate that the American contingent may have alienated some observers. Hay noted similar weaknesses in the film that introduced the American presentation, which on first glance appeared to be a masterful creation in the finest Hollywood tradition, including an eloquent appeal from President Kennedy. Some in the audience saw beyond the showmanship American arrogance and even propaganda. The simple plot of the film had a group of three teenagers driving around Detroit, playing on the obvious connection between Detroit and the auto industry. The three youths included a white male, a white female, and a black male. It was an attempt to demonstrate the diversity, and yet the harmony, of the city of Detroit, but it struck some in the crowd as cheap pandering. The racial unrest in the United States was well known, and few in the audience were convinced that all was well by a simple film clip. And if the intent was to show the diversity of the city, what about including an Asian? A Latino? The racial mix in the car was a small point—after all, *someone* had to be in it—but another small point that detracted from the presentation. Perhaps more grating than the three passengers in the car were the stops they made along the way. They pulled into the local burger shop, with its sign looming in the background. They stopped at the Texaco station, again making note of the company logo. They drank Coca-Cola, waving the bottles within obvious range of the cameras. These shots were intended to demonstrate the vibrancy of the American economy and the variety of elements in Detroit's corporate culture. But many in the room found the peddling of American goods unsettling, and near the end of the film one anonymous observer shouted, "What nice propaganda!"[100]

To counter the arrogance of the Americans—real or perceived—the Mexicans built their entire candidacy around the idea that the Mexicans were simple, humble people with a rich past and a bright future. They mentioned often the appeal of the Olympics to the Mexican people, especially the children, rather than some corporate goal. This message of simplicity, and promises of a toned-down Olympics, appealed to many delegates, including Avery Brundage, who hoped to avoid another extravagant, grandiose Olympics, which Tokyo was shaping up to be. In keeping with this theme, the Mexicans tried to avoid the lengthy, pompous-sounding introductions of the Americans. As they were about to be introduced, Dr. Hay grabbed the card with their titles printed on it. After a few quick changes, the voice came over the speakers, "Architect Pedro Ramirez Vasquez, President of the Mexican Olympic Committee; Mr. Martin Gomez, member of the Mexican Olympic Committee; Dr. Eduardo Hay, member of the Mexican Olympic Committee . . ." and so on. In lieu of fancy titles, the Mexicans took an "everyman" approach to the introductions, and it endeared them further to voters from more marginal nations.[101]

The Mexican campaign was not perfect and did undergo some humorous glitches along the way. Prior to leaving for Germany, the Mexican committee had planned to match the American film with one of their own. Their film, though, never made it to the screen before the IOC. The delegation had left Mexico City before the film was finished, and they trusted that the completed version would be useful. At last, the night before the final presentations, the film arrived. Excited, the group sat down to watch the movie. Out of the initial pops and scribbles of the reel-to-reel picture came dust-blown images, in black and white, common to spaghetti Westerns and many Mexican films. There were horses and cacti and gunshots and re-enactments of the Mexican Revolution. Before the film ended, the group agreed that it could not be used. In Hay's words, it was a "very nice, very typical Mexican movie." But it was not the stuff with which to impress the IOC.[102]

Instead the Mexicans relied on a series of speakers, which stood in stark contrast to the theatrical efforts of the American group. It was an effective gambit, even if it was forced upon them by necessity. Each of the speakers was an accomplished orator, and the subject matter appealed to the audience. The panel of five addressed such matters as the financing of the Games, the staging of sporting events, the facilities available, the history and culture of Mexico, and the issue of the altitude. Alejándro Carrillo offered one of the most well-received speeches, which was about the Mexican people. He had been educated at the University of Texas, where he won awards in speech contests. Many in the crowd appeared genuinely moved by his discussion of simple, humble, hardworking, and honest people. These were not selfish folks out to make a buck from the Games; they were a determined people who had transformed their nation after the Mexican Revolution, and the Olympics would symbolize the success of that transformation. The audience applauded him loudly.[103]

The Mexicans also shrewdly accentuated their more socialist attitudes while downplaying associations with American ways of life. Their speeches emphasized the people, the youth, who would benefit from the promotion of sport that the Olympics offered. Such ideals correlate directly with Russian sporting traditions, in which sport was most often used to strengthen the working masses, to encourage them to work smoothly and efficiently as one. The Mexicans also openly opposed the capitalist nature of the Olympics, the obvious economic boon that it offered, instead promoting its social and cultural values. Dr. Hay emphasized such points in the conclusion of his speech, saying "[We seek the Games] not for us, not for our business, but for our youth. That is why we are asking for this. Not to have another title." Hay delivered the speech in French, rather than English, as all other speakers had done. By speaking French, Hay reached another segment of the delegation without alienating anyone; it was a sly maneuver. In distancing themselves from the United States, the Mexican committee probably did not lose any votes—supporters of the United States would vote for Detroit anyway. But this distance helped make Mexico City an attractive alternative for the Soviet bloc.[104]

Appealing to the Soviet bloc was also a significant part of the second factor related to the Mexican victory, the political realities of the Cold War. The Mexicans were reasonably assured of winning the votes of the Russians and their supporters, at least a portion of the Latin American vote, and perhaps some African votes. Mexican newsmen, before the final presentations, were skeptical that they could win over enough votes. Africa and Europe seemed to be supporting Lyon, and the Latin American vote was likely to be split by Buenos Aires, Detroit, and Mexico City. At least one prediction considered the swing votes to be from Latin America and hoped for a tie on the first ballot, with the supporters of Buenos Aires swinging to Mexico City on the second. Even those staunchly behind the Mexicans did not know what to expect in the final vote, and in the words of one Mexican newspaper, "Mexican children are prepared for a horrible mistake."[105]

The delegations were scheduled to meet for the final presentations and official vote on 18 October. After a long night of final preparations, the Mexican delegation awoke to find a shock on the front page of the newspaper: the U.S. Senate had approved a $4.2 billion aid fund. The package promised to continue sending aid to developing Latin American nations but also hoped to extend aid to communist countries such as Poland and Yugoslavia, part of the Soviet bloc that the Mexicans had wooed so zealously. This announcement threatened to undermine all the dealing the Mexicans had done, as many nations now had a real financial incentive to support the United States. The team went into one last damage-control campaign, seeking out the Russian delegates. Did the aid package change anything? Could they still count on the Soviet vote? The Russians assured them that nothing had changed; their votes would still go to Mexico.[106]

Even with Soviet support, the Mexican bid would have failed had not the bulk of the Olympic body decided that the time had arrived for a Latin American nation to host the Olympics. While the final ballots are secret, and it is impossible to know precisely which nations voted for Mexico, everyone agreed that Mexico's support was rooted among Latin American nations and newer additions to the IOC. In the words of IOC President Avery Brundage, "What helped Mexico was that it is one of the smaller-scale countries, and some members felt they could do more for the Olympic movement on the whole by giving encouragement to such a country. Such encouragement, in this case, amounted to the Olympic Games."[107] Falling outside the preserve of the Euro-American sphere also helped the Mexicans in a more practical way: NATO's boycott of East Germany was an unpopular policy with Brundage and other Olympic policy makers. Both Detroit and Lyon suffered by association with this policy, as Brundage noted after the final vote. Finally, Mexico was the standard-bearer for all Latin American and Spanish-speaking nations, none of whom had hosted the Olympics before; for delegates from similar nations, it was an easy decision whether to grant the Games to the United States or France—again—or to one of their own.[108]

While politics certainly played a role in Mexico's selection on a grand scale, each vote is cast by one individual, and individuals can be swayed by influences other than national or international politics. The Mexican delegation earned their victory with hard work and skillful negotiation, plying the desires and massaging the egos of each representative. Josué Sáenz, head of the Mexican Olympic Committee, began lobbying for votes as early as 1960, visiting the Shah of Iran in an attempt to secure the Iranian vote. Even before the convention began, the Mexican committee assigned individuals to specific regions and worked to win support in each region. One member took Latin America, another Europe, and so on. They focused on the Russians and the entire Soviet bloc, which held a total of eight crucial votes.[109]

They also contributed to negative conversation about their rivals. Much talk amongst the delegates concerned racial discrimination in the United States, and in Detroit in particular. There was also some concern about the commercialism in Detroit's exhibit and the likelihood that a

U.S. Olympics would be even more grandiose than the Tokyo Games, a prospect that most delegates hoped to avoid. While Mexican papers seemed to think more favorably of the French presentation, one editorial noted that while Mexican sports installations were ready for the Olympics, those of Lyon were still in piles of bricks.[110]

Simply fraternizing with representatives from swing-vote nations may not have been enough. They studied the IOC representatives in each region, learned their eccentricities, their hobbies, their favorite foods. To ensure that their efforts would be successful, the Mexican contingent engaged in a time-honored Olympic committee activity: bribery. While committee members are still reluctant to speak openly of the process, it is clear that some "greasing of the wheels" took place. In getting to know members of other committees, they took special note of artistic interests. If a rare Aztec artifact or finely polished glass sculpture made its way into the hands of a collector of such pieces, perhaps the beneficiary would remember where it came from on the day of the vote. The extent of this bribery is unclear, and the outcome may not have hinged on it. It is also entirely possible that the Americans and French dealt under the table as well. In any case, it is one more way that the Mexicans assured their selection.[111]

Another key factor in the Mexican victory was the ability to explain and defuse the altitude question. Many observers believed the Mexican bid was doomed from the beginning, as rumors swirled that the thin air could kill an athlete pushing himself to his physical limits. The Mexicans had invested in dozens of studies of the effects of altitude on athletes and presented ample evidence that the altitude was a nonfactor. In some events, yes, the altitude would serve to weaken an athlete's performance, but these effects would be shared by all athletes equally. Athletes traveling from afar, if given time to acclimate themselves to the altitude, would not be at a disadvantage. A central component in overcoming the question of elevation was a speech given by Dr. Eduardo Hay during the final presentation. Hay, in eloquent fashion, not only defused the rumors but even made the altitude a positive point. He argued that the climate in Mexico City is the best in the world, as the high air makes the weather pleasant and cool year-round. The speech included an impressive list of events and festivals that Mexico City had hosted previously, never with any serious altitude-related incidents.[112]

The Mexicans turned the altitude issue to their advantage, as all the other delegations seemed to harp on it rather than promoting their own strengths or attacking other, more serious, elements of the Mexican candidacy. As General Clark told one reporter, "If our opponents use that argument, it means they . . . can not reproach us with technical and financial deficiencies."[113] By the end of the convention, this point had been so effectively made that even non-Mexicans spoke out on the issue. At the end of the Mexican presentation, when one last question about the altitude was directed at the Mexican team, General Vladimir Stoitchev of the Bulgarian delegation jumped up and said, "Horses never have trouble getting acclimatized down there. And if horses can stand it, so can the humans."[114]

Finally, the Mexicans brought an impressive array of facilities and programs to the table. Their bid was a strong one, even without considering the factors mentioned above. Mexico City had hosted major sporting festivals before, including the 1955 Pan-American Games, and it was capable of housing the athletes and spectators of the Olympics. The city was dotted with sporting facilities, including aquatic centers, soccer fields, indoor courts and arenas, and even bullfighting rings. The University Stadium could seat 80,000, and the Mexicans promised to build an even larger stadium, with a capacity of 150,000, should they win the bid. The city had hundreds of hotels for visitors and would build a massive complex of apartments for the athletic village. It was a rapidly growing city of some eight million residents that could absorb hundreds of thousands of tourists with ease. Mexico City also boasted cheap lodgings. The Mexican team offered to house the Olympic athletes at a rate of $2.80 per day, which bested Detroit's rate of "$3.00 or less" per day. On the final day, the Mexican delegation came through with other financial incentives. They promised to open the Olympic Village seven days early at no extra charge to allow the athletes extra time to adapt to the altitude, to grant each athlete a stipend of $100, to charter airlines for athletes from various regions of the globe, and to lower airfares for visitors to the Games.[115]

The International Committee assembled to hear the presentations on 18 October. Buenos Aires, the Argentinian nominee, opened the proceedings at 10 a.m. Detroit followed at 10:45. After a break, Lyon resumed the hearings at 3 p.m. The Mexican presentation was scheduled for 4:15, so the group spent the better part of the day listening to the other presentations and searching for last-minute improvements in their own speeches. When the speeches and the politicking and back-room dealing was finished, all the contending nations had to wait for the final vote. At last, Otto Mayer, Chancellor of the IOC, stood to announce the results. "Buenos Aires 2, Lyon 12, Detroit 14, and Mexico 30," he said, and the rest was lost in bedlam. The magic number for a majority, and victory, had been 29. The Mexicans tallied 30 of the 58 votes cast, just over the 50 percent required to secure the nomination on the first ballot.[116]

With the announcement, Hay and the rest of the Mexican delegation, along with others, erupted in applause and shouts of joy. Mexico had come to Baden-Baden as a long-shot candidate. Most observers expected Mexico City to finish third, behind Detroit and Lyon. The reality of their accomplishment, and the enormity of the task they had undertaken, would sink in later. For now, there was time only for celebration. While other delegates could only kick the floor in frustration, the Mexicans danced a conga line around the room. It was a well-earned victory and a landmark in Olympic history. Following the vote, the Americans and French prepared to leave Baden-Baden while the Mexicans prepared for a great party. Prior to the convention, Mexican delegates had inquired about the possibility of a victory celebration in the unlikely event that they secured the nomination. There was no room, they were told—the Americans and French had both already booked the ballrooms for their own victory celebrations. Food and spirits had already been ordered and paid for. However, the hotelier told them, if by some miracle you do win, you will enjoy a lavish celebration on the house. The Mexicans made good on that offer, enjoying a five-star spread of food and wine, paid for by the defeated teams. It was a final touch of irony to a weekend that saw the Mexicans outwit their competitors on many fronts.[117]

That Mexico won the "Battle at Baden-Baden" came as a shock to most observers at that time, but in hindsight the victory is not so surprising. Not only was the international community ready to bring the Olympics to new regions but also the Mexicans simply out-maneuvered their opponents. They successfully crafted an image combining the most appealing aspects of Mexican history and culture with its modern facilities and cosmopolitan atmosphere while at the same time distancing themselves from the Americans. Their bid featured a combination of eloquent speeches and skilled answering of difficult questions, as well as deft management of the political tensions of the time. This marriage of diplomacy and sport, combined with a masterful campaign and presentation, allowed the Mexicans to defeat rivals who had once appeared unbeatable.[118]

As they left Baden-Baden, the Mexicans rightfully congratulated one another on their surprising victory. In the era of superpowers, they had negotiated the murky waters between the United States and the Soviet Union and emerged bearing a great prize: the right to host the Olympic Games. In the weeks and months after, though, the realities of their accomplishment would set in. They felt, as one writer put it, "like a man who entered a raffle for a tiger, and won."[119] There was much work to be done: buildings to be constructed, events to be planned, finances to be sorted out. But as 1968 grew nearer, even more pressing issues threatened the very existence of the Games. Fears concerning the elevation of Mexico City became more pronounced. The Olympic organization was racked by internal issues, such as doping and the debate over amateurism. And as the 1960s rolled on, the Civil Rights Movement in the United States and around the world became an issue too prominent to ignore; race would become the issue at the center of the storm in 1968.[120]

Image Preserved

Early Controversies

and the Cultural Olympics

two

In 1965, the top two middle-distance runners in the world were Billy Mills and Ron Clarke. The Australian, Clarke, was the best in the world at the 5,000 meters, having beaten his own world record several times. Mills, the American, was better in the 10,000 meters, having won the gold medal in the Tokyo Games at that distance. He hoped to beat Clarke in both races at the 1968 Games. On 21 October 1965, the two met in a much anticipated 5,000 meter race. At the gun, all the runners were off, and the race proceeded as might be expected, with Mills and Clarke pacing each other and hanging with the main pack of racers. Midway through the race, Mills appeared to tire and fell off the pace, dropping farther and farther behind with each lap. Clarke took advantage and led the field as it approached the finish. The best in the world, though, was beaten that day by Mahomed Gammoudi of Tunisia, who made an inspired charge at the finish. The pace was tortoiselike by world-class standards, a minute and fifteen seconds slower than Clarke's world-record number. Mills was even worse, stumbling home thirty seconds behind the leader and nearly dropping from exhaustion at the end. It turned out that Mills was suffering from a stomach virus and was racing sick, which explained in part his miserable performance. But what of Clarke and the others?[1]

The race that day was of no importance as far as their prestige in the international racing community was concerned. It was an exhibition, and everyone involved agreed that who won was not important. But Mills' falling out and Clarke's poor time raised eyebrows among sportsmen around the world, for the race was held as part of an event that came to be known as the "Little Olympics," a series of contests that the Mexican Organizing Committee arranged to demonstrate to the world that the Olympics could be held in Mexico City with no ill effects on athletes' performance. But poor times and severe exhaustion for many athletes belied that claim. Anyone who looked at Mills at the finish of that 5,000 meter race had to be concerned that the Mexicans were not telling the whole story.

Mexico City is located on a dried lake bed, surrounded by a rim of mountains, all of which rests on a plateau over 7,000 feet high. How this altitude might affect the most highly trained athletes in the world was a mystery and the source of the earliest major controversy of the 1968 Games. Low-lying nations would be at a disadvantage, some complained. Scores and times would be lower, unimpressive, others noted. Athletes will *die,* the bleakest skeptics thought. In hindsight, the altitude proved to be a minor issue during the actual contests. But before the Games began, these kinds of questions had to be answered, both to make a successful bid for the Olympics and to convince the world that it would be a show worth watching.

Thin air was but one of many controversies that swirled around these Olympics, at times threatening to put the Games themselves in jeopardy. Another pressing issue in 1968 was the matter of amateurism. The International Olympic Committee's insistence on a stringent amateur standard had grown antiquated, as modern athletes required full-time training to achieve the highest levels of success. This issue, too, was complicated by Cold War tensions, as East and West seemed to view the definition of amateurism in completely contradictory ways. By 1968, the two sides were exchanging accusations and insults, and there was some concern that the Olympics could no longer exist as a purely amateur undertaking.

Finally, the question of the representation of South Africa in the Olympics reached a head in the summer of 1968. Despite the apartheid system and obvious inequities in the opportunities offered to athletes of different races in South Africa, the International Olympic Committee determined that enough progress had been made to allow South Africa to compete in Mexico City. An international firestorm ensued as nations from all over the world organized a boycott movement. Only the restoration of the South African ban prevented the boycott, but the movement continued to percolate among black American athletes and ultimately inspired the famous protest of John Carlos and Tommie Smith in Mexico City. For organizers of the Mexican Olympics, resolving such issues in a satisfactory manner was of critical importance for the preservation of the national image. The Olympics were to be the ultimate expression of Mexican modernity and organizational capacity; if the Games did not go smoothly, the reputation of the Mexican government and nation could suffer. As such, each of these issues forced the Mexican Olympic Committee to assuage intense feelings on both sides and raised the diplomatic stakes of the Games.

The Question of Thin Air

The altitude question surfaced long before Mexico City was even awarded the Olympics and had been the trump card of the cities challenging Mexico City for the Games. The 1955 Pan-American Games, so important in Mexico's successful bid to host the Games, became an Achilles heel as the Games approached because detractors could point to many examples of the altitude sapping competitors' energy, even endangering them. Several athletes had collapsed during those Pan-Am Games and not only those who finished poorly. In one celebrated incident, the American Lou Jones fell to the track after the 400 meter race, unconscious, learning only later that he had just broken the world record. Jones was hardly alone in suffering the ill effects of the altitude, and the Pan-Am Games were held up as evidence by skeptics that an Olympics in Mexico City would be unsafe.[2]

Complaints ranged from justified concern to outright panic. Most were genuinely concerned about the athletes' safety, as there was little understanding about the real dangers of intense exercise at high altitudes. The darkest predictions were indeed dire: "There will be those that will die," announced Finnish trainer Onnie Niskanen.[3] While his views were hardly the consensus, many wondered just how much the human body could withstand under such conditions. Equally legitimate were fears that the altitude might favor certain nations over others. Not everyone had access to training facilities at high altitudes, and those athletes without such access would surely be at a disadvantage. While the IOC and various national Olympic committees made an attempt to allow such athletes to train in other nations that did have high-altitude sites, this compromise was limited by the financial resources of the low-lying nations. One prominent figure in the controversy was Roger Bannister, perhaps the most famous runner in the world and the man who had first broken the four-minute barrier in the mile in 1954 and, by the 1960s, an esteemed doctor of sports medicine. He represented England, a nation without high-altitude facilities, and was an outspoken proponent of literally leveling the field. He noted, "Opportunities to acclimatize will be left to the differing wealth of the countries and to the ingenuity, even ruthlessness, of their coaches."[4] Another unanswerable question was whether the thin air gave an advantage to certain individuals. The battery of studies conducted prior to the Games found that the altitude affected each individual differently but was inconclusive as to exactly how those effects were determined. Each nation had to decide how it would select its representatives and hope for the best. In retrospect, it is clear that the thin air *did* favor some individuals while damaging others.

Complaining about the Olympic site was one thing; proposing a reasonable alternative was another. One factor that made the issue so difficult was that no one seemed to have any better ideas. Bannister proposed that some events be held at lower altitudes, such as Acapulco, where the yachting events were to take place. This solution, though, would create a host of new problems. It would mean dividing the Games between several distant sites, and it would throw the plans and preparations assembled by the Mexican Olympic Committee to that date into disarray. It would also bring massive problems to towns such as Acapulco, which were unprepared to handle the traffic and crowds an Olympics would bring. Bannister's idea was unworkable. Another proposal came from an American physiologist, who proposed that the Americans establish a "base camp" on the coast and fly athletes to Mexico City hours or even minutes before their events, before the effects of the altitude set in. The problems with this idea are obvious, and there is no evidence that it was seriously considered by the United States Olympic Committee.[5]

In an attempt to quiet the growing clamor over the altitude, the Mexicans arranged the "Little Olympics" in 1965, almost exactly three years before the actual Olympics were scheduled to begin. The exhibition was designed to give some unity and direction to the teams of scientists who were flocking to Mexico to test the effects of the environment. Rather than keeping track of dozens of separate teams, why not invite all nations to one athletic meet, where athletes and scientists could do their tests during a contest that would simulate Olympic conditions? Sixteen nations responded to the invitation, and they amused the Mexican spectators with their insistent and never-ending testing, even in the midst of the competition. Athletes ran in special suits and special masks, gave blood before and after races, and answered nearly endless questions. Over fifty doctors from various nations trotted along after the athletes, chasing them down for testing immediately after contests ended.

What they discovered was not always pleasing. Almost without exception, the visiting athletes expressed concern about the thin air. "It was like walking uphill," American Ron Laird groaned after the 20 kilometer walk.[6] Billy Mills, who had faded in the 5,000 meter race, explained the toll of the altitude more precisely: "There is this awful sensation of breathing deeply and not being able to pull enough air into your lungs. When you run, you feel like you've never run before. I'm cruising along on the practice track and I get ready to give it the final kick and I turn on that last big burst—and that last big burst isn't there. I don't know where it went, but it isn't there."[7] Athletes around the world were concerned that their abilities, too, might vanish into the thin air at Mexico City, so the battery of tests and studies continued.

Clearly, with athletes dropping out of long races and even winners passing out as they crossed the finish line, the altitude *did* have an effect on world-class athletes. But what, exactly, did these scientists discover, and what did they hope to do about it? Perhaps the most poetic explanation was provided by the sportswriter Bob Ottum: "The altitude will have an effect, but it won't make any significant difference."[8] He explained that the altitude might sap the performance of some athletes and might increase the overall times in the longer events, but on the whole the best athletes would still win, with an allowance for the occasional upset. The results, in short, would be just like those in any previous Olympics. Ottum's explanation did not satisfy the athletes, coaches, and scientists from the many nations sending athletes, since they all wanted to make sure they were not the "exceptions" who would be adversely affected by the altitude. So groups from around the world continued to produce studies and publish their findings, and while the language was a bit more formal and the scientific basis a bit more grounded, the findings of these groups differed little from Ottum's theory.

According to the French delegation, for instance, the key to maintaining performance at altitude was acclimatization. French athletes would need to train at high altitude "for at least three weeks prior to their departure."[9] If possible, too, they should make short trips from high to low altitude, since it was shown that such intervals would both allow the athlete's body to grow accustomed to training in thin air and would increase overall performance. The French study also announced that performance in events lasting less than a minute would not be damaged, but performance in longer events would suffer. It also noted a phenomenon called the "climatic crisis," during which one's performance decreased slightly between the sixth and tenth day at altitude. Finally, the study outlined other concerns for these Olympics, which were problematic but never particularly controversial, including the dryness of the air, the pollution, the time difference and jet lag, and the unpredictable impact of the food, including the dreaded Montezuma's revenge. In sum, according to this report, claims that athletes would die in these conditions were exaggerated, but considerable time and effort needed to be put into the athletes' acclimatization process to ensure optimum performance.[10]

The Belgians carried out their own tests and reached similar conclusions. Finally, the Americans conducted seemingly endless studies, the results of which were released in March 1966 at a symposium held in Albuquerque, New Mexico, entitled "The Effects of Altitude on Physical Performance." The symposium, sponsored in part by the U.S. Olympic

Committee, made several suggestions to both the USOC and the IOC as how best to handle the altitude issue. Most were accepted, if not in full, then to some degree. While a few of their findings were obvious, such as "Athletes should be in top condition," others were more noteworthy. The panelists reached the important conclusion that "The Olympic trials should be held at [high] altitude," since individuals respond differently to the rare air. An athlete who excels at sea level may suffer at altitude and thus would make a poor choice to represent his team in Mexico City. The symposium recommended even more careful scrutiny of athletes, such as examining family history and certain physiological traits such as sickle cell or cardiopulmonary disease. While they could make no definitive statement about how these traits might increase or decrease an athlete's chance of success at high altitude, their studies did note slight differences in performance among athletes with such characteristics. Depending on the length of the race or contest, these traits might slow the athlete down by a few hundredths of a second, enough to render a world-class athlete merely average in the intense competition of the Olympics. Finally, the symposium agreed with other suggestions to lengthen the prescribed period allowed for training at high altitude, a point that the IOC conceded with its October 1967 change of policy, to be discussed shortly. The USOC symposium decided that while there was little physical danger for the competitors, there was much potential for selecting the wrong athlete to represent the nation in the Olympics.[11]

Mexico and the international sporting community had little choice but to deal with the altitude issue. It was on the table when Mexico City won the bid, so there could be no change of venue. Even acknowledging that they would have to accept the thin air, they came up with a number of compromises that eased the tension over the issue. In one instance, seen by many as ironic, the Mexican Organizing Committee decided to remove the equestrian competition from Mexico City to Oaxtepec, nearly 3,000 feet lower. As one representative of the International Equestrian Federation explained, "Horses are inclined to go on well beyond the prudent limit of effort." Another added, "They do not have the common sense that humans do."[12] While many observers noted that this change was a wise one, they also viewed it with some skepticism. If running in the thin air is unsafe for horses, how dangerous might it be for humans?

In fact, the IOC was very much concerned with the safety of its human competitors and even altered its rules to account for the unique conditions. According to the Olympic Eligibility Code, an athlete is only allowed four weeks a year for "special" training at a camp; training at a special camp at high altitude would presumably fall under this category. To account for the altitude in Mexico City, and to provide some additional time for acclimatization, the IOC announced in October 1967 that it would allow an extra two weeks of "special" training in 1968 for a total of six weeks, with the caveat that only four of the six weeks could fall within the three months leading up to the Mexico City Games. How intently most nations took this rule to heart is up for debate, as virtually every nation that could afford special training facilities at high altitude constructed them. The Russians had expansive training sites at Alma-Ata in Kazakhstan and Yerevan in Armenia, both over 10,000 feet. The Japanese trained at Mount Norikura, the French in the peaks of the Pyrenees, and the Americans in the Rocky Mountains. Those who could not afford their own facilities made arrangements to visit a nation that had such facilities, as the West Germans did in joining the French in the Pyrenees and many other nations did in coming to the United States in the weeks before the Games.[13]

The changes in IOC rules offered the United States a unique opportunity for advancing foreign relations. The United States had hammered Mexico on the altitude issue while making a competitive bid for the Games, but it was quick to capitalize on it once Mexico won the bid. The U.S. State Department issued a memorandum to all diplomatic posts on 3 July 1968 encouraging other nations to come to the United States for training at high-altitude locations. Volunteering training facilities in mountainous states such as Arizona, Utah, and Wyoming offered a number of benefits for the United States, two of which were stated in the memo. First, the State Department hoped, "substantial favorable publicity and prestige [would] accrue." Second, the teams of visiting athletes would "undoubtedly enjoy traditional American western hospitality and a beneficial exposure to the United States," no doubt preferring American ways to their own. There were unspoken benefits as well. Inviting their rivals to train with them gave American athletes and coaches an opportunity for the United States to keep a watchful eye on their competition and gauge their own abilities. There might also be psychological benefits as well; if American techniques and performance proved superior to their opponents, it might establish a nagging feeling of doubt or inferiority in the minds of the opposition, potentially a critical advantage in events measured in fractions of a second. In an era when both superpowers attempted to manipulate culture for diplomatic gain, and when everything and everyone from dancers to musicians to chess players became symbols of economic and societal dominance, it is not surprising that the U.S. government may have tried to gain advantage by offering its training facilities to visiting athletes.[14]

The circular met with a wide range of receptions, from gracious bemusement to cold indifference. The Ecuadorian response was especially interesting; they politely declined the invitation to train in the United States as much of Ecuador lies well above the altitudes of Mexico City, and Ecuadorian athletes routinely train at altitudes in excess of 9,500 feet. In their reply, the Ecuadorian officers explained that they "were amused at the Department's reference to the 'extremely high altitude of Mexico City (7,430 feet)' . . . [they] should come up and see us some time!"[15] While Ecuador and others declined the invitation, many other nations accepted eagerly. Before sending their teams to Mexico City, West Germany, Norway, India, Sweden, Austria, and others sent athletes to the American West to train. Even as it hosted other nations for training, neither the United States nor any other nation could be completely certain how their athletes would fare in Mexico City. The pressures of performing under the duress of the Olympics could not be simulated in any training, so it was not without some trepidation that teams headed off to Mexico City in October 1968.[16]

The Debate over Amateurism

Even as athletes around the world contemplated the sinister effects the altitude might have on their bodies, a second controversy was brewing. The debate over amateurism had been present at the creation of the Olympic Games and remains a problem even today, but in the late 1960s it was the single most divisive issue between sporting groups of communist and capitalist nations. The altitude might have presented a problem, but it was one that all athletes would have to contend with equally. Allowing some nations to send "professional" athletes to the Olympics while others were compelled to meet an elusive "amateur ideal" was not so benign an issue.

Amateurism was the core element in what had become almost a religion for some, the religion of Olympism. Originating with Pierre de Coubertin and developed and defended in the twentieth century by Avery Brundage, the amateur ideal ostensibly held Olympic athletes to a higher standard. It evolved from the class-based sporting traditions of the Victorian era, when sporting federations and competitions were largely the reserve of the upper class, who were wealthy enough that much of their time could be spent at play rather than at work. As historian Andrew Strenk explained, "Play without pay was a mark of status."[17] Such athletes could have spent their time elsewhere but dedicated themselves to athletics out of a love of competition, unspoiled by the corruptive force of reward. It is from this tradition of amateurism that the Olympics reemerged in 1896, and it was under such an amateur ideal that the Olympics were governed.[18]

The early rules of eligibility in the Olympics reflected this ideal. In order to maintain amateur status and thus compete in the Olympics, an athlete could not be paid for his/her involvement in athletics. An athlete could not be paid for competition in any sport (even a sport other than the one he contested in the Olympics), nor could he accept payment for coaching or sponsoring athletic competitions. One who accepted pay for athletic pursuits was no longer an "amateur" but was instead a mere "employee" or "entertainer" and not worthy of the Olympics.[19]

The IOC enforced these rules with draconian strictness, and a long line of suspensions and expulsions from the Olympic movement indicated the vagaries of defining amateurism, which grew even more difficult over time. One of the earliest and most celebrated expulsions was that of Jim Thorpe, winner of two gold medals at Stockholm in 1912. Thorpe was stripped of his medals and his amateur status when it was revealed that he had played professional baseball in 1909 and 1910. He had been paid for playing a sport—never mind that it was a different sport than that which he medalled in—and thus was unworthy of the amateur label. The list of athletes who could not measure up to amateur standards, or who could not tolerate going hungry, was much longer, and even the greatest of Olympians were not immune. Paavo Nurmi, six-time gold medal winner between 1920 and 1928, was barred from the 1932 Olympics after accepting expense money "in excess of his costs." Babe Didrikson, one of the great female athletes of all time and the star of the 1932 Olympics, allowed her likeness to appear in an advertisement and was summarily stripped of her amateur status. And Jesse Owens, the American sprinter who dominated the 1936 Berlin Olympics, found the stresses of life as an amateur too demanding. After appearing in several exhibitions for which he was paid, he was suspended from the Amateur Athletic Union (AAU), surrendering his amateur standing.[20]

The list of "non-amateurs" grew longer with each passing year, but the IOC refused to budge on the issue. Part of its stubbornness was derived from respect for the Olympic tradition but even more might be attributed to Avery Brundage, himself the son of a stonemason, who insisted that if he could make it to the top of the athletic world, anyone could. The possibility that he should be the exception rather than the rule never seemed to cross his mind, and his tunnel vision regarding amateurism became almost laughable. "In fifty years," he claimed in 1968, "I have never known one boy too poor to participate in the Olympic Games; in fact, it can be established that 90% of all Olympic medals have been won by poor boys."[21] This claim was unfounded, of course, but the unfortunate truth for dozens, even hundreds, of athletes was that Brundage headed up the most important amateur sporting body, and the rules would be difficult to change unless he yielded.

In time, though, even Brundage had to admit that clinging to the old rules of amateurism was not working. While it is impossible to indicate a date when amateurism died, it was not far along the Olympic time line before an athlete could no longer be purely an amateur and hope to be competitive as well. The competitions grew fiercer, national allegiances more pronounced, publicity and fame greater, and the lures of contracts and appearance fees more tempting. Events became more specialized,

coaching and training techniques more advanced, and training and tournament schedules too demanding. Athletes were forced to buy uniforms,
insurance, equipment, and food and yet could not be paid—for the
Olympics were the preserve of the amateur athlete. The stresses on amateurism were not only caused by physical demands but also by broader
changes in the very nature of sport. With the advance of technology, particularly television, sport was no longer simply a local issue, viewed by
those in attendance. As viewership ballooned into the millions for many
sporting events, money began funneling in from television networks and
sponsors. Sports, especially mega-events like the Olympics, became big
business, and with big business came heightened temptation for athletes
to reap some rewards. Athletes were offered appearance fees to participate
in certain events, athletic scholarships from colleges, cash handouts by
supporters or agents, and bonuses from shoe companies, apparel manufacturers, and other sponsors—all of which were considered illegal by the
IOC and could get an athlete suspended or banned for life. Under the
strictest definitions of amateurism, almost no athletes could be eligible
for the Olympics. Something had to change.[22]

While such pressures strained the amateur ideal almost to its breaking
point, they do not take into consideration the deepening divide between
communist and capitalist nations, a divide that strained the unity of the
Olympic movement altogether. With the restoration of Soviet Olympic
participation at the 1952 Helsinki Olympics, the amateur ideal was confronted with a new problem: the "state-athlete." On the surface, athletics
in socialist and communist nations represented the very epitome of the
amateur ideal: sport was designed to advance social, educational, and
public goals, rather than to achieve private gain. As argued by Sergei
Pavlov, chairman of the Soviet Committee on Physical Culture and Sport,
there were essentially no "professional" sports in the Soviet Union,
rather, all sports were "amateur," open to everyone, and conducted without profit as a motive.[23]

Increasingly, though, Western athletes and organizers did not see it
that way. Perhaps communist athletes did not compete for profit, but
they were given the full support of the government for training and competition. Did they not have their meals paid for? Housing? Transportation? Were there not incentive bonuses and rewards from the government for top performers? Did these athletes not train year-round, being
effectively "employed" as athletes, rather than working some other job
and training at other hours? Whereas defenders of communist sport
might claim that it was the very essence of amateurism, opponents
claimed that it was, in effect, professionalism.

But the issue ran even deeper, inspiring genuine animosity between
spokesmen from both sides of the Iron Curtain. For amateurism, according to its classical definition, was a reflection of more than simply economic

status and interests. It was a reflection of moral character, honesty, and sincerity of purpose. A professional athlete was a mercenary, literally selling out the pure enjoyment and pleasure of play and sport for the selfish end of making money. An amateur, on the other hand, was driven by the purest motives: love of the game, self-sacrifice, the thrill of victory, and physical health. As Avery Brundage explained, "Amateur sport is a delicate and fragile thing. Its values are intangible. They come from the delight of physical expression, the broadened outlook, the deepened experience, the self-satisfaction and joy of accomplishment to the participant. It is an enlargement of life but it must be pure and honest or it is nothing at all."[24] The amateur ideal drips with value judgments, insinuating that the amateur is fair and honest and decent while the professional is greedy, dishonest, and hypocritical. If, then, the Soviets were professionals, they were cheaters as well.

It was this moral condemnation that especially bothered the Soviets, and in the mid-1960s the debate over amateurism became a heated dialogue between East and West. The accusations from both sides sounded remarkably similar. The Soviets alleged: "[Sport in the West] is a big business and athletes are exploited without regard to their health or whether it is good or bad for them"; "Sport is manipulated," becoming a substitute for political awareness and even for religion; and in response to allegations of professionalism, "What about the college-football scholarships and the industry-sponsored athletic teams in [America]?" The Soviets defended their system and insisted that it met the guidelines for amateurism. On the opposite side, the Americans complained: "The Russians . . . are in effect well-paid state officials"; "They included political agents on their teams, and . . . used sport for political purposes, propaganda and national aggrandizement"; and the Soviet sports system was "harsh and severe . . . both Spartan and puritanical, [and] most of the spirit of fun [was] bled from it."[25]

Part of the animosity was caused by the startling transformation in Soviet sport and the fear that the Soviets might soon leave the rest of the world behind. The development and perfection of athletes had become an industry, one that received support and attention from the government far beyond that of other nations. The Soviet sport system had its origins in the revolution of 1917. The communists assumed power in a nation mired in a health crisis. The devastation of war combined with the typically harsh Russian climate had left the populace racked by disease and malnutrition, and the new leaders launched a health program initially to rehabilitate the flagging health of the nation. From the first, this program was tied to politics, and the Soviets would never concur with the Western pretence that sport and politics should not mix; on the contrary, sport was a political tool. The fitness programs quickly assumed a military bent, as indicated in one explanation of the purpose of the Soviet program, which read, "The aim is achievement of a high level of physical development and physical preparation of the population for highly-productive labor and for carrying out the sacred duty of defense of the Homeland."[26] By World War II, the Soviets had established a massive national fitness program, infused the masses with an interest in and passion for athletics, and constructed many sports complexes and arenas to promote physical activity.[27] The physical fitness program was lauded by the government during World War II for generating a fit and well-trained fighting force.

Still, it was not until after World War II that the Soviets took an interest in the Olympics; in fact, they had avoided contact with what they perceived to be "bourgeois" sports of the West. But with the onset of the Cold War, athletics took on a wholly new character, becoming not only a "[vehicle] for Soviet cultural diplomacy" by building relations with neighboring countries but also a powerful tool for waging the Cold War.[28] Barring the outbreak of a true "hot war," victory in the international sports arenas became the best way to "demonstrate the vitality of the Soviet system," and besting "bourgeois" nations on the fields of sport became an obsession for national leaders.[29] In this period, sport was but one of many forms of culture that became a forum for competition between the superpowers, and each side struggled with vigor to produce the "best" musicians, dancers, composers, playwrights, chess players, and athletes.[30]

The massive Soviet sport program shifted its focus from national health and fitness to a single-minded mission to churn out the finest athletes in the world to defeat Western athletes. The Soviets pursued this goal with a zeal unmatched in the West, scouting opponents for weaknesses and scheduling only matches they knew they could win, obsessively training athletes in events that needed improvement, and seeking out budding athletes at ages as young as seven for intensive training. Within a few years, the Soviet system had blown past all reasonable interpretations of the amateur ideal, producing athletes who pushed even liberal definitions of "professional."[31]

This quest for dominance in international sport led the Soviets naturally toward the Olympics. They sent a group to the 1948 London Games to observe, or rather to scout, their opponents. They would not join the Olympic movement if they could not win, plain and simple. By 1951, the Soviets petitioned the IOC for admission, a break with their past policy of avoiding "bourgeois" events. As James Riordan, a scholar of Soviet sports, has noted, this change in policy occurred for a number of reasons: the waning influence of Stalin, who opposed participation in the Games; the decline of the global workers' sport movement, which left the Soviets "no one to play with"; the added security of the Soviet detonation of an atomic bomb; and the growing assurance that they could win.[32] The IOC heard the petition of the Soviets but not without debate. Brundage and others recognized the conflicts between the Soviet system and the amateur ideal, but in some ways Brundage had talked himself into a corner after twenty years in the Olympic movement. To avoid mingling sport with politics, as he had always contended, and also to prevent an uprising in communist nations, Brundage led the movement to admit the Soviets, which was done in May 1951. Even as he did so, Brundage conceded that the IOC had only promises that the Soviets would follow the rules of amateurism but that they had little idea what "took place behind the Iron Curtain."[33]

What did go on behind the Iron Curtain would be a source of controversy for the next forty years. The national fitness program, still designed to strengthen the masses for potential military service now served also as a massive talent search. Not only promising athletes but also dancers, musicians, chess players, and others were selected as children for special training. Those chosen for such programs were sent to boarding schools, where they received free tuition and coaching, room and board, travel to various camps and competitions, and some education. For many, this meant being separated from their parents at a young age and dedicating their lives to a pursuit before they even realized the implications. Soviet leaders countered that none of the students were forced to go, but in a society with few mechanisms for elevation, virtually no one turned down such an opportunity. Education at such schools focused on the development of the young body, with increasingly rigorous athletic training as the student aged, but also unflagging indoctrination in the superiority of the Soviet system. The budding athlete was constantly reminded of the mission at hand: to defeat the forces of capitalism. By the time an athlete reached maturity, he was consumed—or so the government hoped—with a passion for beating the West.[34]

After training in such institutions for years, the top athletes were enrolled at various military or club teams for international competition. To better their odds of victory, the Soviets often padded "amateur" teams with all-stars from the club leagues, as in a 1949 soccer match against Hungary, when a so-called typical team of amateurs from a local factory actually consisted of the top Soviet players, carefully chosen from teams around the nation.[35] The Soviets made every effort to conceal the obvious implications of this system for amateur eligibility. Top athletes were enrolled in military units or other professions, often showing up for "work" only once a month to collect a paycheck. In some cases, such associations drove them even further from the ranks of amateurism, as with those "soldiers" who were elevated to officers ranking as high as captain or major or "auto workers" who received brand new cars as a bonus for their performance. Other perks were less subtle, as athletes breaking world records, attaining a certain athletic title or rank, or winning major events received cash bonuses. Top athletes were hailed as national heroes, recognized throughout the nation and often honored on billboards and posters.[36]

If the Soviet system itself made a mockery of the amateur ideal, Western coaches, sponsors, and athletes were not much better. As historian S.W. Pope has demonstrated, "nineteenth-century amateurism was an invented tradition."[37] Athletic competition was always rooted in some variation of professionalism, including prizes and rewards, gambling money, cash payments, and more recently, sponsorship, college scholarships, and stuffed envelopes. The "amateur ideal" was an invention of the upper class to preserve a purity in sport that had never really existed. It was born in the elite colleges of the eastern United States, advanced by such men as Walter Camp, the great football coach at Yale, who said, "A gentleman does not make his living from his athletic prowess. He does not earn anything from his victories except glory and satisfaction. . . . A gentleman never competes for money, directly or indirectly."[38]

This ideal found a welcome home within the budding Olympism being formulated across the Atlantic, and an American "amateur tradition" was born. The fact that it masked a sporting tradition mired in "professionalism" was lost on those who wrote the canon of early Olympism, and that canon was recited by such followers as Avery Brundage until the realities of the life of an elite athlete were lost. As historian Ronald Smith explains, the very football players to whom Walter Camp preached violated the strictures of amateurism in many ways, including competing for money and prizes; competing against professionals; accepting gate receipts; benefiting from nutrition, meal plans, and tutors not available to all students; and playing for professional coaches. Many such breaches were also true of early Olympic athletes, often harvested from the ranks of top college athletes. True amateurism may *never* have reigned in the Olympics ("amateur" American athletes commonly participated in summer semi-professional leagues, barnstorming tours, or exhibitions for pay), but certainly by the 1912 Olympics the pitfalls of maintaining pure amateurism were clear. The expulsion of Jim Thorpe from the Olympic movement was the most publicized example of an athlete struggling to meet the amateur ideal, but, realistically, few if any top athletes could survive without additional income, a problem that was discussed openly in Olympic circles by the 1950s. The corruption that had always accompanied sport was again tainting the Olympics, making Western nations guilty of "professionalism" as well.[39]

The case of Wes Santee, the top American miler in the mid-1950s, exposed the ubiquity of cheating in American "amateur" sport. Expected to survive on meager meal allowances and reimbursements that barely paid for travel expenses, Santee was expelled from the Amateur Athletic Union and thus the Olympic movement for accepting too much expense money in 1956. Santee described a hectic and demanding lifestyle, constantly on the wing from one track meet to another. To hold down a full-time job would have been impossible, given the time he devoted to training as well as travel. How else to survive, other than to break the rules? Santee found that at virtually every track meet he attended, a brown envelope stuffed with cash awaited him. Meet organizers in need of marquee names or sponsors in search of a marketable name made sure that Santee ate fine meals, wore decent clothes, and had a car to drive—any one of which was enough to cost him amateur status. Santee was not a wealthy man and certainly was no superstar by any modern measure of the word. He was simply an athlete trying to survive. Doing that, while meeting the demands of the "amateur ideal," was simply impossible.[40]

By the early 1960s, these issues cried out for some kind of resolution. While both sides flung accusations across the ideological divide, no one near the debate believed that athletes could subsist while trying to remain "amateurs." As the debate heightened, calls came from many quarters to abolish the old "amateur ideal" and recognize that athletics at its finest requires a full-time commitment. "Why should we be so reluctant to admit that [the champion athlete] is a professional?" asked Rene Maheu, director-general of the United Nations Educational, Scientific, and Cultural Organization (UNESCO). "We deny the obvious fact that the champion is obliged to live the life of a professional athlete."[41]

As pressure for a change mounted, at its 1962 meeting in Moscow the International Olympic Committee revised Rule 26, on amateurism, to read: "When a competitor can prove that his dependents are suffering hardship because of his (or her) loss of salary or wages while attending the Olympic Games, his national Olympic committee may make a contribution to these dependents, but under no circumstances may it exceed the sum which he (or she) would have earned during his (or her) actual period of absence, which in turn must not exceed 30 days."[42] While the restrictions regarding the rule were still strict, a precedent had been established, and Brundage's firm grasp on the international definition of amateurism was loosened. Still, as the Mexico City Games approached, athletes from both East and West viewed each other with suspicious eyes. Even if the rules were relaxed, the chasm between the Soviets and the Americans had not been bridged, and it remained as wide as ever in 1968, with the issue of amateurism at the heart of the gap.

The Issue of Apartheid

No issue posed so real a threat to the 1968 Olympics as the controversy surrounding the participation of South Africa. What seemed a simple question—should the IOC exclude a nation whose government practiced apartheid—quickly became an issue confronted by every athlete, white and black, around the globe. After years of debate, by 1968 the IOC was left with only two choices: ban South Africa, thus conceding that sport and politics are intertwined; or allow South Africa to participate and face what promised to be a firestorm of protest. Before the matter was settled, the IOC had tried the second option, and when the firestorm of protest proved to be more than they could bear, they resorted to the first. In the interim, the decision to reinstate South Africa flung open the Pandora's box of racism and drew unto the IOC the rage and frustration of black athletes everywhere.

According to the IOC's Fundamental Principles, while individual nations may select their athletes as they choose, they must do so according to the "high ideals of the Olympic Movement." Those ideals are expressly stated: "no discrimination is allowed against a country or person on grounds of race, religion, or political affiliation."[43] Beyond these brief statements, though, the policies and behaviors of the IOC regarding racial discrimination are arbitrary and have been either enforced or ignored over the years both for many reasons and for none.

The South African policy of apartheid had been a source of international concern for years prior to the Olympic controversy but reached a head in the early 1960s as African nations began to participate in the Olympics for the first time. One such nation, seeking to send a team to Tokyo in 1964, was South Africa. The IOC, while hoping to preserve the divide between politics and sport, invoked the spirit of this "Olympic code" to deny the South African petition. Their justifications were not merely political. For apartheid, in addition to installing a fiercely racist system of government and social policy, also upset many of the traditions of fair play in sport that were so cherished by the Olympics. Sports organizations in South Africa unfailingly upheld apartheid policies, ensuring a sports system that was hopelessly unfair to blacks.

South African teams were not selected fairly; the evidence was ample and plain. Within South Africa, blacks and whites could not run on the same fields, play in the same arenas, swim in the same pools, or box in the same ring. How, then, could they hold Olympic trials? Blacks and whites could not room together or eat at the same table. They could not travel together. In short, there was no semblance of an integrated South African team. While there was no law, per se, prohibiting South Africans from competing in multiracial events abroad, many athletes who applied to travel for such a purpose found their passports denied. Even the spectators in South Africa were segregated. At first, they could watch the same events while sitting in separate sections; by the mid-1960s, though, spectators were only admitted to sporting events of their own race. In an attempt at compromise, the South Africans had begun to field two entirely separate teams, black and white, which traveled independently of each other and even had different uniforms. But throwing such a thin veil over their racist system did not appease the

IOC. In 1963, the IOC suspended South Africa, barring it from participation in the 1964 Olympics.[44]

The problem appeared to be settled. While IOC members regretted having to ban a nation for seemingly political reasons, the clear link to racism within the athletic system made the decision easier and not particularly controversial. But the South African government and athletic establishment hoped to gain admittance to the 1968 Olympics, and they began to institute changes to the system. They agreed to assemble one team comprised of black and white athletes, which would wear the same uniform and march under the same flag. The team would be housed in the same quarters and eat at the same table. Rules against blacks and whites playing on the same field would be waived not only for the Olympics but for all international sporting events. These developments were enough to warrant a second look from the IOC, which in September 1967 assembled an investigating committee to examine conditions in South Africa. The three committee members were Lord Killanin of Ireland, Reginald Alexander, a white Kenyan, and Sir Ade Ademola of Nigeria.[45]

This committee traveled throughout the country and was given full access to all sporting facilities and competitions. Their discoveries pointed to only limited improvement. The South African government still refused to allow interracial competition within the country, thus complicating and tainting the trial process. There would still be separate trials for black and white athletes, with the top performers from each competition then eliminated or accepted by a selection committee of four black and four white members. In an event such as boxing, in which only one winner would make the team and interracial competition was unavoidable, those contests would be staged outside of the national borders. And there was the still more complex matter of the sporting infrastructure, in which virtually no national support was given to sporting facilities to be used by budding black athletes while ample support went to those for white athletes. The mirage of separate-but-equal facilities was not supported by the facts. In one celebrated incident, world-class cricketer Basil D'Oliveira was so disappointed with the sporting equipment and facilities offered to black players that he moved to England, where he became a star. Even if the Olympic trials themselves were fair—and there were still plenty of questions about that—how could the Olympics endorse a system in which every obstacle was placed in the way of black athletes while every opportunity was offered to white athletes? These were complicated questions, and the 113-page report ultimately filed by the investigating committee reflected this complexity. Was it the responsibility of the IOC to ensure that a nation offered equal opportunity to every man, woman, and child to excel in their chosen sport or merely to ensure that the selection process itself was fair? The committee hesitated to make an unqualified recommendation, at the same time leaving the door open for admitting South Africa to the 1968 Olympics, noting that the progress made in South Africa provided "an acceptable basis for a multi-racial team to [be sent to] the Mexico Olympic Games."[46]

Meeting in Grenoble, France, in conjunction with the 1968 Winter Olympics, the IOC considered these issues in a heated debate. Complicating the issue was the not-so-secret fact that readmitting South Africa would likely inspire a massive boycott by other African nations, possibly precipitating a boycott by the Soviet Union and others. After weighing these issues, the committee voted 41–30 in favor of allowing South Africa to compete in Mexico City later that year. While the IOC "deplored" the policy of apartheid, it also was encouraged by the changes in the South African system and efforts to select a racially balanced team. The committee also voted to reconsider South Africa's status again in 1970.[47]

Even before the doors had closed behind the delegates leaving this meeting, a wave of international protest began building. The next day, the Olympic committees of Ethiopia and Algeria announced that they would not attend the Mexico City Olympics if South Africa was reinstated, invoking a clause formulated by African nations at the 1967 IOC meeting in Teheran, Iran, that allowed for such a withdrawal. They were joined by Tanzania, Uganda, the Republic of Mali, Ghana, and the United Arab Republic the following day. Abraham Ordio of the Nigerian Olympic Committee summed up the concerns of these nations: "What South Africa does in sports outside her borders is not as important as what she does inside her borders, which is a violation of the Olympic code."[48] Accompanying this early flood of withdrawals was speculation that the boycott might grow far larger—which it soon did, incorporating Nigeria, Kenya, and other African nations with larger Olympic teams.

As the list of nations expanded, so did the likely impact on the final medal count. While the absence of Ghana's athletes was not expected to influence the medal standings, losing Kenya's Kip Keino, one of the world's best milers, or Ethiopia's Abebe Bikila, the defending Olympic marathon champion, would make an impact. Even more ominous were thoughts of a boycott by the Soviets and their supporters and the hundreds of top athletes who comprised those teams. The Soviets traditionally supported the African nations, and they quickly issued statements suggesting that they would support them in this protest as well. One such statement called the IOC decision a "flagrant violation of the charter . . . that forbids discrimination of athletes for political, racial, or religious reasons."[49] Still more worrisome was the speculation that Mexico itself might refuse to hold the Games or that other Latin American nations would boycott as well.[50]

Speculation became reality as more nations joined the boycott, including Kenya, Syria, and Iraq in the following days. Soon after, the Supreme

Council for Sports in Africa, which oversaw sport in thirty-two independent African nations, approved the boycott, meaning that virtually all African nations would not be in Mexico City if South Africa were there. Other nations issued statements supporting the African boycott and condemning the IOC decision, including further rumblings from the Soviet Union and statements from Denmark, Sweden, and Norway. Giulio Onesti, president of the Italian Olympic Committee, publicly called for an extraordinary meeting of the IOC to reconsider the issue, stating that the Italians "deplored the true and proper split" of the thirty-two African nations and hoped to patch the IOC together again.[51]

Caught in the middle of this swirling controversy were black sportsmen in South Africa who had rejoiced at the announcement that their Olympic dreams might come true. A few black athletes and officials stood on the doorstep of the Olympics, but at what cost? What they perceived as a victory, the rest of Africa and much of the world saw as a concession to a racist nation. Fred Thabede, a black boxing official in South Africa, expressed the frustrations of other black athletes. "The African states," he argued, "know as well as any that for the past seven years South Africa's committee has been struggling to have an integrated team at the Olympics. And now what do these African states do? They slap us in the face in the most blatant showing of discrimination against our whites and nonwhites that I have ever seen."[52] Others in South Africa found even deeper importance in the IOC decision. The *South African Post,* a non-white newspaper, wrote: "The Olympic movement has succeeded where no one else ever succeeded before, namely, to cause a first crack in the monolithic block of apartheid policy. For the first time, the South African government has publicly admitted that nonwhites also are South African citizens."[53] Here was an opportunity for sport to make a real difference, to begin to strike down the walls of racism in South Africa. And yet it seemed that the whole world wanted the IOC to change its mind.

The tension mounted in the first weeks of March, as Belgium, Bulgaria, and Switzerland voiced their disapproval of South Africa's reinstatement, and opposition from the Soviet Union grew even more strenuous: a Soviet boycott appeared certain. Nations within the Soviet sphere of influence also objected to South African participation. The Polish Olympic Committee, perhaps recalling the tortures of Nazi occupation, issued a statement that it "loathed all nationalism and racial discrimination . . . [and protested] the readmission of a country that trample[d] the basic principles of coexistence of citizens of the same state." East Germany, too, joined the Soviets in protest.[54] Even Jamaica announced that its government would not pay for its Olympic team to go to Mexico City if South Africa attended. One commentator joked that the only ones left at the Olympics might be "Avery Brundage and South Africa."[55]

Still, many bristled at the prospect of a boycott, and Avery Brundage was one of many who spoke out. "No matter what countries withdraw, the Games in Mexico will go on," Brundage announced at a press conference. "We are sorry if countries want to withdraw for political reasons . . . the Mexico Games will go on, and they will be a success, like all other Olympic Games."[56] In the weeks after the initial vote, Brundage appeared intractable, insisting that since the IOC had already voted, there was no need to reconsider. He refused to use his powers as chief executive of the body to call for a full meeting of the IOC, even as members of the executive board urged him to do so. He simply would not budge on the issue.[57]

Brundage, while the most vocal opponent of the boycott, was not alone. Even as nations lined up in support of the African nations, others advocated competing even if South Africa attended. Great Britain, Puerto Rico, Greece, Denmark, Turkey, Italy, and Brazil, along with many others, all issued press releases stating that they would attend the Olympics, regardless of South Africa's status. Mexican officials themselves made only one official announcement in the weeks after South Africa's reinstatement: they would not send the South Africans an invitation until the IOC had settled the matter for certain, presumably at a special meeting. The rumors swirling about actions the Mexicans might take must have terrified members of the various organizing committees. There were any number of possibilities: the Games would be held, whichever teams showed up; the Mexicans would boycott the Games along with the Africans, insisting that South Africa be banned; the Mexicans would cancel the Games altogether. In truth, the Mexicans shrewdly refused to show significant concern, choosing instead to await the final decision of the IOC. While the prospect of a boycott was surely a daunting one, Mexican leadership projected an image of calm. In the interest of speeding that decision along, though, General Clark, now vice president of the IOC behind Brundage, sent a letter endorsed by four other members of the executive council urging Brundage to call a full meeting of the IOC to re-open the issue.[58]

Perhaps out of deference to Clark, a longtime friend and ally, and perhaps yielding to the pressure mounting from various quarters, Brundage agreed to call a special meeting of the executive board of the IOC, held on 21 April in Lausanne, Switzerland. While not a meeting of the full committee, the concession was an opening wedge that would ultimately lead to the revocation of South Africa's invitation. The board's nine members issued a telegram to the rest of the IOC strongly urging them to withdraw the invitation. A subsequent vote by mail confirmed this action. While Brundage remained disappointed with the decision, he could no longer deny the overwhelming sentiment against South Africa, and other board members were satisfied with the ruling. Lord Killanin of Ireland, who had chaired the investigating committee that first opened the door for readmission, explained the decision to the press. In addition to the threat of a boycott or even of Mexico's refusal to support the Games, Killanin cited the possibility of violence against South Africans and their supporters. His comments demonstrated that long-held racist notions were not easily dismissed. "You can't guarantee against embarrassments," he added. "The Mexicans are a proud people. There might have been trouble, you can't guarantee against it."[59]

There were other reasons behind the ruling as well. In the United States, the South Africa controversy had revived a flagging boycott movement among black athletes. Dozens of black Americans, many ranked at the top of their sports, threatened to boycott Mexico City. Their unity with the African nations, the Soviets, and others only added more gravity to the threat of a boycott. Finally, one tragic event united all those concerned in the greater interest of humanity. On 4 April, Martin Luther King, Jr., was assassinated in Memphis, Tennessee. The executive board and others considering the South African petition noted the event with sadness, and many said that King's death played a role in their debate. Ought not the board, now more than ever, be sensitive to the union of race and sport and strive for the same measures of fairness and equality that King died for? Only a few weeks after King's death, and with his memory heavy on everyone's mind, the IOC simply could not justify readmitting a nation built upon racism and repression. South Africa was out.[60]

Constantin Adrianov, the Russian representative to the board, was especially pleased with the outcome. He left the meeting smiling broadly, knowing that the ruling saved the Soviets from having to make a difficult decision. The Soviets had walked a delicate line without stumbling. They had supported the boycott movement from its inception but had not made a firm commitment to boycott themselves. Had they committed too early, the Soviets would have damaged their reputation within the IOC, a reputation that had been improving steadily since joining the Olympic movement in 1952. Had they not supported the African cause, they would have given ground to China, with whom they competed for the favor of Third World nations. Balanced between these opposing possibilities, the Soviets dangled the prospect of a boycott without making any definitive statements. This prospect of a Soviet boycott, including many other nations, contributed to the pressure that forced the reversal, although Andrianov denied such an influence. When asked if the threat of a Soviet boycott had forced the decision, he seemed startled. "Threat?" he asked. "At no time have we made a threat of boycott. What we have said was that if South Africa were admitted, we would have a meeting and reconsider our attitude toward competing. We made no threat."[61]

The prospect of a Soviet boycott had been more imminent than even the press suspected. Leaders of the Soviet Olympic Committee, not long before the final vote of the executive board, exchanged memos with the Soviet government in Moscow—memos that nearly forced a Soviet boycott regardless of the South Africa ruling. As one government official asked, "If it is possible not to compete if South Africa does, why shouldn't we stay away anyway, to save all that hard currency?" "National prestige," came the reply. The Soviets had grown accustomed to using sport as a mechanism for demonstrating the superiority of their people, their government, and their organizational capabilities, and the Olympics was the grandest stage for such a demonstration. But a poor showing in the Olympics would have just the opposite effect.

The exchange continued: "Can the Soviet athletes defeat the Americans at the Games?" One can almost feel the Soviet Olympic Committee gulp, recognizing where this line of questioning was heading. If the government was eager to save the money to be spent on the Olympic team and was not convinced that Soviet athletes would make a good showing, the entire Soviet Olympic enterprise was in danger. The Olympic committee hastily drew up "scientific proof" that they could indeed defeat the Americans at the Games: lists of athletes, times, scores, and measures demonstrating Soviet superiority. And, ultimately, the Soviets did not boycott the Olympics. This exchange is but one more example of how closely the Soviets and the Americans watched each other during this period and the aspirations they held for sport as a mechanism in "winning" the Cold War.[62]

Such a boycott would only have heightened Cold War tensions between the Soviets and the Western nations, in addition to erasing the possibility of waging the Cold War on the fields of sport. With the executive board's reversal, not only would they not have to boycott the Games but they could appear to have won a standoff with the West. If their support of the boycott had been a bluff, it was a successful one, and Adrianov's smile was justified.[63]

While there were many who supported the ruling, others were disappointed with it, even despondent. The decision to readmit South Africa had been based on a number of policy changes that, however superficial they might have appeared to outsiders, had cracked the severity of racism in sport. With South Africa now banned, what motivation would the South African government have for easing racist policies? Making compromises with the IOC was pointless, so why not restore apartheid measures in sport? The black athletes and officials who had rejoiced at the initial decision were crushed by the reversal. Their hopes of equality had been dashed, and the prospects for further change appeared grim. A suggestion from USOC member Asbury Coward, that such athletes (and white South African athletes as well) be allowed to compete in the

Olympics as independents, marching under the Olympic flag, went un-heeded. The South African Olympic Committee, too, was outraged at the decision. Perhaps having pent up roiling emotions in the months while the decision was under debate, after the reversal the South Africans no longer restrained their anger. Reg Honey, South African representative to the IOC, called for the resignation of the entire executive board and de-clared the ruling "illegal and immoral." Frank Braun, president of the South African Olympic Committee, added bitterly, "We will accept the il-legal position as it stands now in a gentlemanly manner."[64] And John Vorster, Prime Minister of South Africa, jabbed, "[we are] back in the jun-gle, [and we might as well have] tree climbing events as Olympic Games."[65] But while most in South Africa ranted about the decision, some South Africans hoped to gain something positive from it. In Cape Town, the press largely accepted the decision, hoping that the ruling "will cause a fresh wave of soul-searching in the national party."[66]

Perhaps most stricken by the decision was Avery Brundage. Steadfast throughout the controversy, after the ruling the eighty-year-old Olympic president began to show his age. Appearing weary, beaten, and at times teary-eyed, Brundage hinted that he might retire in the wake of the con-flict. During the Mexico City Olympics, the IOC would hold elections for the presidency and other offices. As he addressed the press in Lausanne, Brundage said he wondered "whether [he] would accept the invitation to take another term if the invitation [was extended]." The defender of the separation between sport and politics had suffered a grave blow.[67]

Brundage anticipated that changing policies in sport based on political reasons would start the Olympics down a slippery slope, the bottom of which was a long way down. He argued that no nation is without its flaws, so sport must be kept above such considerations, or every interna-tional competition will be plagued with protests and boycotts. As if hear-ing such complaints from Brundage, on 23 April, the same day in which the vote banning South Africa became official, Jack McDonald, U.S. Rep-resentative from Michigan, called for the exclusion of the Soviet Union from the Olympics. Were not Jews in Russia persecuted as harshly as blacks in South Africa? "Is Russia's long record of persecution of the Jew-ish religion less obnoxious than South Africa's policy toward its black people?" he asked. Similar questions were raised again in September, as many pointed out the hypocrisy of banning South Africa while not ban-ning the Soviet Union after its invasion of Czechoslovakia. Czechoslova-kia's top Olympic athlete, runner Emil Zapotek, appeared on Czech tele-vision shortly after the invasion, demanding that Russia and its allies be banned from the upcoming Olympics. The slope grew more slippery with such pronouncements.[68]

While few took McDonald's resolution seriously, the South Africa con-troversy did have an interesting footnote further proving the entanglements between sport and politics. South Africa's neighbor Rhodesia was ultimately banned from the Olympics as well. While Rhodesia's government was based on similarly racist policies, it had made more compromises on the field of sport and through a fairer system of trials would bring an integrated team to the Olympics. On 12 June, however, the Mexican Olympic Committee announced that Rhodesia would not be allowed to participate. The Rhodesians, it seemed, were under a travel ban enforced by the United Nations, who would not issue passports to the team. They had hoped to make the trip by using Olympic documents, but the Mexicans refused to overlook the U.N. ban. Was the Rhodesian exclusion motivated by the same political and racial factors driving that of South Africa, or were the Mexicans simply obeying the U.N. travel ban? Whatever the reasons, Avery Brundage again bemoaned the ties between sport and politics. One Rhodesian newspaper described the slippery slope even more eloquently: "The Mexican politicians may win in the end, but first let Rhodesia try to shame Mexico into realizing the paradox of excluding a nonracial Rhodesian team so as to teach Rhodesians nonracialism."[69]

The Cultural Olympics

Even as the clamor over a variety of controversies carried on, preparations for the Games continued in Mexico City. With the Opening Ceremonies still a year away, one important part of the Olympics began as the Cultural Olympics were inaugurated with a spectacular show. On 12 October 1967, as darkness fell over the pyramids at Teotihuacán, their silhouettes hung eerily against the orange backdrop of sunset. Then piercing lights shot from the ground into the night sky, dancing between the structures, around and over them. The biblical voice of Charlton Heston boomed from the dark, telling tales of ancient peoples building the pyramids. The voices of Vincent Price, Burt Lancaster, Charles Bronson, and others picked up the narrative, speaking of the *Mexica,* a nomadic people who discovered their sacred symbol, an eagle perched on a cactus, a snake in its mouth, at the site where the pyramids stand. Music rose and fell behind the voices, much of it played on pre-Columbian instruments. For several hours, a small crowd of mostly American tourists watched the presentation, drinking in both the spectacular light show and the Mexican history and mythology. As the lasers fizzled to a stop and the music died down, dim floodlights lit the pyramids, and the visitors concluded the evening with a hurried walk back to their cars and buses in silence, surrounded by the chill of late October air and the ghosts of Mexico's past.[70]

The sound and light show at the pyramids was one of the first events of the year-long "Cultural Olympics," a celebration of international customs and artistry that rivaled the athletic contests in scope and scale. The

Mexicans took to heart their status as the first Latin American nation to host the Games, and they genuinely sought to make their Olympics the warmest, broadest, and most egalitarian sporting event ever held. In preparing for the Games, organizers struggled with a difficult dilemma: how best to present Mexico as a modern, progressive nation while still preserving the charm and simplicity of Mexican life? It was a difficult task to deliver the grandest Olympics yet while faced with grim financial realities and limitations. Under the aegis of López Mateos, who first chaired the organizing committee, the Mexicans sought to emulate the Tokyo Games of 1964, for which the Japanese had spent billions of dollars in delivering a lavish sports festival. In 1966, after López Mateos resigned his position due to poor health, the architect Pedro Rámirez Vázquez assumed leadership of the organizing committee and restored fiscal responsibility in the process. While still spending far more than the original planning committee had anticipated, under the guidance of Rámirez Vázquez the Mexicans managed to stage an outstanding competition for less than 10 percent of what the Japanese had spent. Part of achieving such cost efficiency was an attempt to emphasize Mexican culture and pragmatism rather than gaudiness and grandeur.[71]

A major part of their agenda in that regard was the Cultural Olympics, the first of its kind but now an accepted part of Olympic tradition. The cultural festival was the brainchild of Ramírez Vázquez. Under his skillful guidance, the Cultural Olympics equaled, and in some ways surpassed, the athletic contests: more nations—and more individuals—participated in the cultural events; the artistic achievements were warmly received by spectators and critics and played out before huge audiences; and in some cases the artwork produced for the Games still stands while few of the athletic records lasted more than a few years. If the Olympics themselves became for many a symbol of the government's shortsightedness and poor fiscal policy, the Cultural Olympics was an accomplishment without blemish, a testament to all that was right in Mexico.[72]

The Cultural Olympics served several purposes, though organizers could scarcely have imagined they would be so successful. First, they served as a form of advertising for the Olympics. The cultural events began in the fall of 1967 and continued throughout the year, thereby constantly not only exposing Mexicans to the artists themselves but also reminding them of the athletic festival to come in October 1968. Newspapers were filled with mention of the Olympics long before the athletes started to arrive. It seemed that every play, every dance, every art festival or poetry reading was advertised under the Olympic logo. Mexican television ran programs describing the events, encouraging attendance at local theaters, musical performances, and the ballet. Local businesses got into the spirit, advertising not only Olympic dinners, Olympic parties, and Olympic weddings, but Olympic hairdos and Olympic watches, Olympic houses and Olympic brandy, Olympic banks and Olympic dresses. If there were Mexicans who were unaware that the Olympics were coming, they were few in number; by October, they flocked to Mexico City in droves.[73]

Second, the Cultural Olympics advanced understanding and appreciation of other peoples and cultures. The spokesman of the program, Oscar Urrutia, summarized this aim of the Cultural Olympics by citing an ancient Mexican poem, "Yet even more do I love my brother Man."[74] Hearing poetry of the ancient Greeks and modern Africans, watching dances of Chinese girls and German boys, viewing modern art from the United States and classical art from Britain, reading the Dead Sea Scrolls and listening to the Duke Ellington Orchestra could not help but broaden the thinking of Mexicans, many of whom rarely left their home villages or cities.[75]

Third, the Cultural Olympics would level the playing field, allowing smaller or poorer nations to compete in the same arena with the superpowers. In the words of President Díaz Ordaz, "In physical strength, size, sources of wealth, economic development, and in other areas, certain countries may be outstanding . . . [but] in loftiness of thought, no nation, no one group of people can consider itself superior to the rest."[76]

Finally, the Cultural Olympics would send a message to the rest of Latin America and the world that Mexico was a modern and progressive country, no longer mired in the *mañana* and *machista* attitudes of the past, an element of the Cultural Olympiad's significance that has been well described by Eric Zolov. The cultural festival featured not only modern works of art and sculpture but also displays featuring architecture and design, space exploration, and nuclear power. Such displays, even if they were borrowed from other nations, conveyed a message of modernism, telling visitors that Mexico was in tune with the latest trends in not only fashion, music, and entertainment but also technology, transportation, and energy.[77]

In more subtle ways, the Cultural Olympics indicated to the world that Mexico was advancing philosophically and politically, as the sweeping scope of the exhibits incorporated contributions intentionally drawn from all regions of the world, representing all major religions and political systems, and including men, women, and children. The idea of gender equality was one that permeated several aspects of the Games and led to a noteworthy accomplishment in the Olympic torch bearer, Norma Enriqueta Basilio, the first woman so honored. At the same time, the ubiquitous presence of the Olympic hostesses, or *edecanes*, who bore a striking resemblance to 1960s airline stewardesses, undermined this progressive message. Even more pertinent, there were no women in the highest ranks within the Mexican Organizing Committee, and none participated in the bidding presentation, while vast numbers of them labored in the organization as secretaries and translators. Even as they tried to advance an image of gender equity, organizers struggled to overcome deep-seated traditions of male dominance.[78]

The triumvirate overseeing the cultural events was comprised of Ramírez Vázquez, Urrutia, an architect who had worked with him often in the past, and Mathias Goeritz, a German native and restless artist who fled the Holocaust before World War II and worked in many media, including painting, sculpture, and architecture. Urrutia served as the program coordinator and spokesman, and in a press conference on 15 July he explained many of the upcoming events and exhibits. The largest exhibit was the "Route of Friendship," a collection of eighteen modern sculptures lining a ten-mile stretch of highway approaching the city and ending at the Olympic Village. Organized by Goeritz, the exhibit featured original works from some of the top sculptors in the world, at least one from each continent, with sixteen countries represented. It intended to unify artists from all regions, ethnic groups, and political trends to one artistic purpose. Such limitations meant that the final group consisted of not necessarily the finest artists from each continent but rather those best qualified while still meeting the demands for diversity. Each artist delivered a scale model of the sculpture to the organizing committee, and then local workers constructed each sculpture to full-scale in concrete along the roadside. While some compromises of the original artists' intent were made to fit the financial and environmental realities of the project, none of the artists withdrew their submissions, and ultimately all were completed to generally positive reviews. The smallest of the sculptures was 20 feet high. The tallest, nearly 80 feet high, was the crown jewel of the collection. "Red Sun," designed by renowned English sculptor Alexander Calder, still stands in front of the Aztec Stadium.[79]

The program included hundreds of significant artists, writers, and performers from all over the world, including Eugene Ionesco, the playwright; The Bolshoi Ballet from Moscow; The Martha Graham Dance Company from the United States; Van Cliburn, the pianist; an international film festival; a festival of Mexican folklore; dozens of plays and orchestral performances; and a massive World Youth Camp at the Olympic Village, estimated at 20,000 Mexican children and an equal number from around the world.[80] It also included exhibitions and displays of paintings and artwork, including works donated by the Avery Brundage Foundation in San Francisco and noted art collector Richard Brown Baker of New York; works from English artists J.M.W. Turner and Francis Bacon; a display of classical Japanese art; a "Festival of Children's Painting"; a show of architectural plans and models; a collection of postage stamps from around the world; a painting by Salvador Dali, "The Cosmic Athlete," and one by Paul Gauguin, "Vairu Mati"; and a huge mural by the great Mexican muralist David Alfaro Siqueiros.

The Americans zealously supported the Cultural Olympics and seemed intent on dominating the cultural festival as well as the athletic competition. Perhaps due to proximity, but also wealth and commitment, the United States contributed more to the Cultural Olympics than any other nation. President Lyndon Johnson explained U.S. involvement in the program: "If we have never learned it before, we humans would be wise to learn it now: we are brothers, we live in one world, and we will survive in peace on our planet only if we know and appreciate each other."[81] As such, the United States sent, among others, the Phoenix Singers, a New Orleans jazz band, and several dance troupes, as well as exhibits on nuclear energy, the space program, contemporary art, Navajo sandpainting and weaving, architectural design, and the history of the Olympic Games. The United States was particularly interested in the Olympic Nuclear Exhibits, demonstrating not only U.S. domination of this critical field but also American generosity in sharing equipment and technology, on a limited basis, with Mexico. The exhibit was a popular and diplomatic success, and it was supported by a visit of Vice President Hubert Humphrey to Mexico City in April. Humphrey toured Mexican Olympic facilities and in a series of meetings and luncheons discussed American and Mexican cooperation regarding nuclear energy and the American exhibit. His tour concluded with a well-publicized visit to the Mexican Olympic Sports Center, which he said "probably reached the Mexican public more effectively than any other" part of the tour. In an era when cultural exchange was a significant spoke in the diplomatic wheel, the United States clearly saw the Olympics, and the exhibits accompanying them, as an opportunity to win supporters in Mexico City.[82]

The Cultural Olympics met—even exceeded—the expectations of its organizers. But some commentators noted an unforeseen drawback to the festival: the rich and fascinating culture of the Mexicans themselves was overshadowed by hundreds of imports from faraway lands. During the Olympics, spectators listened to the music of Beethoven and watched the plays of Arthur Miller and observed the sculptures along the highway built by artists from around the world. They witnessed a Mexico City striving to be modern, structured, and organized, with the most up-to-date technologies and buildings. To some observers, such as Octavio Paz, the undertaking was a façade, masking the realities of Mexico from the millions of visitors. Paz wrote, "The Mexican seems to be a person who shuts himself away to protect himself. His face is a mask and so is his smile. . . . He builds a wall of indifference and remoteness between reality and himself, a wall that is no less impenetrable for being invisible. The Mexican is always remote, from the world and from other people. And also from himself."[83] The Cultural Olympics exemplified this remoteness. The Mexicans welcomed foreigners who came to see the Games, and they put on a vast cultural festival, but observers came away knowing more about Europeans than Mexicans. Travelers noted that the Mexicans, especially Mexican youth, had a great admiration of American culture and sought to emulate it whenever possible. The Mexicans, it seemed, were perpetuating the Latin American tradition, seeking legitimacy through the imitation and satisfaction of foreigners. Thus the Cultural Olympics celebrated European and American culture, relegating Mexican culture to a lesser stature.[84]

The Cultural Olympics picked up its pace on 12 September, one month before the Opening Ceremonies, as several events got underway, including "The History and Art of the Olympic Games," a gallery of art devoted to the Olympics from their ancient origins to the present; "Space for Sports and Cultural Activities," a show of the latest gymnasiums and stadiums, concert halls, and the like; a "Festival of Children's Painting"; and "Kineticism: System Sculpture in Environmental Situations," a show of modern sculpture depicting sport and movement. As the Cultural Olympics steamed ahead, other happenings indicated that the start of the Games neared. Tourists, international media, and athletic teams began to arrive, and the bustle surrounding the Olympic Village and the sporting arenas increased. And the Olympic Torch made its way from Greece, its gradual approach building the excitement.[85]

Even as the start of the Games inched closer, the international media —and Mexicans themselves—wondered if the Mexicans could pull it off. A recurring theme in stories about the upcoming Olympics was the so-called *"mañana"* attitude among Mexicans, a general laziness and tendency to procrastinate that surely would doom an undertaking of such magnitude. But organizers knew that if the city was not ready, it would not be laziness that was the problem: getting ready for the Olympics was simply a huge undertaking. In making their successful bid for the Games, committee members had stressed the athletic facilities already available in the city. After several members visited the 1964 Olympics in Tokyo, Japan, they were shocked to see that the Japanese poured some 2.7 billion dollars into preparing for the Games, including construction of a high-speed train and massive urban improvements. The Mexicans were not prepared to spend that kind of money. The committee re-examined the facilities available and drew up new building plans, borrowing ideas from the Japanese. Their "shoestring" budget of improvements came to $84 million U.S. dollars in federal spending, coupled with some $75 million from private investors, for those projects directly related to the Olympics. It is difficult to gauge exactly how much the nation spent in preparing for the Games, since auditors did not include such projects as a new six-lane highway connecting the facilities, considering them either regular expenses or permanent improvements. Among the improvements the committee deemed necessary were a massive series of building projects, including the Olympic

Village, improvements to roads, water supply lines, and sewage facilities, and most controversial, a subway system. While it was hoped that such projects would ease the horrible congestion and pollution in the city, during construction such problems only became worse. Visitors to Mexico City in the months prior to the Games were understandably skeptical that the projects could be completed in time.[86]

In addition to these major projects, the committee undertook many lesser ones as well. The Olympic stadium was marked with huge orange balloons, visible from miles away, and balloons and banners throughout the city marked the way to various venues. A white line was painted on the streets leading to the Olympic stadium. "Street fixtures" incorporating streetlights, benches, mailboxes, street signs, telephone booths, and the like adorned the street sides. For visitors still not comfortable making their way around unchaperoned, 3,400 special taxis rode along the Olympic routes, and nearly 1,000 "Olympic girls" were hired for the Games. These pretty, multilingual young women in miniskirts walked amongst the Olympic venues offering directions, assistance, or simply conversation to visitors. Gardens and walkways throughout the city were improved, over 40,000 flowers adorned major landmarks, and over 10,000 trees were planted along major thoroughfares. Hotel construction, expansion, and renovation, which was moving at a frenetic pace even before the Olympic bid, quickened all the more after it. So rapid was this construction that Mexico City was expected to outpace—by 10,000 or more—the 50,000 rooms it had promised in its initial bid for the Games. The largest and most luxurious hotel, the Sheraton Maria Isabel, added 400 rooms, and at least four other major luxury hotels were completed by October. To handle the rush of tourists filling such hotels, new agencies were formed to take reservations for transportation, lodging, and tickets to the events, and a new fleet of taxis and buses was prepared especially for the Olympics.[87]

Such improvements did not even consider the vast building projects related to athletic contests, which in mid-summer were far from complete. An international contest among architects produced revolutionary designs for several buildings, most notably the Sports Palace, an $8 million, 25,000-seat arena for boxing, basketball, fencing, and other indoor sports, topped by a spectacular copper geodesic dome. By mid-June, it was nearly complete except for the floor and some seating. The University Stadium, recently expanded from 57,000 to 80,000 seats, was ready and featured a new track. The even larger Aztec Stadium, for soccer, had been completed in 1966, including an eight-foot-deep moat ringing the stadium, a hazard to any potentially rowdy soccer fans attempting a charge onto the field. A velodrome for the cycling events, sporting the steepest incline in the world—39 degrees, to prevent cyclists from flying off the track in the thin air—also neared completion.[88]

Other facilities were far from finished. The high-tech pool, including the first sensitive plates built into the sides for precise timing, was ready, but the new swimming and diving center around it awaited a roof and seats in the stands. A smaller gymnasium for volleyball still had no floor. The Olympic Village itself, 29 buildings of six and ten stories, was a hive of activity as round-the-clock construction continued. Other buildings, including a media center, two commercial centers, an international club, and a medical clinic were in the early stages of construction. The pace of construction on such projects grew more frantic as the deadline approached.[89]

The organizing committee set 31 August as the deadline to have all projects complete—a few weeks before the rush of media and tourists was expected to arrive. That deadline came and went, with workers still toiling furiously to have everything ready. In the first week of September, there remained much to be done. The floors in the basketball and volleyball centers were still under construction. The lights in the volleyball center were taken out, as it was found they were too bright for the players to tolerate, and a new system was being installed. The swimming pool, already filled with water, required new tiles. The Olympic flame was not ready to go. Walls around the Olympic stadium were too high. The press booths had no furniture. Roadsides awaited landscaping. Perhaps not one of these details was catastrophic, but in general, with little over a month until the Opening Ceremonies, the city and the Olympic facilities had a rough, unfinished look and feel about them.[90]

Even with work still under way, President Díaz Ordaz made his tour of the facilities on 12 September and inaugurated many of the new buildings. In his estimation, Mexico City was ready for the Games to begin. There were still some glitches to be taken care of, and work would continue until the very eve of the Games. They may have cut it close, but with only a few exceptions the preparations were completed. The media center never quite made it—during a rain storm the roof leaked so badly that a corps of Mexican boy scouts ran between the typewriters with garbage cans to catch the water streaming from the ceiling. Aside from a few such problems, though, the city was well prepared.[91]

As the date of the Opening Ceremonies approached, Mexico appeared to be living up to its promise as a modernizing nation. While questions lingered regarding the thin air, the amateurism debate, and the boycott movement, it seemed that the crisis had been averted and the Olympics would proceed as planned. The Cultural Olympics generated excitement and momentum in Mexico and abroad, and as the Games drew near there was great international anticipation. Olympic organizers would have shuddered to think that the greatest challenges to their Olympics were still to come, as black American athletes contemplated still more action, and a nascent student movement in Mexico swelled in the summer heat.

Mexican hostesses, such as Lourdes Ochoa and Martha Glés de Costo pictured here, were ever-present during the Olympics. Such hostesses simultaneously represented an attractive, modern, independent Mexican woman and reminded observers of the traditional, male-dominated, machismo culture. National Archives and Records Administration, College Park, MD, Still Pictures collection, RG 306-OG-122 (hereafter referenced as NARA).

Mexico's attempt to present itself as both a modern, cosmopolitan nation and one with a rich cultural history is well represented by Olympic hosts such as José Ambrosio, pictured here dressed in the costume of a charro horseback rider. NARA, RG 306-OG-50-10.

The giant sculptures of the "Route of Friendship" were one of the most impressive aspects of the "Cultural Olympics," none more impressive than Alexander Calder's "Red Sun," outside the Aztec Stadium. NARA, RG 306-OG-45x.

Observers take in the Children's Art Exhibit, one of the favorite exhibits of the "Cultural Olympics." NARA, RG 306-OG, proof sheets.

The pageantry and symbolism of the Games are evident in this photo, showing the array of flags at the Olympic Village, with "Signal Du Village Olympique," a sculpture from the Route of Friendship by Belgian sculptor Jacques Moeschal, in the background. U.S. Olympic members stand at attention at the Olympic Village. In the background stands Moeschal's sculpture. NARA, RG 306-OG, proof sheets and RG 306-OG-20.

The United States considered its Space Exhibit one of its most important contributions to the "Cultural Olympics," and a means to impress both allies and rivals with its impressive technology. This series of photos shows, first, the entrance to the U.S. Space Exhibit on the day of its opening, Oct. 19, 1968. The exhibit attracted many interested observers, including Soviet Astronaut Gherman Titov, shown here viewing an Apollo capsule. He is accompanied by U.S. Ambassador Fulton Freeman and Mexican Olympic Organizer Pedro Ramírez Vázquez. Finally, U.S. hopes of impressing foreigners with the Space Exhibit had the desired effect on at least one Mexican boy, pictured here next to a full-scale model of a U.S. space satellite. NARA, RG 306-OG-67-4; RG 306-OG-66-12; and RG 306-OG-65-3.

Despite the intense competition in the various sports arenas, the athletes often put aside their Cold War rivalry in quieter moments. Here, Soviet and American athletes share such a moment in the Olympic Village, as Yevgeny Lapinsky and Eduard Sibiriskov watch Vincent Matthews and Al Robinson in a game of chess. In another such instance, Soviet athletes Vladimir Sochin and Eduard Sbodnikov watch a game on television with American wrestler Larry Kristoff. NARA, RG 306-OG-55-5 and RG 306-OG-132.

The athletic contests were so compelling that many observers forgot about the various controversies preceding the Games. The thin air, once thought to be a detriment, contributed to an unprecedented barrage of records in the track and field competition. Dick Fosbury, shown here, captivated spectators of the high jump competition while winning the gold medal. The other photo shows Kip Keino and Ben Jipcho at the conclusion of the 1500 meter final, in which Keino prevailed over American Jim Ryun. Some attributed Keino's victory to the thin air, as Keino trained at high elevation in Kenya, while Ryun struggled to adapt to the conditions. NARA, RG 306-OG-237 and RG 306-OG-228.

The signature moment of the Closing Ceremonies, when the scoreboard changed from "Mexico 68" to "Munich 72." Despite organizers' efforts to maintain order, athletes, spectators and performers gathered on the track in a joyous crowd. NARA Still Pictures, RG 306-OG, proof sheets.

Image Tarnished

The Revolt of the Black Athlete

three

September 18, 1968, should have been one of the best days of John Carlos' life. He was at the end of a four-week stay at Echo Summit, a top resort in Lake Tahoe, California. The first hints of fall sent cool breezes through the tall pines, and the weather invigorated him. He had spent the month training with the finest athletes in the country, jabbing and jockeying with each other in friendly competition, a daily regimen that left Carlos in the best shape of his life. He was 23 years old, and he was about to qualify for the Olympic Games.

As his race, the 200 meters, approached, Carlos breathed in the crisp air with confidence. He jawed at the other competitors, explaining in detail how he would defeat them. This was his time. At his best, John Carlos had the fastest start of any sprinter in the world, and for this race, he was at his best. After only a few steps, he could no longer see the other competitors at either side. A few more steps, and he could not even hear them. It seemed he was alone on the track. As he streaked across the finish line, Carlos knew it had been a great race, a perfect race. The time reflected as much: 19.7 seconds, a world record. For about five seconds, Carlos drank in the most satisfying victory of his life.

It took only about five seconds for U.S. Olympic Committee officials to meet him on the track and to begin souring this, his finest moment. For this race,

Carlos had worn a new product sent by his shoe company, Puma, a sprinting shoe called the "brush" shoe. Rather than having six lengthy spikes, as did the standard sprinter's shoe, the "brush" shoe had some sixty tiny spikes, or brushes. In theory, the new design impeded the runner's step less than a standard shoe and was the ultimate design for the popular faux cinder Tartan tracks, like the one at Echo Summit. Whether or not the shoe actually aided Carlos' heroic run is unclear, but Olympic officials, who knew he was wearing the shoe before the race began, hurried to inform him that the world record would not stand.

While disappointed, Carlos was not surprised. He felt it was but one in a string of injustices perpetrated against him—and against all black athletes in America. Had not white officials, that same week, informed all the black athletes that, should they qualify for the Olympics, they were required to perform "in honor of the United States," or they would be sent home from Mexico?[1] Had not those same officials, for reasons unexplained, ruled that Carlos, who had missed a key qualifying event with a torn hamstring, could attempt to qualify for the Olympics in the 200 meters but not the 100, his best event? Had not those same officials allowed an unusually large pool of qualifiers to come to Lake Tahoe, hoping—or so many black athletes believed—to ensure that plenty of white competitors would be available in case the black athletes decided to boycott the Olympics? No, it was no surprise that white officials soiled his proudest moment. It merely ensured that, rather than leave Tahoe happy and proud to represent his nation, Carlos left bitter and more determined than ever to make some sort of statement during the Olympics.[2]

The Black Athlete in America

John Carlos was among the angriest in a group of black American athletes who were frustrated not only by the actions of white officials listed above but also by an entire society and athletic establishment dominated by whites at the expense of blacks. In 1967, these athletes, energized by the shift in the Civil Rights Movement toward the aggressive, confrontational tactics of Black Power, began to organize, creating a sort of union of black athletes. On the eve of the Mexico City Olympics, their threats and protests, coupled with the boycott controversy over South Africa's participation, threatened to permanently scar an already wounded Olympiad. As it was, these struggles indelibly marked the Mexico City Olympics: the raised fists of two of these athletes became the most enduring image of the Games rather than the countless joyous images of Mexican citizens and tourists enjoying the festival. At the same time, those raised fists spoiled hopes within the U.S. government that the 1968 Olympics would be a triumphant moment in the Cold War for the United States.[3]

In the wake of the World War II, the realm of sport was on the cutting edge of the Civil Rights Movement. Most famously, Jackie Robinson captured headlines not only in the sports pages but also on the front pages of newspapers across the nation when the Montreal Royals, a minor league team owned by the Brooklyn Dodgers, signed him in 1946. His signing was seen as a monumental event, a harbinger of racial equality that would surely follow. Roy Wilkins, president of the NAACP, voiced such aspirations, saying that, by taking the field with white ball players, Robinson "will be saying to [black Americans] that his people should have their rights, should have jobs, decent hours and education, freedom from insult, and equality of opportunity to achieve."[4] Others felt even more strongly. "He was our Messiah," recalled Ed Charles, the third baseman for the Kansas City Athletics, in 1968. "He was Moses to our people. He gave us all pride. It wasn't just baseball, it was everything. We had a dream and he made it come true. Now, we could dream about everything."[5]

Robinson's success opened the door for other black athletes to follow, still seven years prior to the 1954 landmark Civil Rights decision *Brown v. Topeka Board of Education*. In July 1947, the Cleveland Indians signed Larry Doby, making him the first black player in the American League. Following Robinson to the Dodgers were John Wright, Don Newcombe, and Roy Campanella by 1950. Other teams followed soon after, and by the time of the *Brown v. Board* decision, only four major league baseball teams remained segregated; all would be desegregated by 1959. Similarly, professional football teams began to sign black players, beginning with Marion Motley, who signed with the Cleveland Browns in 1946. While it would take until 1962 for the final NFL team to sign a black player—Bobby Mitchell of the Washington Redskins—most had integrated prior to 1954. In fact, in that year the top three rushers in the NFL were African American. Professional basketball teams, too, integrated in the post-war era, with William "Pop" Gates and William "Dolly" King opening the door in 1946 and six others signing in 1948. It seemed that sports had indeed shown the way to racial equality well before advances in other aspects of life.[6]

But sport, once at the forefront of the drive for African American rights, soon lost its opening-wedge status and by the late 1960s had become more a symbol of inequality than equality. The black athlete actually furthered stereotypes and hindered black advancement, encouraging black adolescents to pursue the myth of athletic excellence while eschewing much-needed academic development. While a few black athletes did achieve fame and fortune, the vast majority toiled in a system ruled by white owners, coaches, and sponsors. Many black athletes came to feel they were used and abused by a white-dominated sporting infrastructure. This argument has been made eloquently by the historian John

Hoberman in *Darwin's Athletes,* in which he writes, "[sport] has preserved traditional white hierarchies in an era of so-called black dominance."[7] By the late 1960s, many black athletes were speaking up about the racist nature of sports in the United States.[8]

The claims of injustice advanced by the black athletes were hardly hollow. An examination of the black American athlete in the 1960s reveals a life of not only physical turmoil and constant training but also one filled with challenges in gaining an education, financial stability, satisfying relationships, and respect. Black athletes at white colleges were ostracized from normal social events. Often one of only a few blacks at a university, the athlete was unwelcome in the fraternity system, had difficulty finding dating partners, and found solace only in the athletic arena. The black athlete often encountered discrimination in the housing market, where he was often denied access to apartments or rooms readily rented to whites. He was frequently placed into easy courses, unchallenged academically, and graduated—or worse yet, failed to graduate—with an empty diploma. "At the University of New Mexico I got a sweater," noted one black athlete, in summarizing his college experience. "At Cameron State College in Oklahoma I got a blanket. At Southwestern State I got a jacket and a blanket."[9]

Worst of all was the ubiquitous racism that surrounded the black athlete. Professors asked challenging questions of other students but only engaged athletes about their scores or times on the field. White students stared and whispered at black athletes, who could only wonder whether the whispers concerned their status as star performers or the color of their skin. Tommie Smith expressed this frustration, saying, "Sit next to a girl with long blond hair and you feel her tense up and try to move over. Talk to a couple of white girls in the cafeteria and see what happens. People are reading papers, and first thing you see the papers drop and eyes peering over. For quite a while, Lee [Evans] and I were so naïve we thought, 'Man, we're just great athletes, that's why they're staring at us.'"[10]

The plight of the professional athlete was not much better. He may have escaped the college system, but he was still the victim of racism. Black athletes suffered from the stereotype of being physically gifted yet mentally deficient. They were relegated to positions that accentuated their athletic prowess yet required little thought. In the late 1960s, there were no black quarterbacks in the National Football League, only a handful of black pitchers or catchers in baseball, and no black point guards in the National Basketball Association. Typically, black athletes were "stacked" at a single position. There might be three or four black wide receivers on a football team but none at other positions, thus limiting the playing time and influence of black players overall. Furthermore, black athletes were paid far below the standards of white athletes with similar abilities (with the notable exception of superstars such as Willie Mays or Hank Aaron). Endorsement dollars, too, were limited for black players since, as one advertising representative put it, "If a black man peddles it, regardless of who he is, whites won't buy it."[11] A similar disparity was apparent for athletes celebrating Olympic success; the media seemed drawn to white gymnasts, swimmers, and track stars, who often landed major endorsement deals, while successful black boxers, runners, and others received no offers. And there were the taunts and racial slurs from fans, athletes, and even coaches, who continued their insults long after Jackie Robinson's initial season. Finally, these athletes performed at the command and whim of almost exclusively white managerial staffs. There were no black owners, only a single black head coach (Bill Russell, named player/coach for the Boston Celtics in 1966), and few black assistant coaches. What it all added up to, according to one black athlete, was that black "super-animals" were used by whites as if they were a "piece of equipment," performing as long as they were able and then discarded like so much garbage.[12]

Black Athletes and the Civil Rights Movement

The protest-rich decade of the 1960s was the perfect time for black athletes to demonstrate their anger at the discrimination and inequalities they encountered in sport. The idea of an Olympic boycott by African Americans had been proposed before, though it had never attained broad support among athletes. In 1960 rumors swirled about decathlon champion Rafer Johnson, who mentioned that a boycott of that year's Rome Olympics had been discussed. In 1963, comedian and Civil Rights activist Dick Gregory suggested a boycott of the 1964 Tokyo Olympics. Three-time gold medallist Mal Whitfield elaborated on Gregory's comments, and he quickly became the most prominent black athlete to advocate a boycott, a precursor to Harry Edwards in 1967. Whitfield noted many of the same complaints as Edwards, especially regarding treatment of black athletes away from the sports arena. "The Negro champion and the white champion may stand equal on a dais as they each receive gold medals," he said, "but when they leave the dais only the white champion's accomplishments assure him a stable and successful future."[13] It was time for "the Negro to launch the dramatic offensive."[14] Black athletes did not boycott the Tokyo Games, as there was not much interest beyond the few comments of men such as Gregory and Whitfield, neither of whom were active competitors. It took three years of changing currents in the Civil Rights Movement, the assassination of Martin Luther King, Jr., the advance of Black Power, and the continued struggle of black athletes for equality off the field for the boycott movement to win the support of many top athletes.

By the mid-1960s, as the Civil Rights Movement made its way into the urban centers of the north, a growing number of blacks challenged the effectiveness of nonviolence and called for more militant forms of protest. In June 1966, Stokely Carmichael, leader of the Student Nonviolent Coordinating Committee (SNCC), gave voice to this militant movement at a rally in Greenwood, Mississippi, when he announced, "We need Black Power!"[15] In the ensuing months, Carmichael and his successor, H. Rap Brown, deepened the divide between themselves and Martin Luther King, Jr. In June 1967, Brown called for a complete break with King's nonviolence, saying, "The white man is your enemy. You got to destroy your enemy. . . . I say you better get a gun. Violence is necessary—it is as American as cherry pie."[16] By the end of 1967, the Civil Rights Movement was fractured, with several factions vying for the support of the black populace. King remained the most important figure, though his influence over the black masses was waning quickly. A second group was the Nation of Islam, who followed Elijah Muhammad and preached separatism between the races. Finally, there were the Black Power advocates, increasingly influenced by the openly violent Black Panther Party. Each of the three factions found followers among black athletes, and as divided as the Civil Rights Movement was, athletes were equally divided.[17]

By early 1968 the march toward equality seemed permanently sidetracked, as the proponents of violence and separatism eclipsed King as the leaders of the Civil Rights Movement. The final report of the Kerner Commission, which explored the condition of blacks in the inner cities, was released in February 1968 and verified this rift between the races. "Our nation is moving toward two societies, one black, one white—separate and unequal," the report read, statistically proving what many Americans knew intuitively.[18] In April, Martin Luther King, Jr., was assassinated in Memphis. He had always insisted on nonviolence, and while his influence had been challenged, it still held sway with many black Americans. But at the last even King wondered whether violence could be contained. Only days before his death he said, "Maybe we just have to admit that the day of violence is here . . . maybe we have to just give up and let violence take its course."[19] With King's death, the greatest symbol of nonviolence was removed—and removed by violence, no less—seemingly confirming his doubts. Blacks took to the streets in violent demonstrations around the nation. Stokely Carmichael advised his followers, "Go home and get a gun!"[20] There were riots in major cities across the nation, with racially motivated murders in Washington, D.C., Minneapolis, Detroit, and Memphis, among others.

Drifting along on the changing tides of the Civil Rights Movement were black athletes, many of whom were involved in the movement, others of whom remained detached, obsessed with their athletic pursuits. The most prominent black athlete was Muhammad Ali, formerly Cassius Clay, an avowed follower of Elijah Muhammad. Ali, first introduced to the Nation of Islam in 1958, changed his name after winning the heavyweight title in 1963 and formally announced his conversion to Islam in 1964. The host of white reporters who questioned his sincerity were proven wrong in April of 1968 when Ali refused to respond to an Army induction officer who called for "Cassius Clay." He was indicted for failure to submit to the draft, but he remained steadfast, saying, "I am not going ten thousand miles from home to help murder and kill and burn a poor nation simply to help continue the domination of white slave masters over the darker people."[21] For this action, he was sentenced to five years in prison (but remained free pending numerous appeals), the World Boxing Association stripped Ali of the heavyweight title, and he immediately became a martyr and hero among black athletes.[22]

After being stripped of his boxing title and removed from the ring, Ali remained a central figure in the public eye for his outspoken opposition to the war in Vietnam as well as his support of the boycott movement among black athletes; however, Ali remained aloof from the broader movement of black athletes. He led with his words but was unconcerned whether anyone followed him. He did not incite his fellow black athletes to action but, rather, pursued his own goals. "We who follow the honorable Elijah Muhammad believe in the separation of the races," he intoned during one interview. "In no way black and white will get along." Yet he never advocated violence and disavowed any ties to the Black Panthers. "I'm only Muslim. I'm with nothing else," he said.[23] And so Ali achieved an interesting duality during 1968, serving as an inspiration to black athletes while not seeking followers as other Civil Rights leaders did.[24]

The majority of black athletes, rather than following Muhammad Ali and the Nation of Islam, supported the Black Power movement. There were echoes of the Black Power movement in the words, tactics, and symbols employed by Harry Edwards and other athletes. As Black Power advocate Charles Hamilton explained, "There comes a point beyond which people cannot be expected to endure prejudice, oppression, and deprivation, and they will explode."[25] Black athletes had reached such a limit. Tommie Smith expressed this tension well, saying, "As far as being spit on, being stepped on, being bitten by dogs, the first dog that bites me I'm going to bite back. We're not going to wait for the white man to think of something else to do against us."[26]

The influence of Black Power was evident in other aspects of the so-called revolt of the black athletes. Edwards, who had participated in many Civil Rights protests, borrowed tactics from such protests and employed them to great effect for black athletes. Among such methods were boycotts, sit-down strikes, and walkouts. While the boycott movement against the Olympics was the most obvious example, black athletes participated in dozens of lower-profile boycotts at meets and colleges around the country. Several black athletes refused to play for their teams until conditions changed; while a few were cut from the roster by their coaches or colleges, many times some effort was made to address their concerns. The athletes, like Black Power advocates, practiced intimidation and threatened violence. An athletic squad could hardly be expected to enter a stadium wielding machine guns; however, they intimidated observers in other ways. Many of the athletes wore dark sunglasses, berets, and black jackets in addition to perpetual scowls on their faces. A picket line of such athletes was a fearsome sight, not only to white observers, but also to other black athletes who might otherwise have avoided protest. The black athletes also insinuated that they would resort to violence by repeating the Black Power mantra, "by any means necessary," a phrase found throughout newspapers, books, and pamphlets of the period.[27]

Finally, black athletes borrowed that favorite symbol of the Black Power movement, the so-called Black Power salute, a raised fist. The salute, in some ways another element of intimidation, might more properly be considered a symbol of independence. No social setting acknowledges such a gesture as appropriate, so black protesters delivering the salute told all who saw them "we are going to do things our way." The fist was a common symbol printed on posters and in pamphlets and literature promoting Black Power. Black students and protesters raised their fists at strikes and rallies. Black soldiers of the era were known to deliver a derogatory Black Power salute to their commanding officers rather than a standard military salute. Black athletes witnessed such displays, read about them, and used them in the months prior to the Olympics. Some must have asked themselves, What better time to use such a salute than during that solemn moment on the medal stand at the Olympics when most victors stood at strict attention? By 1968, the language, tactics, and symbols of Black Power were everywhere and were especially prominent in the colleges and universities where most Olympic-caliber athletes lived and trained. That black athletes ultimately adopted such techniques and formed their own movement is hardly surprising.[28]

The Rise and Fall of the Olympic Boycott Movement

Virtually all of the top black athletes aiming at a spot on the 1968 Olympic team had felt the sting of racism at one time or another. Bob Beamon, who broke the world's record in the long jump at Mexico City, lost his scholarship at the University of Texas at El Paso for refusing to jump against the team from Brigham Young University, a Mormon institution. When Beamon and other black athletes learned that the Book of Mormon "castigates the black race as inferior and descended from the devil," they felt the boycott was justified—and sacrificed their scholarships for it. Ron Copeland, an Olympic hopeful in the hurdles, recalls that apartments that denied him a spot suddenly became vacant when he had a white friend call for him. Basketball star Lew Alcindor was virtually silent and reclusive by the time he reached college, so scarred was he by a series of incidents in his youth, including one in which his high school coach had berated him with racial slurs at half time of a game. John Carlos himself had been expelled from East Texas State for telling the school paper about his former coaches, who consistently referred to black athletes as "nigger" or "nigra."[29]

Having endured such incidents, many black athletes had contemplated some sort of protest action on their own. In late 1967, though, such individual sentiments began to coalesce into a broader movement, fueled by the charged atmosphere of the late 1960s and inspired by other protests staged by students and civil rights activists. The leader of the athletes came to be Harry Edwards, a sociology instructor and track coach from San Jose State University. Edwards was the perfect leader for such a movement. He was an imposing figure, standing 6'8" and usually wearing a beret and black sunglasses. He was outspoken, at times outrageous, in his denunciation of the white race, referring to popular white leaders with nicknames such as "Lynchin' Baines Johnson," "The Dishonorable Hubert Humphrey," and "Cracker Dick Nixon." Edwards was also a former athlete who had set many meet records in the discus, exceeding 180 feet in competition and approaching 200 in practice, had been a star on the San Jose State basketball team, and reportedly received offers to play for the Minnesota Vikings and San Francisco 49ers of the NFL without having played a down of college football. But he had also lived the life of a black athlete off the field and found that his athletic prowess was not enough to gain him entry into white fraternities, most restaurants, or much off-campus housing. He had suffered for his outspokenness. To his horror, one morning he found that his two dogs had been chopped into pieces and dumped on his front porch, accompanied by the letters "KKK" painted on his house. It was experiences such as this one that motivated Edwards.[30]

Through personal experience and years of cataloging the troubles of his students, Edwards developed a lengthy list of complaints against the white establishment in sports and was determined to do something to change it. He read carefully Bill Russell's autobiography, *Up for Glory,* which depicted not only one of the greatest basketball players of all time but also a man and a life rent apart by racism and abuse from white coaches, fans, and fellow players. He took note when, in 1965, black players in the American Football League boycotted the All-Star Game in New Orleans, Louisiana, where most of those same players were not allowed to eat or drink in many restaurants and clubs. Edwards, as did virtually all Americans, both black and white, also followed closely the saga of heavyweight boxing champion Muhammad Ali and was inspired by his determination and courage.[31]

The protest grew much more immediate for Edwards after two events in the fall of 1967. First, Tommie Smith, a top black sprinter on Edwards'

San Jose State team, sparked a storm of controversy when he answered a reporter's question about a possible boycott of the 1968 Olympics: "Yes, this is true. Some black athletes have been discussing the possibility of boycotting the games to protest racial injustice in America."[32] The media grabbed the story, and Ṣmith found himself at the center of a "boycott movement" that he did not even realize existed. Still, Smith embraced the challenge of heading the nascent movement and, along with the great 400 meter runner Lee Evans, he continued to make statements alluding to a potential boycott, all the while with Edwards as the intimidating front man.[33]

Even as the national media tried to absorb the impact of Smith's comments, another protest, this one directed by Edwards himself on the San Jose State campus, led to the organization of the very boycott suggested by Smith. As the fall semester was just getting under way, Edwards and one of his graduate students, Kenneth Noel, arranged a protest for the first day of classes. It was a simple rally, beginning with some thirty-five black students and one hundred whites waving signs and chanting to protest racism on the campus in housing, social organizations, and athletics. Within a few hours, over seven hundred students, faculty, and administrators had assembled. They drew up lists of demands and made plans for further protest. A movement was born almost instantly. Its first target was to be the opening game of the football season, and thus the student movement at San Jose State was tied to athletics from the beginning.[34]

Ultimately the boycott movement mounted by athletes and students alike led to the cancellation of that first football game, and Edwards learned that such mobilization could lead to change. He shifted his focus from the tiny theater of campus life at SJSU to the behemoth of global racism and decided that the ideal stage for protest would be the 1968 Olympics. Along with a core group of athletes from SJSU, including Tommie Smith, Edwards formed the Olympic Project for Human Rights in October 1967 and arranged for a meeting with athletes from around the nation at the Los Angeles Black Youth Conference that November. The meeting featured speeches by many top athletes, among them Alcindor, Smith, Carlos, and Evans. A few speakers were opposed to the boycott, arguing that sports had provided many opportunities for black advancement in America, and boycotting such an event was counterproductive. Such voices were shouted down by the audience, which grew increasingly enthusiastic as the meeting went on. At its conclusion, the group voted to plan a boycott of the Olympics—no active athlete voted against it—and the boycott movement was officially under way.[35]

In the months that followed, Edwards refined the group's agenda, settling on six specific demands, which he announced at a press conference in December. First, they sought the restoration of the heavyweight title to Muhammad Ali. Second, they demanded that Avery Brundage be removed from the International Olympic Committee for his alleged association with the Nazis, among other infractions. South Africa and Rhodesia must be banned from international competition, according to Edwards. The demands also included the addition of blacks to key administrative and coaching positions, including at least two coaches to the U.S. Olympic track team and two representatives on the USOC. Finally, the athletes demanded that the New York Athletic Club, a prominent sponsor of many track meets, be desegregated.[36]

Among the first significant actions of the Olympic Project for Human Rights was a boycott of the prestigious track meet at the New York Athletic Club, the same club they demanded be desegregated. The NYAC struck some as a curious target. While its membership was admittedly all white, it had made many contributions to inner-city track clubs and youth organizations, in addition to hosting a fully integrated track meet each season. Boycotting this particular target demonstrated that black athletes refused to be simply performers, that they must be eligible for membership in the club if they were to compete. The boycott was also an important test of the group's ability to organize a protest that would be both nonviolent and successful. Early signs indicated that the movement was having some success, as several prominent athletes announced that they would stay away from the meet. As word of the protest spread, athletes—and entire teams—from the New York area and elsewhere elected to skip the event. Black athletes rallied to the boycott cause, and many white athletes, too, stayed away, out of either sympathy with the boycott or fear of being involved in a violent incident. Traditionally black colleges around the nation supported the boycott and declined invitations to participate. Several other schools, including the track powerhouses of Villanova and Georgetown, joined them. The military academies decided it was too risky to send their students into the fray and thus added to the boycott. Even some international squads, most notably the Russians, withdrew. So widespread were the withdrawals that the NYAC launched a national campaign encouraging teams to attend the meet, with all expenses paid. The call was answered by, among others, the "third-rate" mile relay team from the traditionally liberal University of California at Berkeley, which drew a chorus of criticism from the liberal press. Yet even after this publicity campaign, the NYAC meet appeared headed for disaster.[37]

By coincidence, on the day the meet was to be held newspapers ran the headline that the IOC had readmitted the South African team, an announcement that energized the already mounting black movement. In response to the news, Edwards vented to the press, "Where are all the people who say the Olympics should be above racism? Who can say the Olympics shouldn't be the target now? The committee has shown the black man just what it thinks of him. I think things will really begin to heat up."[38] Indeed, the news of the boycott by African nations lent a new sense of empowerment to the NYAC boycott, and the crowd of black athletes picketing the event stole the spotlight from the athletes inside. Several blacks who tried to cross the picket line ultimately yielded to threats of bodily harm from the picketers and joined the boycott while a few others crossed the line unimpeded. All told, only nine black athletes participated in the meet, most notably Bob Beamon, who won the long jump. The vast majority remained outside, waving such banners as "RUN, JUMP, OR SHUFFLE ARE ALL THE SAME, WHEN YOU DO IT FOR THE MAN!"[39]

The evening was not without tense moments. The crowd of demonstrators joining the athletes attempted to storm the arena at one point, only to be forced back by policemen wielding nightsticks. A bit later, a group of protesters attempted to block one of the entrances used by the athletes, forming a picket line and marching by the doors, in spite of police orders to move. Harry Edwards, attempting to prevent violence, grabbed a bullhorn and encouraged the crowd to move to another entrance, which it did, allowing most of the competitors to enter the building freely. One group of athletes, representing teams from Holy Cross and Providence universities, pulled up just as the crowd was reforming and had to sprint from their bus to the entrance, pursued by protesters chanting and screaming at them. The scene frightened black athletes crossing the line as well. Once inside, Bob Beamon turned to one of his teammates, Dave Morgan, and said, "I'm scared, man." "You're not as scared as me," Morgan replied. "I never been so scared."[40] In spite of their fears, the meet carried on with no serious incidents, and the protest was achieved with only a few minor scrapes and bruises; the potential violence had been averted. The boycott itself was a success. Entire sections of Madison Square Garden, usually filled to capacity for this event, remained empty. The protest left many of the top athletes in the world either outside on the sidewalk or far away from the arena, so there were few outstanding achievements during the meet. The press declared the contest was essentially empty without black competitors, and black athletes left the event energized and ready for further action.[41]

Fueled by the success of the NYAC boycott, the Olympic Project for Human Rights quickly organized a succession of protests on college campuses. These protests ranged from sitting on a track to prevent a meet to the simple threat of boycotting, and their goals ranged from the removal of racist coaches to excusing players from competing against Brigham Young University. At the University of California at Berkeley, a notice from the group announced that black students would picket and disrupt all athletic events at the university and that black athletes would boycott all competition until their demands were met. The university met, even exceeded, their demands before any such threats were realized. Two coaches labeled by the movement as racist resigned; two black coaches were hired; a program was implemented to encourage black students to attend the school; and a new black studies program was created.[42]

Similar protests were carried to the University of Washington and the University of Texas at El Paso. The latter was the scene of one of the most bitter confrontations between black athletes and white administrators, in part because the protest fell soon after the assassination of Martin Luther King, Jr., and the black students involved sensed that their own protest was carried out in homage to King. It was bitter, too, because UTEP administrators were utterly intransigent in their policies. In this case, black track stars refused to participate in a meet against Brigham Young University based on the racist elements of Mormon ideology. For this protest, the black athletes, including Bob Beamon, were stripped of their scholarships. The protest did not end there, however, as many black students calmly walked to the track and sat down, refusing to allow the meet to continue. The sit-in was eventually broken up by the local police but not before the protest had demonstrated a clear connection between athletics and the student body in general; the students had carried out a peaceful protest that would have made Dr. King proud.[43] As protests continued throughout the summer, with impressive frequency universities yielded to the demands of protesting student-athletes. All told, the Olympic Project for Human Rights assisted student-athlete protests at over thirty universities.[44]

Participants in these protests drew the ire of white critics everywhere, and the lives of the athletes at the forefront of the movement bordered on unbearable at times. Public displeasure came in the form of everything from simple boos to hate mail and threats. At the Los Angeles Invitational Track Meet in January 1968, Tommie Smith was greeted by boos from the crowd when he was introduced. As he fell behind in the 440 yard dash—a race he had never lost indoors—the crowd cheered raucously. The cheers grew to a roar when he finished in third place. Smith interpreted the boos as a sign that his message was finding its mark. "If they felt upset enough to boo me," he said, "I guess I must have had a pretty strong effect on their consciences." Hate mail poured in to Smith, Lee Evans, and other athletes and included countless insults, racial slurs, and threats as well as some generally painful comments, such as, "Dear Traitor: . . . I'd rather have our country finish last, without you, than first with you." The hate mail piled up for Lew Alcindor, too, who had never stated directly that he intended to boycott but who had said in one well-publicized interview, "Well, if you live in a racist society and you want to express yourself about racism, there's a lot of things you can do, and a boycott is one of them." After this interview, Alcindor received letters saying he was an "uppity nigger," that he was a traitor to the United States, and that he should be thrown out of UCLA and barred from professional basketball.[45]

While the list of critics of the boycott seemed endless, there were those who voiced their support. In one celebrated case, the Harvard crew team, after qualifying for the Olympics, issued a formal statement of its sympathy for the black athletes. "We . . . have been concerned with the place of the black man in American society and his struggle for equal rights. . . . Everything about the plight of the black man in this country is regrettable. . . . We feel strongly that the racial crisis is a total cultural crisis." In response to this statement, Edwards stated, "It [is] beautiful to see some white cats willing to admit they've got a problem and looking to take some action to educate their own."[46]

In addition to the slights of countless white critics, the boycott movement endured considerable dissention from both former and active black athletes themselves. Many athletes balked at the prospect of surrendering years of training in a protest that would mean little, especially if the U.S. team succeeded without them. One of them was Ralph Boston, world-record holder and defending Olympic champion in the long jump, who said, "What boycott? I've put too much time and effort into track and field to give it up. If I felt there was sufficient reason I would boycott, but I don't even know what the reason is. At least Negroes have this much: we can compete in amateur sports and we can represent ourselves and then the country."[47] Charlie Greene, a favorite in the 100 meters, refused to accept the unpatriotic rhetoric of the movement. "It comes down to a matter [of] if you're an American or if you're not," he said. "I'm an American, and I'm going to run."[48]

Former athletes were equally divided on the boycott question. Jesse Owens, the great sprinter who had dominated the Berlin "Nazi Olympics" in 1936, opposed the boycott. "We shattered this so-called Aryan supremacy then by our own supremacy and by standing and saluting the American flag," he recalled. "I feel that the deeds of an individual are far more potent than a boycott. There is no politics or racial prejudice in the Olympics. I believe you contribute more by entering than by staying out."[49] A few straddled the fence, wary of sounding too "angry" or "militant," yet also hesitant to appear unsupportive of the black athletes. Jackie Robinson, interviewed often during this period, fell into the latter category. Publicly, Robinson refused to bad-mouth the athletes or the boycott movement. "The tragedy is that the Negro athlete is more concerned with gold medals than the advancement of his people," he said, indicating his support for the boycott. He continued, "I am proud of these fellows willing to sacrifice something dear to them. . . . I support the athlete." In the same breath, though, he added, ". . . but I don't think there are enough athletes to make it worthwhile. I wouldn't do it myself." While Edwards and others dismissed such doubters as "Uncle Toms," it grew increasingly difficult to hold the splintering Olympic Project for Human Rights together as the summer wore on.[50]

The realities of athletic life also contributed to the decline of the boy-cott movement. Virtually none of the athletes, even those heading the boycott movement, were willing to abandon their training altogether. They trained as hard as ever, participated in meets and contests, and flocked to the preliminary qualifying session in Los Angeles. If they were serious about a boycott, it was suggested, shouldn't the athletes abandon these formalities as well? As the final Olympic Trials ap-proached, observers were hard-pressed to notice any real difference in the activities of the athletes. While many athletes maintained the boy-cott rhetoric, it looked to the rest of the world as if the athletes were ready to go to Mexico City.[51]

The athletes, already divided, discussed the issue constantly through-out the summer, especially after the decision to include South Africa in the Olympics was repealed in late April. At the end of July, a rift tore through the movement when Lee Evans and a group of athletes voted to drop the boycott and attend the Olympics. While Edwards tried to keep up appearances, after another month of debate and division in the ranks even he was ready to capitulate. On 31 August he announced, "The ma-jority of athletes will participate in the Olympics." And with that, the boycott died.[52]

The boycott failed for a number of reasons. Chief among them was the lack of unanimity among the athletes. Explaining the final decision, Ed-wards said, "Of the 26 athletes who held an excellent chance of making the team, 12 and maybe 13 were not willing to boycott under some cir-cumstances."[53] To boycott under such circumstances would likely have been an empty protest, a meaningless sacrifice for those who chose not to attend. If only a few black athletes boycotted, their positions could be easily filled by other Americans, black or white. If John Carlos skipped the Olympics, Charlie Green would have been just as likely to win a medal. If Tommie Smith boycotted, Jim Hines may have won in his place. If the boycott were to be of any significance, it had to be unanimous.[54]

The fragmentation of the boycott movement might also be attributed to another characteristic that it shared with the broader Black Power movement—its constituency. Like the Black Power movement, the Olympic Project for Human Rights was comprised almost entirely of young black males, which contributed to tension surrounding the boy-cott. First, the OPHR was entirely black. As the 1960s progressed, many organizations within the Civil Rights Movement had grown frustrated with the presence of whites in their groups. White people always seemed to wind up in supervisory or important roles, which irked black activists. Many blacks began to question whether whites could truly understand black needs, and the Black Power movement rejected white participation. The OPHR, too, had no white members. The only white person currently associated with the OPHR is Peter Norman, the Australian sprinter who appeared on the medal stand in Mexico City in front of Tommie Smith. Photos of Norman in that medal ceremony lend a white presence to public perception of the athletes' movement. While it is unlikely that the most militant black athletes would have accepted whites in their ranks, outside observers would likely have given more credibility to an integrated movement. White sympathizers within the movement may have served as valuable spokesmen to the largely white media or to white coaches, owners, and organizers who controlled the sports structure that black athletes were trying to change. Instead, black athletes were forced to assume a defensive stance with the media, which no doubt contributed to their difficulty in finding supporters.

A second way in which the OPHR's constituency resembled other Black Power organizations was in its youth. Edwards himself was only 25 years old. Most of the members were younger. As top athletes in peak condition, they ranged in ages from eighteen to a year or two older than Edwards. Much as the Black Power advocates rejected the "elder statesman," Martin Luther King, Jr., these younger athletes rejected former black heroes such as Jesse Owens. The media pressed such former athletes for their views on the boycott and often found that they disagreed with the boycott movement. Had they been able to present a united front to the media and the world, the movement might have been more successful.

The revolt of the black athletes was also an overwhelmingly male undertaking. Women such as Elaine Brown have written of their frustrations within the Black Power movement in general. Women were often made to do traditional "women's work" in the office, such as cooking or cleaning, and were never considered for leadership roles within the movement. Female black athletes suffered similar treatment within the OPHR. In spite of their growing success on the fields of sport, highlighted by Wyomia Tyus' gold medal performance in the 100 meter sprint in Tokyo in 1964, it was understood that the women would support male athletes in the boycott, even if women were rarely asked their own opinions. Women in the movement were virtually invisible to the media; their opinions and interests regarding the movement were just not mentioned. As with the potential to build a broader coalition by including whites and elders, the opportunities available by including women were lost. What remained was a movement driven solely by young black males, and even many of them did not support the boycott. Fractured along so many lines, the movement could not hold itself together.[55]

In the end, too, the boycott failed because athletes are driven to compete. Lee Evans, one of the most vocal leaders of the boycott movement, has conceded that he always wanted to compete in the Olympics, privately hoping that the others would vote down the boycott because he wanted to race as much as the others. He attributes similar feelings to Smith, Carlos, and other athletes. But even as they abandoned the boycott movement in favor of participation, black athletes dropped hints that they might carry out some protest during the Olympics. While a formal boycott had been abandoned, individuals continued planning protests on their own. Lew Alcindor, so fiercely attacked after merely mentioning the possibility of a boycott, never did attend the Olympics. He skipped the qualifying camp and spent his summer in New York, working with Operation Sports Rescue, a program dedicated to inner-city children. Alcindor insisted that his time had been well spent; it was more important to him to try to "change ten would-be junkies into useful citizens" than to win an Olympic medal.[56] He suspected that the Olympic basketball team would be just fine without him, a suspicion that was confirmed when the United States won the gold medal in Mexico City. Other athletes intended to make some sort of protest. Among them was the triple-jumper Art Walker, who said, "I think we still ought to do something anyway to let black America know we identify."[57] Harry Edwards insisted that all athletes going to the Olympics would wear black arm bands and might refuse to walk in formation, to acknowledge the American flag, or some other form of protest. As the athletes went their separate ways and headed to Mexico City, even they didn't know what kind of protest might lay ahead.[58]

One such athlete was John Carlos, who spent the days prior to his departure thinking about the boycott, about his teammates, and about what he might do should he reach the medal stand. The night before he left for Mexico City, he considered these things as he watched news coverage of the upcoming Olympics. On the screen, he saw students chanting in the background, thousands of them, waving banners and shaking their fists. He had been to the city before and understood a little about the poverty, the disparity of wealth, the ever-present police force, and the possibility of discord. He hoped that the Olympics and the money it brought in might change things in Mexico City, alleviating some of these problems. Apparently the people were still not satisfied. "Good for them," Carlos thought, "using the Olympics to publicize their issues." He watched for a few moments, remembering his earlier visit to the city and pondering again the protests of black athletes. Then he turned off the television and headed to bed, an early flight to Mexico awaiting him the next day.[59]

Image Shattered

Tlatelolco

four

John Carlos, who arrived in Mexico on 3 October, in all likelihood was watching footage of a protest held by Mexican students in the historic Plaza de las Tres Culturas in the Tlatelolco district of Mexico City. The Plaza is a site of singular significance for Mexicans, as it represents all three of the major eras in Mexican history. There are Aztec ruins, partially excavated and seemingly growing from the grass and slopes; nearby is a cathedral, built by Spanish missionaries; and surrounding the whole area is a cluster of apartment buildings and a highway, vestiges of the modern era. According to legend, it was on that site that the Aztecs mounted their final, heroic resistance against the conquistador Hernando Cortés, thwarting his advance temporarily. It was there, across the ruins and on the vast slate square that filled the bulk of the Plaza, that Mexican students gathered on the afternoon of 2 October 1968.

The meeting capped several months of student agitation, protesting the harsh treatment of students by Mexican authorities and demanding the expansion of the democratic process in Mexico. The assemblage was entirely peaceful, and over the course of the evening enthusiastic cheers interrupted a pleasant, picniclike atmosphere. The students, who made up the majority of the crowd, were joined by their families, parents, and many children who ran about in the ruins. Local police and the military hovered at the fringes of the crowd, but the students had grown accustomed to their presence after months of similar protests. The hum of helicopters, too, seemed little cause for concern.[1]

Suddenly, at about 6:20 p.m., two helicopters swooped low over the square. A few moments later, thousands of army troops, who had quietly observed the protest for most of the afternoon, moved to seal off all exits from the square. A third military group, the Olimpia Battalion, which had been raised and trained as a security force for the upcoming Olympics, opened fire on the crowd from a number of balconies that lined the square. The crowd was helpless. The unarmed students formed a panicked human wave, rushing from one end of the square to the other, seeking desperately for some escape. They trampled one another, a reckless stampede that left some students crushed in their wake. From every side the students met death: from bayonets, from gunfire, from helicopters, even from tanks. The killing continued for over an hour, subsided for a few minutes, then resumed. Until eleven o'clock the firing was nearly constant, and stray shots were heard even into the next day. Students fled into the apartments that ringed the square, huddling on the floor with strangers who took them in. Soldiers and tanks saturated these buildings with bullets and grenades, blowing out windows and wounding many people inside. The barrage burst many of the pipes in the building, soaking the terrified residents and contributing to their discomfort and confusion. The troops then stormed the apartments, arresting not only anyone who looked like a student but many of those who had tried to help them. Those arrested were sent through a gauntlet of soldiers and police, beaten and groped as they were pushed toward the trucks awaiting them.[2]

It is unlikely that we will ever know precisely how many students died in the Plaza. There were rumors of dead bodies—even some living victims—being cremated by police to prevent the true extent of the slaughter from being known. The government wholly denied these charges, challenging graveyard workers and hospital staff to come forward if they had witnessed such cremations. The official figure was thirty-eight dead, including four soldiers. Observers insist that the total was much higher, some estimating as many as three thousand killed. Most agree that the true total is somewhere in between, probably about 300. Several thousand student leaders were taken into custody. Many were tortured by methods including beatings, electric shocks, mental torture, food deprivation, and simulated castration. It would be years before most of the students could consider public protest again, and many were too scarred emotionally to participate in any protests after that night.[3]

October 2, 1968 is a landmark date in Mexican history. On that night, Mexico, which had been lauded internationally as the paragon of stability and progress in Latin America, revealed grievous flaws while the world's media watched. The motto of the Mexico City Olympics, "Ante los Ojos del Mundo" ("Before the Eyes of the World"), only reminded Mexicans that this tragedy unfolded before millions of viewers, shattering the myth of peace and stability. Its mask pulled aside, the government at last had to confront issues that had been swept under the carpet for decades. The Mexican government had hoped that the Olympics would signal to the world that Mexico was a modern nation, prosperous enough, motivated enough, and organized enough to stage the largest sporting festival in the world. Instead, the student massacre announced to the world that much of that image of prosperity was a façade, concealing a nation rife with social problems and dissatisfied citizens. The massacre renewed interest in reform, reviving a liberal tradition that had lain dormant since the end of the Lázaro Cárdenas presidency in 1940. Since 1968, the presidents of Mexico have slowly allowed voices of discontent to be heard in public forums, have expanded the role of minority parties in the political process, and have looked more earnestly at the problems facing most of the population.[4]

Origins of the Student Movement

The Mexican government, even as it had achieved the "Mexican miracle" in the 1940s and 1950s, and even as it was lauded by the rest of the globe for its political stability, had always had its detractors. Various strikes and protest movements over the years had inspired specific mechanisms within the government for handling such problems, and by the time the students began their protest in 1968, the government was practiced in dealing with troublemakers. With rare exception, violence was not the *modus operandi* of the Mexican government; it preferred to extinguish opposition in quieter and more devious ways. Since the beginnings of the Mexican Revolution, opposition groups operated only so far as the government allowed, never seriously challenging the established system and yet never entirely snuffed out. Leaders of groups that started to speak too loudly were usually co-opted into the Institutional Revolutionary Party (PRI) and thus silenced. Often such groups found their voices squelched by a publicity infrastructure that was entirely controlled by the government; paper and ink for printing pamphlets or newspapers, space on billboards, airtime on radio or television, and virtually any other means of reaching a wide audience were either government owned or sympathetic to the PRI.[5]

Any movement that managed to circumvent such obstacles confronted still greater problems in challenging the government. Propaganda campaigns, launched in those same government-owned newspapers or over the radio, were vicious and ruthless, humiliating and emasculating individuals at the head of such movements. The president and his aides, too, thwarted opposition groups by either ignoring them or refusing to meet with their representatives publicly, ensuring an "our word against theirs" debate that the government would surely win. Finally, and only if all of the above mechanisms had failed to quiet the protest, the government might resort to force. The most vocal dissenters were made to disappear swiftly and completely. This had happened in the Revolutionary era rarely—so rarely that the incidents barely dented the Mexican reputation for stability.[6]

These methods for controlling protest had been tested several times prior to 1968, and always things had ended badly for the protesters. In 1940 troops fired upon labor leaders who sought improved working conditions, leaving eleven dead. The worst massacre prior to 1968 took place in 1952, when the army attacked a group protesting the policies of President Ruíz Cortines, killing over 200 people. Not all protests were put down with violence. When railroad workers struck in 1959, the government arrested the leaders of the union, many of whom spent years in prison, and fired thousands of workers. And in 1964 and '65, when young doctors protested for increased wages and benefits, the government employed a variety of tactics to defuse the movement. Empty promises and backroom deals, never fulfilled, were favorite tactics of the president. Perhaps the most devastating ploy was a clever propaganda and slander campaign against the doctors. The government purchased dozens of full-page ads in local papers, pretending to be doctors who opposed the protesters, and described them as a splinter group with little support in the medical community. After months of these kinds of attacks, the doctors found they had virtually no popular support, that many doctors did not know what their medical leaders really wanted, and they still had not had an honest meeting with the president. The movement crumbled, its proponents beaten and demoralized.[7]

Students in Mexico faced other obstacles in mounting a protest, some common to students everywhere, others peculiar to Mexico. Students in general provide an ideal source of protesters. They are generally not of the lowest financial class, so they have the means and wherewithal to support a movement. They are educated and literate and also more politically aware than other groups. They are young and energetic, looking for outlets to vent their energy. Most are at an age when they seek to assert independence and establish their own identity, often by breaking with societal norms or family traditions. They have less to lose than other groups and are rarely tied down by commitments to home, family, and career. Finally, and not insignificantly, students have more time to dedicate to such activities—most even relish the opportunity to skip class for something so exciting as a protest march. Yet even with so many advantages, student movements often fail to materialize. For while they may have the time and the means to stage a protest, students sometimes suffer from apathy, laziness, and spottiness of commitment. For many, their political awareness and interest is only just developing, and they may not identify with the ideals of a broader movement. While the most focused and driven of students provide leadership, the masses of students may not follow them or may not remain interested over the duration of a prolonged protest. Drawn in by the excitement and charge of the moment, when the drudgery and work of day-to-day operations set in, many students quietly find their way back to the classroom.[8]

Such general characteristics combined with the growing global ferment to form an international student movement, which fueled the unrest in Mexico in the summer of 1968. Mexican students shared much in common with students in France, the United States, and elsewhere. School and college campuses seemed to promote activism, as students grew more educated about national and international issues, were exposed to revolutionary literature, and had ready access to large groups of their peers. Like students around the world, Mexican students drew inspiration from the activism of Mohandas Gandhi and Martin Luther King, Jr., and they grew restless at the sight of such things as the oppression of blacks in the United States, the cruelties of the Vietnam War, and the authoritarian nature of governments celebrating "progress" and "democracy." They adopted the revolutionary rhetoric of intellectuals such as Albert Camus and Herbert Marcuse, and in Mexico of the historian Daniel Cosío Villegas and writer Octavio Paz. When students waged pitched battles in the streets of Paris and Chicago, those in Mexico were energized to hasten their own revolutionary movement. As has been noted by historian Herbert Braun, however, Mexican students were perhaps more self-absorbed than those in France or the United States. Despite paying some attention to such international influences, they were obsessed with their own nation and its president.[9]

Students in Mexico faced other challenges as well. The movement struggled to win followers aside from students, though they made many attempts to connect with workers, peasants, and others. The grim financial prospects of most Mexicans left them unconcerned, and in many cases even hostile, to the students, whom they viewed as spoiled kids marching in the streets when they should have been in class. Finally, and perhaps most importantly, political careers in Mexico were achieved within the PRI. Thus any student with the drive and focus to lead a protest had to think twice before attacking the government if he had any interest in a career in politics. And so, without having to exert any overt pressure at all, the PRI co-opted many student leaders who realized that speaking out against the government might threaten their futures. Understanding such obstacles, the American ambassador to Mexico, Fulton Freeman, speculated in June of 1968, "It is most unlikely that such conditions [between students and the government] will rapidly develop here to critical proportions, at least until after 1970 when president Díaz Ordaz's term ends."[10]

It was into this atmosphere that the students launched their movement in 1968. The protests began in late July, when students from several schools marched through the streets in celebration of the tenth anniversary of Fidel Castro's revolution in Cuba. A chance encounter between student groups from the Vocational School Number Two of the National Polytechnic Institute and the Preparatory School Isaac Ochoterena—traditional rivals—led to fisticuffs in the street. The scuffle would have been simply another chapter in a long line of street fights between the two rival schools had not the *granaderos,* Mexico's feared riot police, been sent to the scene. They dispersed the students, swinging their clubs and injuring many demonstrators. They pursued both groups back to their schools, where they continued to attack both students and teachers—in one instance blowing down the door of an eighteenth-century building with a bazooka and injuring many students huddled behind it. In extending their brutality onto the school campuses, the *granaderos* breached the barrier of university autonomy that was a tradition in Mexico. Discipline of the students had always been the sacred preserve of university officials. Now, with the government clearly in violation of such a policy, the university students began to protest the brutality of the police, and university officials supported them for the assault on autonomy.[11]

In the days following the initial attack, student groups began marching in the streets. With images of the student protests in France only a few weeks old, Mexican students from dozens of schools and universities began organizing into a broader movement, and within days students throughout the city went on strike. The movement escalated rapidly, and on 26 July a massive student march was again met with violence. *Granaderos* and the city police assaulted the students with clubs and bayonets, injuring many and killing four. This latest spate of violence only heightened the resolve of the students, who organized further and released a list of six demands that included: the release of all political prisoners in Mexico; the repeal of Article 145 of the penal code, which allowed for the arrest and punishment of dissidents under the vague category of "social dissolution"; elimination of the *granaderos*; dismissal of Mexico City's police chief, Luis Cueto, and his deputy; payment of an indemnity to victims of police aggression and their families; and admission of responsibility for the violence committed.[12]

There was much debate in the media, both in Mexico and the United States, about these demands, but in hindsight they seem simple enough. The last four were all directly related to the police aggression toward the students, the catalyst for their protest. The repeal of Article 145 was a broader demand but one not uncommon in protest movements in Mexico. Article 145 had been wielded by the government many times in the past; it gave the police a ready excuse to arrest whomever they saw fit. It was only natural that a protest movement would demand the repeal of such a law.[13]

Only the first demand—the release of political prisoners—indicated any broad political intent of the students, and it, too, seems like a natural demand for a "protest" group. Journalists speculated that such a demand indicated that communists had infiltrated the student movement, for most political prisoners in Mexico were connected with communism in some way; however, the Communist Party denied any involvement with the students. Members of the Communist Youth, who agitated for a more militant movement, later complained that the Communist Party itself did not play a more prominent role in the student movement.[14]

The rank-and-file of the student movement consisted of a diverse group whose motivations ranged from radical political beliefs to mild political interest to the thrill of challenging authority and skipping school. At the center of the movement was a determined and energetic leftist group, who for that summer made a career of protest. A small number of these were veterans of the recent clashes in France. For the majority of protesters, though, it was the activity of the movement more than its political objectives that engaged them. Demanding such things as the release of political prisoners was an exhilarating thing for the students to do. It gave a revolutionary feel to the movement, uniting them with students in France, the United States, Ireland, Italy, and elsewhere, who spent much of that summer marching in the streets. While they waved pictures of Che Guevara and Mao Tse Tung, Mexican students were not calling for a revolution as some other students around the world were, and they did not call for a significant overhaul of the political system. It is worth noting, too, that they made no mention of the Olympics in their formal demands. At its genesis, what the student movement wanted most was an apology and to be left alone by the authorities.[15]

It is possible that Díaz Ordaz could have defused the movement at this early juncture, perhaps by issuing such an apology and making a few concessions to the students. Instead he chose to escalate the cycle of oppression, leading to more student protests, and the pattern continued throughout the summer. Newly released government documents reveal that Mexican government officials formulated a strategy to handle the student movement in much the same manner as the railroad strike and the doctors' strike. On 26 July government officials created a strategy committee headed by Secretary of the Interior Luis Echeverría, who played the central role in directing government response to the students. This early strategy allowed the movement to carry on its activities largely unchecked while the government planted subversives within the movement to weaken it from within, at the same time hoping that student enthusiasm for the movement would wane. They purchased full-page advertisements criticizing the student movement and attempted to alienate the students from the rest of the population by leveling accusations of communist agitation. The police arrested many student leaders—several of them foreigners older than typical students—contributing to rumors of communist involvement. Among the thousand or so protesters arrested were two Spaniards, an Algerian, five Frenchmen, and Mika Satter Seeger, daughter of the American folk singer Pete Seeger.[16]

Such government efforts were counterbalanced by student publicity campaigns, as growing armies of students distributed fliers, conversed with people on the street, and emblazoned buses and walls with their slogans and demands. The protests continued to grow in number and intensity, and as the movement grew, its ideology began to crystallize and broaden. Initiated as a reaction against police brutality, the movement quickly came to incorporate demands for expansion of the democracy, university reform, and efforts to ease poverty. The students began to talk about political domination by the PRI and about overcrowding in the universities. They began "questioning the political system and demanding a greater role in the decision-making process."[17] They also began to attack the Olympic Games. On 30 July banners revealed one of many new slogans, "NO QUEREMOS OLIMPIADOS"—"We don't want the Olympics."[18]

By the beginning of August, student marches routinely included 50,000 or more protesters, with thousands of observers gathering at the roadsides to watch. While the students were always peaceful and unarmed, such masses of humanity were more than just a cause for concern for government officials: they also began to exacerbate traffic problems in a city already known for its traffic jams. The student-activists began to reach out to other groups, such as workers, the urban poor, and Indian peasants. While they did not achieve great success in winning broad-based support, such efforts did not go unnoticed by the government. Mindful of the May rebellion in France, the Mexican government could ill afford a similar sweeping attack with the Olympics so near. Also, as noted in a number of U.S. government intelligence memos, the expansion of the movement indicated that it was not likely that it was directed by only a handful of extremists, or directives from Moscow, but rather was indicative of a movement that had struck some chord with the broader Mexican population.[19]

Even more noteworthy, the students began to take the protest directly to Díaz Ordaz, chanting and jeering outside the presidential offices in the Zócalo, and demanding a public meeting with him. They waved banners suggesting that the president was an "assassin" and parodied his empty offer of an "extended hand" with cartoons of an extended claw. Other posters depicted Díaz Ordaz using the Mexican Constitution as toilet paper.[20] Such attacks cost them potential support from other groups, as many felt their actions were in poor taste.

In a demonstration on 27 August in front of the presidential palace, the students grew increasingly rowdy, until by the end of the display they had desecrated many symbols central to national pride, spray-painted the palace, and pulled down the Mexican flag. They shouted insults at the president and chanted, "*Sal al balcón, chango hocicón*"—"Come out on the balcony, monkey with a big snout."[21] These attacks struck Díaz Ordaz on a particularly tender nerve: his physical appearance. The object of jokes and derision throughout his life, he was always on guard against such attacks as president. Other students broke into the cathedral on the Zócalo, rang the church bells, and set off fireworks in the cathedral. Their actions on that night had two deleterious effects. First, they cost the students many supporters, who were offended at the desecration of the palace. Second, they deeply offended Díaz Ordaz, who was insecure about his appearance, sensitive to any insult, and suspicious of any number of conspiracies against himself and the country. It was, in part, the virulent insults launched by student-protesters that drove Díaz Ordaz to consider a violent solution to the problem.[22]

Such violence resurfaced at the end of August, after a month of peaceful and undisturbed student marches. On 28 August the students launched their largest protest yet, including some 200,000 students, teachers, and parents. While again the march stopped traffic and filled the Zócalo, the police were nowhere to be seen. That night, long after most of the protesters had gone home, a few thousand students returned to the square, apparently intent on spending the night and planting some sort of permanent pickets in front of the presidential residence. It was then that the police arrived, at first chasing off the protesters with only minor resistance. When the students returned, armed with bottles, rocks, sticks, and other makeshift weapons, the confrontation descended into violence. Dozens of students were arrested, and four were killed in the melee.[23]

Perhaps in an attempt to avoid having to resolve the issue violently, in his fourth annual presidential address, delivered on 1 September, Díaz Ordaz dedicated much of his speech to the student protest and the coming Olympics. In hindsight, the speech is a classic example of a tactic used many times before by the government in handling protest: empty promises. Díaz Ordaz specifically addressed two of the six student demands. Regarding the release of political prisoners, he maintained his position that there were no prisoners held solely for their political beliefs and that all those incarcerated had committed other crimes (such "crimes" in many cases fell under the aegis of Article 145, "social dissolution"). He intimated, though, that he might be willing to release some prisoners if the protests ceased. Regarding Article 145, Díaz Ordaz explained that he had initiated a study of the article and suggested a public debate within the Congress. Such assurances appear even more transparent in hindsight than they did in 1968, and few students were assuaged even then. Regarding the use of violence, Díaz Ordaz was even more intransigent. Not only was no apology for prior acts forthcoming, but he insisted that the government was ready to use armed force to prevent further disturbances. Unbeknownst to the students, Díaz Ordaz was making preparations for such a conflict, requesting —and receiving—radios, riot gear, and heavy weapons from the U.S. State Department. The warning foreshadowed the events of a month later, though no one recognized it at the time. Student leaders were disappointed that Díaz Ordaz addressed only two of their demands—and those inadequately—and they vowed to continue their protests.[24]

The first weeks of September passed relatively quietly. The students respected the observance of several national holidays by refraining from protests. In addition, classes were starting up again, and some students talked of ending the strike. A minority, though, agitated as actively as ever for change. They formed "brigades," meeting each day to distribute literature in the streets and encourage workers and peasants to join their movement. They preached of a corrupt government, ruled not by democracy but an entrenched oligarchy, and an economy grossly divided between the wealthy few and the impoverished many. These students took up headquarters at the National University, where they used the campus grounds for planning upcoming protests and organizing the brigades for their daily marches.

It was this improper use of the university campus that prompted the most significant government attack thus far, when army troops attacked the National University and seized control from the students on 20 September. At about 10 p.m., trucks and armored cars swarmed over the campus, breaking into the student offices and arresting hundreds of students, faculty, and administrators. The military repulsed several efforts by students to retake the campus, insisting that the students had been using the grounds illegally. U.S. officials wondered whether this explanation was simply an excuse for the government to occupy the university, where a number of important Olympic facilities were located. It was later reported that the attack was a preemptive strike to thwart a student march on the Olympic Village, though it is impossible to know whether such a march was actually in the works. While university staff balked at this ultimate breach of autonomy, those few who openly defended the students' actions soon joined them in jail, and the total number arrested quickly topped one thousand. The university would be restored to its normal operation procedures, explained the Minister of the Interior, Luis Echeverría, but probably not until after the Olympics were completed. The Minister of Defense, General Marcelino García Barragán, was less optimistic, saying that the university would be restored only when he was certain there would be no more student disorder.[25]

The students took refuge at the other main campus in the city, the National Polytechnic Institute, surrounded by the army but not seized immediately. In the ensuing days, they engaged in numerous street battles with the army and the police, exchanging volleys of rocks and bottles with the tear gas launched by soldiers, and continued their agitation as best they could, leaving fliers in the streets and painting their slogans on city buses.[26] The battles between students and authorities ebbed and flowed, stirring up ceaseless debate in the Mexican papers and much uncertainty whether the problem could be solved before the Olympics. On 22 September, even as flocks of doves were released in a rehearsal of the Opening Ceremonies, across the street students and soldiers engaged in a pitched battle on the university campus. Injuries were common in such battles, and the death toll mounted. In the battle that day, students overturned buses and set fire to them and threw rocks, bricks, boiling water, and Molotov cocktails at authorities, who responded with tear gas and occasionally gunfire. This kind of violence led to the police storming the students' stronghold at the Polytechnic Institute, an action that led to the resignation of the rector of the National University, Javier Barros Sierra, a resignation that was rejected by the university's governing board, which still hoped to convey an image of normality. Still another battle raged on the night of 24 September, in which students for the first time responded to the violence with gunfire of their own, contributing to as many as fifteen deaths. Students were heard to ask passing motorists for donations of gasoline, "for the people of Mexico," to use in the making of their bombs.[27] Such entreaties met with little success, though students still hoped their protests might win acceptance with a broader audience. "It is no longer a student fight," one said, "but a fight by all the people."[28] In spite of such aspirations, the students struggled on largely unaided by other groups, pitted against the authorities in nightly battles.[29]

The U.S. government and media watched the proceedings in Mexico with more than simply passing interest. Cold War tensions contributed to their concern, as early reports seemed to indicate that the student movement of Castro-friendly Mexico had been infiltrated by communist radicals. For years, the U.S. State Department had kept tabs on communism in Mexico and was leery of the left gaining influence. As the student movement grew, State Department documents reflected almost a paranoia that communists controlled the movement. But such claims more accurately reflected the Mexican government's perspective than reality. As September wore on, diplomats seemed to recognize that the role of communists within the movement was limited, and they became concerned instead that the student movement might win a larger audience, eventually driving the government itself to the left.[30]

A second cause for concern was that the student movement—or government reaction to it—would threaten the Olympics, the athletes, or traveling spectators. U.S. diplomats were unimpressed with Díaz Ordaz's handling of the affair long before the massacre itself. On 28 August, one such diplomat assessed his methods to that point, writing, "The evidence thus far is that Díaz Ordaz has not distinguished himself in handling the student crisis. He apparently has (1) under-estimated the depth of student hostility toward the GOM [Government of Mexico]; (2) overestimated the role played by alleged 'Communist' agitators; and (3) failed to follow up on possible opportunities to settle the problem."[31]

Then, five days prior to 2 October, on 28 September, calm set in. Students and the government alike began speaking óf a rapprochement and making concessions, however mild. With the Olympics less than three weeks away, and both sides exhausted by intense fighting, it seemed that a compromise was in the offing. Rector Barros Sierra returned to his post after his resignation was denied and insisted that he would come back to work only if the army vacated the National University. Shortly thereafter, the army did indeed begin making preparations to end its occupation, painting over the many murals and slogans created by the students and generally cleaning up the mess of the past few weeks. At least one editorial in the Mexican daily *Excelsior* speculated that the withdrawal of troops from the university would bring an end to the student protests. Díaz Ordaz replaced a member of the Congressional Committee on Student Affairs whom the students had named as unsympathetic to their needs. For their part, the students reiterated their commitment to nonviolence, and while they refused to cancel the strike, they vowed repeatedly not to disrupt the Olympic Games in any way. The only notable demonstration during this period was a low-key "Mothers March" on 30 September, consisting of some 3,000 women. Finally, the military rolled out of the National University, sweeping away all signs of an occupation that had lasted nearly two weeks. Not long after, the students pensively resumed their customary places on campus. It felt for all the world like things were heading back to normal, and everyone hoped the Olympics might arrive with no further incidents. Covey T. Oliver, the U.S. ambassador in Mexico City, wired home, "Tensions seem to be easing in Mexico City." It was 1 October.[32]

The Massacre at Tlatelolco

The following day, leaders of the strike movement continued their trend of recent days: organizing smaller gatherings and treading carefully to avoid police violence. At about 5:30 p.m., some 10,000 people gathered at the Plaza de las Tres Culturas—students, parents, women, children, and elderly among them—for their latest rally. The throng had planned to march to a nearby campus for a demonstration, but strike leaders announced to the crowd that those plans had been scrapped for fear of inciting the troops who had surrounded the Plaza.

Scholars disagree as to the exact nature of the attack in Tlatelolco, but it clearly involved some planning by the military and was much more than a spontaneous outbreak of violence. In a press conference given late on the night of the attack, Mexican Presidential Press Secretary Fernando Garza delivered the official government version of the story to a crowd of foreign journalists. Among other things, Garza explained that the fighting began when one group of students began firing at another. A conflicting report claimed that students initiated the firing from a balcony on the third floor of one of the apartment buildings. The evidence does not support either story. Witnesses in the square recall seeing men wearing white gloves—afterward understood to be a sign that they were members of the Olimpia Battalion—spaced strategically throughout the square. Moments prior to the attack, these men rounded up many of the student leaders and forced them to a second-floor room in one of the buildings fronting the square. From the balcony of that room, these soldiers were able to fire on the crowd from an ideal vantage point, and they did so indiscriminately. At the same time, two military helicopters circling the area began circling lower and lower over the square. Two flares, green and red, flashed from one of the helicopters moments before the attack began, later described as a signal to the ground troops to seal off all exits from the square. The helicopters, the tanks, and the spacing of the troops all suggest a pre-planned attack.[33]

One mysterious element of the massacre points to an even deeper conspiracy. One of the earliest injuries was to General Hernández Toledo, who suffered a wound from a .22 caliber weapon, which soldiers would surely not be using. Toledo, who oversaw the troops in the immediate area of the square, insisted that his troops resorted to violence only when fired upon by snipers from the top of the apartment buildings and held up his wound as proof. But why would the students, after weeks of essentially unarmed and peaceful protest, suddenly choose to engage in the systematic sniping suggested by Hernández Toledo, especially after the lull in violence of the past week? More likely is a theory advanced by historian Enrique Krauze that the whole affair was premeditated, including the shot on Toledo (which was not fatal). Krauze speculates that a military sniper, armed with the smaller gun to add to the deception, fired the shot at Toledo—who himself was not aware of the plot—to make it seem that the students had fired the first shot. A more recent study by Mark Kurlansky presents a similar story. According to new interviews and evidence, Kurlansky explains that members of the Olimpia Battalion accessed the balconies of the apartment buildings even before the shooting began and behaved as "snipers" throughout the attack; witnesses say that the shots continued for over two hours without pause. These snipers wounded not only students but also regular military personnel in the crowd below.[34]

Student leaders did their best to prevent panic in the crowd before finally succumbing themselves. They beseeched the crowd not to run, shouting that the flares were only designed to scare them, that the shots were only fired into the air. In fact, the shots were fired straight into the crowd, and as the troops closed in, in a pincer movement, the crush of protesters fled first one way and then the other, facing fire from both sides. While the government claimed that several soldiers were killed by shots from the students, it is likely that they were shot in cross fire from the various military units firing in all directions. In the days and weeks following the massacre, students insisted that none of them carried guns. Even if one or two did have a pistol that night, the suggestion that many students fired on the soldiers is not borne out by the evidence or by their own statements. Guns had never been the weapons of choice in the many skirmishes prior to 2 October; instead, students had thrown sticks, bottles, rocks, and Molotov cocktails, none of which were employed at Tlatelolco. Especially after a week of peace, it is unlikely that the students would have chosen that evening to fire upon a mass of heavily armed soldiers that had them surrounded in an enclosed area.[35]

Students were rounded up for arrest by the hundreds, lined up against the walls of the cathedral, the housing unit, the ruins. Those who had taken refuge in the apartment building, including many leaders of the strike, suffered the worst abuses. Huddled on the floor in hiding, many of the students did not realize until later that they were soaking wet from the ruptured pipes. The police who searched the building grabbed virtually anyone resembling a student, including several foreigners and laborers. They were treated as one, herded in groups of a dozen or two into several apartments designated as holding areas, where many were made to strip and subjected to searches—witnesses recall that many students were naked even as they were marched to transport vehicles. The police screamed at them, badgered them, and beat them. The march from the apartments to the trucks was even worse, a gauntlet of sorts with soldiers lining the whole walk. The abuses here were even harsher, as these soldiers targeted their blows at the prisoner's unprotected faces and groins. Most were doubled over in pain by the time they reached the trucks. The students were then hauled away to prison, where many would suffer days and even weeks of extended beatings, deprivation, mental abuse, and torture.[36]

The mess created in Tlatelolco was difficult for authorities to clean up, both literally and figuratively. A school adjacent to the square served as a triage center to aid the wounded, and it remains to this day a walk-in clinic. The next day, the rain-soaked, blood-stained Plaza was littered with shoes, bits of clothing, purses, and hats. The bodies were gone, and since soldiers had confiscated every camera they saw, the media and witnesses could only guess at the body count. The Plaza was understandably deserted. Now and then a family shuffled out from one of the apartment buildings; many families left the buildings after a night of questioning by the authorities. The students were all gone. Dozens had been killed, and even conservative estimates suggested that thousands had been arrested.[37]

While the square was silent, the prisons and hospitals of Mexico City resounded with the moans of the wounded and the cries of those being tortured. Many of those held in captivity after the massacre were brutally tortured by soldiers searching for clues as to the leadership, direction, and finances of the movement. The accounts of Luis Tomás Cabeza, González de Alba, Álvarez Garín, Heberto Castillo, and scores of others describe horrible tortures endured, first in a military camp and later in the notorious Lecumberri penitentiary. Such accounts are the centerpiece of Elena Poniatowska's gripping book *La Noche de Tlatelolco,* later translated as *Massacre in Mexico.*[38]

The arrests continued for a few days after the massacre as authorities hunted down student leaders. The students themselves were shocked and horrified at the brutal repression, and only the most foolish of them set foot in the streets during those days. Those in the student leadership who were left made several statements to the press, describing in detail the effects of the massacre. Such statements describe a student movement that, after the massacre, was terrified, immobilized, confused, and without leadership. Other such press releases assured the public that the student-protesters would not hold any more meetings and would not disrupt the Olympics, though they urged an end to repression and freedom of the students in captivity. Olympic organizers and government officials declared that they were "discussing" the situation with leaders of the movement and soon after announced that the students had agreed to postpone any further activities until after the Olympics. In truth, continued protest would not only have been difficult, with so many of their members either dead or in jail, but it would have been extremely dangerous as well. Díaz Ordaz and his administration had made the decision to end the protests by whatever means necessary. Renewed protest would surely have been met with similar violence. The student movement was, for all practical purposes, dead.[39]

The Student Movement and the Olympic Games

Historians have yet to adequately assess the relationship between the student movement and the Olympics. Accounts of the 1968 Olympics almost always mention the students, and vice versa, and without question the two together have attracted more scrutiny from historians than either would have independently. But were the two so connected at that time? The day after the massacre, the U.S. ambassador to Mexico wrote, "there [did] not seem to be any connection between [the] shootings and [the] Olympics."[40] While there could have been a student movement without the Olympics, we must wonder whether it would have ended in such disastrous fashion. If the students initially showed no interest in any ties to the Olympics, by the time of the massacre, the two were so closely linked that without the looming Opening Ceremonies there may not have been a massacre at all. There were at least five significant ties between the two: 1) timing; 2) student rhetoric; 3) the security force that repressed the students was raised for the Olympics; 4) heightened media coverage; 5) the perception in international circles that the students were protesting the Olympics.

The first connection between the two movements is timing. In the early months of the student movement, while the Olympics were still seemingly in the distant future, neither the press nor the Mexican government nor the students themselves, for that matter, made much mention of any connection between the two. The government initially had taken a nonviolent approach, employing a combination of delay tactics, smear campaigns, and false promises. Such techniques had little effect on the burgeoning student movement. As the months wore on, the impending Olympics grew more prominent in everyone's consciousness. Leaders of the student movement declared that "time was on their side because the Mexican government had to show [the] International Olympic Committee . . . that political stability could be maintained" leading up to the Olympics. The international media seemed to take the student movement more seriously as the Games drew nearer, less often writing off the students as an ill-guided communist-infested rabble and more often giving serious consideration to their grievances.[41]

The Mexican government, too, and Díaz Ordaz in particular, grew more agitated as the Games drew closer. Díaz Ordaz insisted that order be restored before the hordes of media, athletes, and spectators descended upon Mexico City. By September members of the U.S. State Department wondered if the window of opportunity for a peaceful settlement had passed. The student movement had gained so much momentum that violence and repression seemed the only possible solution. As a State Department memo dated 26 September explained, "All indications are that the Government of Mexico is completely determined to restore order by any means." Díaz Ordaz himself said plainly, "We are not going to let the student protest interfere with the Olympics." With only a few weeks until the Opening Ceremonies, and with international media already arriving, Díaz Ordaz had run out of time. As one American diplomat put it, the "significance of [the] Olympic deadline should not be underestimated. [The] government obviously felt that concessions under pressure would only strengthen [the] hand of radicals and encourage terrorist elements who might jeopardize [the] Olympics." For the Mexican government, swift and violent force was the only way to subdue the students before they could threaten the Olympics.[42]

Student rhetoric, graffiti, cartoons, and slogans are the second connection between the two movements. From the beginning students vowed not to disturb the Olympic Games. They recognized that the Olympics were hugely important to building Mexican pride and nationalism, and the vast majority of Mexicans supported the undertaking. To attack them directly would be self-defeating. Still, the Olympics exemplified much that was wrong with Mexico, and the students increasingly drew connections between their own grievances and this ultimate symbol of Mexican extravagance and waste. While the government spent millions of dollars in construction, beautification programs, and training and organizing for the Games, the masses remained mired in poverty. One student summarized their views: "We weren't against the Olympics as a sports event, but we were against what the Games represented economically. We're a very poor country, and the Olympics meant an irreparable drain on Mexico's economic resources . . . [the president] made this commitment simply to make a big splash, to enhance our country's outward image, which had nothing at all to do with the country's real situation." By the end of July, the first slogans and banners decrying the Olympics had appeared. On one sign, the Olympic rings were replaced with five smoking bombs. Another read, "Mexico: Gold Medal for Repression." The popular Olympic jingle "1968: Year of the Olympics" was replaced with "1968: Year of the Repression." By the end of August, the crowds of protesters waved countless signs against the Games. At a march on 27 August, nearly half a million people joined the students in chanting, "We don't want the Olympics, we want revolution." Similar slogans were spray-painted on buses and buildings, often directly on top of the Olympic logo or Mexico's logo for the Games, which read "Mexico '68."[43]

The third link between the two was the security force that helped put down the rebellion. As with any large event, the Mexicans heightened their security presence in the weeks prior to the Olympics, and a special battalion was assembled to preserve public order during the Games, the Olimpia Battalion. This unit wore plain clothes, with white gloves to denote their special role. Witnesses at the Tlatelolco massacre recall seeing white-gloved soldiers interspersed in the crowd, some in civilian clothes (while still wearing the telltale white gloves). In a newspaper ad purchased by the students some two weeks after the massacre (and largely unnoticed in the midst of the Olympics), student leaders blamed the Olimpia Battalion for the slaughter of innocents in Tlatelolco. One U.S. State Department report explained: "Students did not start [the] violence at Tlatelolco, but rather [a] well-armed group identifying [them]selves by gloved left hand[s] started firing and provided pretext for army firing."[44] Testimony at later hearings indicate that a total of some sixty-five soldiers from these battalions had been sent to the square and played a key role in blocking the panicked students as they tried to flee. They also stormed the apartment buildings surrounding the square, as witnesses recall hearing soldiers calling to one another, "Olimpia Battalion! Olimpia Battalion!" and such things as, "Don't shoot! They're wearing white gloves!"[45]

Surely the Mexican military could have squashed the student movement without the participation of these sixty-five soldiers, but their presence was a telling reminder that the protection of the Olympics was at stake.[46]

A fourth connection between the two was heightened media attention. Just as there was additional security for the Olympics, there was dramatically increased media in the country. With only a few weeks before the Opening Ceremonies, the number of reporters and film crews in Mexico City was growing by the day. Arriving reporters received specific instructions from the Mexican government regarding their coverage of the student movement. Jack Zanger, a writer for the *New York Times,* resigned from the press corps in protest over being censored. "We should have known what was coming at the first meeting," said Zanger, "when an official told us: 'There are no riots. If anyone asks you about riots, say it's not your department.'"[47] Many papers, including the *New York Times,* carried daily updates of both the Olympics and the student movement. Many such reports were critical of Díaz Ordaz's handling of the students and wondered what protests they had planned for the Olympics. Such speculation grew louder as more and more crews arrived. If the student movement was to be put down, it needed to happen before the full media crush that was to arrive in the following days.

One incident in particular exemplifies this theme. After the attack of 2 October, much furor was made in the Italian press over the wounding of Italian journalist Oriana Fallaci. Fallaci, in Mexico City to cover the Olympics and investigate the student movement, was on the third floor balcony of an apartment house during the attack. "She threw herself face down on balcony, was menaced with pistol and seized by hair by Mexican security officer, compelled to stand with hands on wall for two hours in exposed position and hit by three bullets or fragments at that time."[48] In response to this attack, the Italians threatened to withdraw their Olympic team and requested compensation from the Mexican government. Nothing more came of the incident, and Fallaci made a full recovery, but her injury demonstrates that the government did have an interest in "solving" the student problem before the media presence grew even greater.[49]

Finally, the widely held perception that the student movement aimed to damage the Olympics created a connection between the two. If, as the cliché holds, perception is reality, then the student movement was a threat to the Games. The international media began linking the two movements early on, and as the Games drew nearer scarcely an article could be written that did not speculate whether the protests would threaten the Olympics. An article running in the 2 September issue of *Newsweek* quoted one student as saying, "The committee is considering different projects to use the Olympics to embarrass the Mexican Government. Violence is definitely being considered—but right now it would be a last resort."[50] A government propaganda campaign contributed to this misconception. The idea was promoted in Mexican newspapers. On the morning after the massacre, one editor printed this phrase just under the headline: "The Objective: Preventing the Nineteenth Olympic Games from Being Held."[51] These campaigns were largely effective, as most international readers or visitors to the country believed that the students were trying to disrupt the Games. One French tourist commented, "The students' acts of bravado and the turmoil they were causing were threatening to ruin the Olympic Games."[52] Another said, "What happened was that students wanted to steal the spotlight from the Olympics."[53] At its height, such concern over the safety of the Olympics led to discussion of postponing the Games until the student movement was silenced, a rumor that the IOC was quick to dispel.[54]

Coupled with such beliefs were legitimate concerns about the safety of visiting athletes and tourists. The U.S. State Department grew more alarmed in the weeks prior to the massacre and remained so in its aftermath. It issued bulletins speculating that there might be more trouble during the Games, and increased security would be provided. On the day of the Opening Ceremonies, the front page of the *New York Times* ran a large picture of the Olympic Stadium, ringed with hundreds of riot police. But the movement had been thoroughly crushed, its leaders either dead or jailed, and the Games went on undisturbed. As one historian wrote, "By mid-week of the final week before the Opening there was much more threat of turmoil than actual turmoil. Mexico City was outwardly peaceful and serene."[55] Student promises not to disturb the Olympics were upheld, though one wonders if they would have staged some kind of protest had the massacre not occurred.[56]

The student movement, in hindsight, had been thoroughly crushed, its leaders incarcerated and its rank and file demoralized. Díaz Ordaz and his officers, though, still wondered whether there might be some backlash during the Games. Pockets of student resistance carried on in rural areas and might somehow revive the urban movement. The Mexican government arranged for the tightest security ever seen at an Olympic Games, and athletes approaching the stadium might have understandably thought they had walked into a war zone. An Olympics that was supposed to symbolize peace, prosperity, and goodwill instead opened in an atmosphere of fear, tension, and distrust.

The World Watches

October '68

five

At 10:30 a.m. on the morning of 23 August 1968, the Olympic flame sprang to life in the sacred grove of Zeus in Olympia, Greece. A Greek actress dressed in authentic costume sparked the flame by focusing the sun's rays on a dab of resin, and the march of the flame toward Mexico City had begun. As with most other aspects of the Games, the Mexicans had plotted the most elaborate course ever for the flame to follow, and the journey took nearly two months. The theme of the journey was Columbus's voyage to the New World, and so the flame made a lengthy circuit of the Mediterranean through Greece, Italy, and Spain. Along the way, the flame paused for various ceremonies: in Genoa, Italy, the birthplace of Christopher Columbus; in Barcelona, Spain, one of the seats of the Spanish empire; in Palos, Spain, where Columbus's voyage began in 1492. From there the torch made its way across the Atlantic to San Salvador, where Columbus first landed in the Americas, escorted on its journey by a direct descendant of Columbus himself. Finally, on Columbus Day, the torch arrived at Vera Cruz, Mexico. There, adding to the drama, the torch shared its flame with four other torches—in honor of the five Olympic rings—and the five followed different routes to reach Mexico City. Along those five routes, the torches made their way to all reaches of Mexico, and at every stop they were greeted with enthusiastic, curious spectators. At last, on the eve of the Opening Ceremonies, the five flames were reunited at the Pyramid of the Moon at Teotihuacán, thirty-one miles north of the city. There the flames fanned out in many directions as part of the ancient Aztec ritual of the new fire; huge pyres lit up the night sky, and finally the flames were reunited again for the final trek to Mexico City.[1]

At last all was ready. The evening of 12 October arrived, and the city opened its arms to some 135,000 tourists; 80,000 spectators packed into the Olympic Stadium for the Opening Ceremonies, which were brilliant indeed. It was the beginning of the largest Olympics to that date, as 7,226 competitors from 119 nations filed into the stadium. The athletes gleamed in bright colors as the sun began to set: Nigerians in green gowns; Americans in red blazers, and Russians in blue; Australian girls in yellow dresses, Mexicans and Japanese in white. Everyone was smiling, especially Gustavo Díaz Ordaz, who opened the proceedings and watched from his presidential box, thrilled at this triumphant moment for both his country and his presidency. The ceremony exemplified one of the slogans of the Olympics, "Everything is possible in peace." As part of this message of peace, the Mexicans released thousands of doves into the air, and they circled over the stadium, swooping and swirling as a single unit before flying out of the stadium. If only for a few hours, nations put aside their differences in the real world and communed in peace in the world of sport.[2]

The lighting of the Olympic flame was another revolutionary moment. The honor had fallen upon Norma Enriqueta Basilio, a twenty-year-old Mexican woman. She was the first woman to have the honor, and her selection exemplified a number of objectives of the organizing committee. First, it was hoped that the selection of an athlete from a rural area, rather than someone who lived in or near Mexico City, would help unify the entire nation behind the Olympic cause. The daughter of a Mexican cotton farmer from Baja, California, she represented portions of the Mexican population not usually celebrated, and when the announcement came in July that she would light the flame, Mexicans throughout the country applauded the choice. She also represented "a new kind of Mexican," tall, thin, educated, and beautiful, in contrast to the older generation that she called "short and fat."[3] The very fact that she was a woman also sent an important message: that Mexico was not a sexist, male-dominated nation, and that in fact women were making important strides toward equality. Finally, as a competitor in the 400 meters, she also had the long stride and endurance necessary to complete the run around the stadium and up the steep steps to the stadium's rim, no small accomplishment even for a fit athlete. She was the perfect choice, and as she approached the stadium behind a police escort, adoring fans threw flowers into the road before her. She entered the stadium to a huge roar, and as she circled the track and trotted easily up the steps to reach the huge saucer that would house the flame, the crowd's applause and shouts of support grew. The roar was nearly deafening as she reached the final step, turned, and held the torch high for a moment. Then she dipped the torch into the saucer, and flames poured skyward. The Games had begun.[4]

The Athletic Competitions

The athletic contests that followed were spectacular, though the issue of elevation was never entirely put to rest. The first medal event of the Games, the 10,000 meter run, could have been taken as a bad omen. Several athletes collapsed during the course of the race, and only a handful remained in contention in the final laps. All the medals went to athletes who lived and trained at high elevations. Naftati Temu of Kenya won the gold medal, Mamo Wolde of Ethiopia the silver, and Mohammed Gammoudi of Tunisia (who had won the "Little Olympic" race the previous year) the bronze. To the delight of the crowd, a diminutive twenty-one-year-old Mexican, Juan Martinez, finished fourth. Already, though, the media focused on the altitude issue and whether athletes training at low altitudes would suffer.[5]

It did not take long, though, for athletes in the shorter events to perform, and records began falling quickly. The American sprinter Jim Hines, who had run fast times since arriving in Mexico, tied his own world record in the 100 meter sprint in both qualifying heats before breaking it in the finals on the second day of competition. On the same day, American Jay Silvester set an Olympic record by tossing the discus over 207 feet in the preliminary round. Rainy weather on the next day did not stop the avalanche of falling records. Silvester's teammate, thirty-two-year-old Al Oerter, broke the world record by five feet in the medal round, winning his fourth consecutive Olympic gold medal. After a long season of mediocre performances, Oerter explained that he had spent the whole year preparing to make a long throw in the rarefied air in Mexico. Not long after, Wyomia Tyus, a twenty-three-year-old sprinter from Griffin, Georgia, broke the world record while winning gold in the 100 meter dash. The same day, Dave Hemery of Britain broke the world record in the 400 meter hurdles, and Ralph Doubell of Australia tied another in the 800 meter run. Records seemed to be falling in every event, and it became clear that the thin air only aided competitors in nonendurance events. In addition, many competitors cited the synthetic Tartan track, smooth and level even in the poor weather, as contributing to the barrage of records. All told, over the course of the entire track and field program, world or Olympic records were matched or broken in every event save the 5,000 and 10,000 meter runs.[6]

Records continued to fall as the days went by. Tommie Smith won the 200 meters in world-record time, while Peter Norman and John Carlos, who finished second and third, both tied the old record. The American Bob Seagren tied with two Germans, Claus Schiprowski and Wolfgang Nordwig, in breaking the world record height in the pole vault, as nine men vaulted over 17 feet. A Russian, Jan Lusis, broke the world record in the javelin throw. Italian Giuseppe Gentile finished first in the hop, step, and jump (now called the triple jump), ahead of four other competitors who bested the old world record. And that was just on the third day of competition.[7]

The signature feat of the Games, and one commonly attributed to the altitude, was Bob Beamon's spectacular long jump. It was no surprise, really, that Beamon won the event. Blocking out the political turmoil, the racial conflict, and the possibility of a black boycott of the Olympics, he had spent most of 1968 in isolation, training intensely for the Games. He won both the long jump and triple jump at the National Collegiate Athletic Association (NCAA) championships and came into the Olympics having won 22 of his last 23 competitions. It was no surprise, either, that the world record fell in Mexico. In October 1967 at the "Little Olympics," Russia's Igor Ter-Ovanesyan had jumped 27 feet, 4 3/4 inches, tying the world record held by Ralph Boston. So it was no surprise that the record fell, or that it was Bob Beamon who broke it. But the manner in which he did it stunned everyone who saw it.[8]

Beamon nearly failed to make the final round, fouling in two preliminary attempts. He survived, though, in the same way that Jesse Owens had done at the 1936 Olympics. Ralph Boston, his rival and friend, told Beamon to back up several inches and jump conservatively, securing a place in the finals. Beamon did and advanced to the next round. The next day, 18 October, was overcast and humid, but neither the weather nor the cheers of the crowd distracted Beamon. With his first jump, he soared farther than anyone had before. Beamon and the other competitors knew it was long but had to wait several minutes to learn exactly how long—Olympic officials had installed new optical technology to measure the jumps, but it was only programmed to measure 28 feet. An official ran out of the stadium and returned with a tape measure and confirmed that the jump was 8.90 meters, or 29 feet, 2 1/2 inches, crushing the old world record of 27 feet, 4 3/4 inches. Thin air or no, it was an astonishing accomplishment, a record that would stand until Mike Powell broke it by two inches at the 1991 World Championships.[9]

Less than ten minutes later, even as the cheers for Beamon's jump still rang in the air, Lee Evans set another astonishing record. Evans had considered not racing, as part of the continuing Black Power protests during the Games, but John Carlos sought him out and told him, "You run, win, and then do your thing, man."[10] Still high from watching Beamon's leap,

Evans crushed the world record in the 400 meter run. His time of 43.8 seconds was not matched until 1988 by Butch Reynolds. The records set by Beamon and Evans make 18 October 1968 one of the greatest days in track and field history.[11]

If the elevation inspired many exceptional performances, it also contributed to a few collapses by top athletes, most notably the American miler Jim Ryun. Ryun entered the Olympics as one of the most celebrated American athletes, winner of 47 races in a row and the world record holder in the 1,500 meter run.[12] But he had suffered from mononucleosis in the month before the Games and seemed to have some sort of mental block in adjusting to the thin air. His closing kick had not been in evidence during practices and preliminary heats, though he still won the heats. He met a pair of Kenyans in the final, Ben W. Jipcho and Kipchoge "Kip" Keino, whom he had defeated in his semi-final heat. The Kenyans, renowned for their grueling training runs and seemingly endless reserves of energy, were particularly feared at these Olympics for their experience in running at high altitudes.

Of this busy group, Keino was the busiest. By the day of his showdown with Ryun, he had already competed in the 10,000 meter run, two heats of the 5,000 meters, and three preliminary heats of the 1,500 meters, logging over sixteen miles of competition, and many wondered when he would tire. Unbeknownst to many at the time, Keino was also suffering from gallstones, which made him buckle over in pain even as he led the 10,000 meter race, causing him to finish well back in the pack. Over a week later, the pain from the gallstones was so severe that Keino resigned to forfeit the 1,500 meter final, and he stayed in his room at the Athletic Village that morning. But as the race approached, he changed his mind and hurried to reach the stadium. Stuck in a taxi in traffic, Keino jumped from the car and ran over a mile to the stadium only minutes before the race began. The other runners noticed that Keino was winded and sweating, and most expected him "to fall flat on his face at any moment."[13] Keino, though, pressed on, and it was Ryun who suffered in the 1,500 meter final. Jipcho led the early portions of the race. Keino surged to the front on the second lap and maintained a fast pace, while Ryun lagged behind, unable to mount a challenge. Ryun came back in the final lap to finish second, three seconds slower than Keino, still among the best times in Olympic history. Of all the events in Mexico City, this was the one most often held up as an example of the altitude favoring one athlete over another. Ryun's world record, set at sea level, survived the Olympics, but his reputation as the top 1,500 meter runner was eclipsed by Keino, who became a hero in his country and around the world.[14]

All told, the elevation affected performances much as experts had predicted prior to the Olympics: athletes in longer events in running, swimming, and especially rowing failed to approach record times while those in more explosive events, such as sprints and throwing events, frequently matched personal bests and world records. The rowers suffered the most, as at least sixteen different competitors required oxygen treatment either during or after their events. The leading U.S. doctor on hand to analyze the influence of the elevation, Dr. Daniel Hanley of Bowdoin College, summarized the issue, saying, "There is not a shred of evidence that the altitude had any harmful after-effects on the athletes from all the nations who . . . participated here . . . all things considered, altitude was even less of a problem than anticipated."[15]

Not all events were influenced by the elevation, though one of the most memorable did involve height. Dick Fosbury provided one of the most entertaining moments of the Games while revolutionizing the high jump at the same time. Employing a backward, headfirst style, now known as the "Fosbury flop," the twenty-one-year-old senior from Oregon State University dazzled the crowd by setting an Olympic record and barely missing in three attempts at the world record. The crowd shrieked and howled with his every jump, as the unorthodox style was simultaneously effective and dangerous. In describing the technique, Fosbury said, "I take off on my right, or outside, foot, rather than my left foot. Then I turn my back to the bar, arch my back over the bar and then kick my legs out to clear the bar."[16] With every such leap, it appeared that he would crash onto his head, a prospect that mesmerized the crowd. Fosbury added to the tension with his nervous rituals, staring at the bar, rocking from one foot to the other, clenching and unclenching his fists, seemingly interminably. It was written that he once stared at the bar for four-and-a-half minutes before making his jump, and he often tested the two-minute time limit given to each jumper. As he went through this ritual before each jump, the crowd whipped into a frenzy, exploding in amazement every time he cleared the bar without killing himself.[17]

Fosbury was not the only showman at these Games, and stars were born in many other events. Leonid Zhabontinsky, the great Soviet weight lifter, feigned an arm injury while marching as the flag bearer of the Soviet team, then went on to crush the competition—and several world records—in the weight-lifting competition. Vera Caslavska, a Czech gymnast and favorite of Mexican fans, won four gold medals in gymnastics to go along with three she had won in Tokyo in 1964. In winning the overall gymnastic competition, she bested two Soviet competitors, Zinaida Voronina and Natalia Kuchinskaya, a thrilling victory given the political tensions between those two countries. Already a fan favorite, she secured her place in Mexican hearts by performing her final routine to the "Mexican Hat Dance" and confirmed it by getting married in Mexico City the day after winning her four medals. Her wedding was *the* event mentioned in Mexican society pages, and the couple could scarcely make their vows heard above the din of clicking cameras.[18]

Debbie Meyer, a sixteen-year-old schoolgirl from Sacramento, California, struggling with a sore throat and intestinal problems, battled to victory in the 200, 400, and 800 meter freestyle races. A nineteen-year-old boxer from Houston, Texas, named George Foreman slugged his way to the gold medal. It mattered not that his feet were a bit slow and his style somewhat clumsy; he battered the opposition into submission with fearsome power, winning over Mexican fans and foreshadowing his rise to the heavyweight championship of the world. The U.S. team cruised to a gold medal in basketball, continuing a winning streak that dated back to 1936, but the defining moment of the basketball tournament came when Yugoslavia defeated the Soviet Union 63–62 in the semifinals. The game was close from start to finish, physical and emotional, as the Yugoslavians struggled not only to win a basketball game but also to overcome agents of the nation that threatened their independence. After the victory, which their coach described as "vital for the morale and pride of our players and people," the players kissed, embraced, cried, and rolled on the floor in ecstasy. The fact that they lost the final game to the Americans, 65–50, was of little consequence, for they had won the game that mattered most.[19]

Tommie Smith and John Carlos

As extraordinary as the athletic contests were—and they were extraordinary indeed—politics and scandal were never far from the surface throughout these Olympics. The most significant incident was the Black Power salute given by Tommie Smith and John Carlos. The boycott movement among black American athletes had failed, but they had agreed to carry out protests individually as they saw fit. Even after the Games had started, black athletes made statements hinting at some kind of protest. In the first few days of competition, though, there was little sign of discontent. Jim Hines, who won the 100 meter dash in world-record time, informed Olympic officials that he would not accept a medal from Avery Brundage; he was awarded his medal by someone else. But the real test of black militancy came on 16 October, the fourth day of competition, when Smith and Carlos competed in the 200 meter sprint. The boycott movement had originated in statements made by Smith, and Carlos became one of its leaders as the summer wore on. The two were co-favorites in the 200 meters, so it was an ideal opportunity to plan some sort of protest, as two of the most militant black athletes were expected to be standing together on the medal stand.[20]

The two invested only minimal time in planning a precise demonstration. Carlos, bitter after his treatment at the Olympic Trials in Tahoe and deeply committed to the cause of black equality, approached Smith before their semi-final heats, two hours before the final. The discussion was brief and revolved around securing a few articles of clothing to make some sort of statement on the medal stand. Smith had a pair of black gloves. Carlos had some black beads. Both agreed to do something on the stand, but they would work out the details later.[21]

Before making any kind of protest, though, both Smith and Carlos had to get to the medal stand. They were among the favorites to win in Mexico City, and both swept through their preliminary heats without being challenged. Smith, though, endured a thigh injury during his semi-final heat and left the field on a stretcher. He estimated there was only an 80 percent chance that he would run in the final. While lying on the stretcher between the races, Smith determined that he had come too far not to give it a try. He would run the final, even if he had to limp to the finish line. Once Smith had committed to run, Carlos began to contemplate how he wanted to run the race. He discussed it with his coach, Bud Winters. Having run in world-record time in Tahoe and beaten the best in the world repeatedly in the 200 meters, he was convinced that he could not be beaten in the final. At the same time, he knew that winning a gold medal meant more to Smith than to him. He told Winters, "The race don't mean shit to me . . . [and Tommie] would be elated if he won it."[22] Indeed, after winning the race, Smith told the press, "This meant everything to me."[23]

Carlos has written that he decided to "let" Smith win the race, if the opportunity presented itself. He got a fantastic start and led comfortably after 130 meters. He checked to his left to see how far back Smith ran and eased up a bit to allow him to take the lead. He ran the last thirty meters or so on "autopilot" and failed to consider the possibility that another runner might catch him as well. The oversight cost him a silver medal, as Peter Norman caught him at the line. The two finished in a dead heat, but examination of the "photo-finish" showed Norman ahead by inches. Disappointed in his overconfidence, Carlos later conceded, "If a white man can run a 20 seconds flat in the 200-meter, he deserves to win the second place medal."[24] He had blown the silver medal but would still be on the medal stand. And that had been the ultimate goal.

Smith's interpretation of the race, along with some compelling facts, challenges Carlos's story. Smith had been running quicker times in each of the preliminary heats, besting his own world record each time. In the final race, he accelerated dramatically in the final sixty meters and won by several meters over Norman and Carlos. Smith's winning time was 19.83 seconds, a world record that stood for over ten years. Carlos may have slowed intentionally to "let" Smith win, but it is a distinct possibility that Smith would have caught him anyway, considering his finishing time. As Lee Evans later recalled, it was commonplace for Smith to come from behind, to explode past a runner who thought he had the race won, with his remarkable finishing kick. In any case, the race set up the grouping on the medal stand that remains such an enduring image: Smith on the top step, with Norman to his right and Carlos to his left.[25]

In the ten-minute interlude between the end of the race and the medal ceremony, Smith and Carlos, amidst the bustling activity in the stadium corridors, hurried to finalize their plans. Smith's wife brought the black gloves; Smith took the right-hand glove, Carlos the left. Smith threw on a black scarf, and Carlos donned a black shirt and his black love beads. Both men removed their shoes and rolled up their pant legs, revealing long black socks. The pair approached Norman, who would stand beside them on the medal stand, and he agreed to wear a button from the Olympic Project for Human Rights (the button, incidentally, was borrowed from a white member of the Harvard crew team, who had supported the black athletes from the beginning). As the group made the walk to the medal platform, amidst the cheering of the fans, Carlos had one last brief conversation with Smith. He warned him that someone in the stadium might attempt violence during their demonstration. "The people will be shocked to silence and we should be able to hear the clicking of a gun," he said and warned Smith to be ready to hit the ground if he heard such a click.[26] With those thoughts in his mind, Tommie Smith took the top step of the medal platform to receive his gold medal. Asked later what he was thinking at the time, Smith explained, "Praying . . . I was praying underneath the bleachers, I was praying on the walk up the victory stand, and the entire time I was up there."[27]

The moments before the playing of the national anthem were filled with a myriad of emotions and thoughts for both men. They both pulled on their black gloves just before kneeling to receive their medals. They also both carried their shoes, which they placed on the platform next to them, in honor of the Puma brand, since "Puma had been providing them with all of their running equipment."[28] Smith was torn between the obvious tension of the moment and the joy of achieving his lifelong goal of winning Olympic gold. He took a moment to greet the crowd, both arms raised in victory, unwittingly revealing the glove on his hand, setting off nervous whispers between some Olympic officials who spotted it. Track coach Payton Jordan, who had given Smith and Carlos permission to wear black handkerchiefs and black socks beneath their sweatsuits, hoped that the protest would go no further. As the other athletes were introduced, Smith composed himself and prepared for the protest. He later explained the symbolism of their attire: "I wore a black right-hand glove and Carlos wore the left-hand glove in the same pair. My raised right hand stood for the power in black America. Carlos' raised left hand stood for the unity of black America. Together they formed an arch of unity and power. The black scarf around my neck stood for black pride. The black socks with no shoes stood for black poverty in racist America. The totality of our effort was the regaining of black dignity."[29]

With all three men on the stand, the stadium fell into silence as the announcer introduced the American National Anthem. The men turned, with Norman now standing in front of Smith and Carlos, and the music started. As the first notes sounded, they dropped their heads to their chests and shot their clenched fists skyward. Smith, on the top step of the platform, stood rod-stiff, his right arm straight and tall, his eyes clenched shut. Carlos, behind him, stared emptily into Smith's back, his body less stiff, his saluting arm bent a bit at the elbow.[30]

Within moments, eyes that had been averted to look at the rising American flag were riveted on the pair, and cameras flashing throughout the stadium recorded one of the most memorable moments of the era. While there may have been a few gasps of surprise, no cocking of guns was heard from the stands. As Carlos said later, "One could hear a frog piss on cotton it was so quiet in the stadium."[31] The next few minutes were a blur for the athletes. As they were hustled from the field, both delivered the Black Power salute several more times. There were shouts from all directions, mostly insults or angry words, but some cheers of support as well. In the tunnel beneath the stadium, they were assailed by the media with countless questions, which they answered hurriedly or not at all. Eventually they made their way back to the Olympic Village, where they found they had been evicted. Carlos collected his bags from the street outside of his villa, and after a time found lodging at the downtown Hotel Diplomatica, paid for by Puma.[32]

The storm of protest began in earnest the following day, and the significance of their action set in. In an instant, Smith and Carlos had shattered the myth of the pacified black American, renewing fears of a black uprising that hearkened back to antebellum fears of a slave revolt. On the surface, this was merely two black athletes raising their fists on the medal stand. More profoundly, though, it was two black men taking the ultimate opportunity to reject custom, convention, and control. White America gasped, as did the Olympic community. The International Olympic Committee called for some action from Avery Brundage, who needed little prodding—he was already furious. The next day, the U.S. Olympic Committee issued a formal apology to the International Olympic Committee for the actions of the two athletes and warned against further protests. It also announced that the pair had been banished from the Olympic Village and would be sent home. The media generally condemned Olympic officials for blowing the incident out of proportion, thus forcing the story onto the front pages of newspapers around the world. Smith agreed, saying, "We couldn't have done more to publicize our cause than the committee did. We're very grateful."[33]

While the action was swift and appeared forceful, it could have been worse. Both athletes had completed their events, they remained members of the team, and they got to keep their medals. They also ignored the

USOC order that they leave Mexico within forty-eight hours. Carlos explained, "They said we had to get out of Mexico City in 48 hours. They must certainly have realized they did not have this power. Only the Mexican Government can kick us out of Mexico and they have said nothing about it."[34] Both remained in Mexico until 21 October, five days after the protest itself but a few days before the Games concluded. Growing weary of the intense media pressure in Mexico, they agreed to return to the United States. They both missed the Closing Ceremonies.[35]

Over the next few days, athletes both present and former took sides, either supporting their protest or criticizing it. Hammer thrower Harold Connolly said, "Let a Russian try that and see what happens. I know a lot of Russians who don't like what happened in Czechoslovakia, but they can't say a word."[36] A wave of lesser protests and gestures over the next few days supported Smith and Carlos and their cause. A group of Cuban athletes wore black berets on the medal podium. The Mexican women's 4 x 100 relay team, which took second place, sent their silver medals to Harry Edwards as a sign of their support for the African American athletes. Wyomia Tyus and the rest of the American women's 4 x 100 relay team dedicated their gold medals to Smith and Carlos. Lee Evans, Larry James, and Ron Freeman, who swept the top three spots in the 400 meter run, wore black berets and raised their fists during the medal presentation. The moment was especially difficult for Evans, who, along with Smith and Carlos, had been considered both one of the leaders of the boycott movement and among the most militant of black athletes. Recognizing that Smith and Carlos had already made a powerful gesture, and mindful of the swift punishment that befell them (in fact, the USOC had banished Smith and Carlos only a few hours before the 400 meter final), Evans opted for a less controversial protest. His fist was raised for only a few moments and was not accompanied by the bowed head and serious countenance; he smiled throughout the ceremony. As he said later, "After what Tommie and John did, what anybody else did was like little or nothing."[37] Perhaps most surprising, Ralph Boston, the black American long jumper who had been staunchly opposed to the boycott, went shoeless on the medal stand out of deference to his fellow black athletes.[38]

Contrasting such supportive acts were the comments of Jesse Owens, once a role model for many of the black athletes. Owens was outspoken in his criticism of the boycott effort and equally critical of Smith and Carlos. He called the pair to task, saying, "We don't need this kind of stuff. We should just let the boys go out and compete."[39] Other black athletes refused to offer their support as well, most notably George Foreman. After winning the gold medal in heavyweight boxing, Foreman paraded around the boxing ring, brandishing a tiny American flag and chanting, "United States Power." Some witnesses considered this act a parody of the solemn and, to some, unpatriotic gesture of Smith and Carlos.[40] Foreman, then and now, declared himself an American athlete first and foremost, rather than a black American athlete. He also expressed some displeasure at having been excluded from the discussions about the boycott because he was not a college athlete at the time. In any case, Foreman continues to be criticized by historians and participants in the movement like Tommie Smith for not supporting the others. Other black athletes branded both Foreman and Owens as "Uncle Toms" for such actions.[41]

Regardless of whether other athletes supported or condemned their actions, Smith and Carlos created a storm of controversy and strengthened the bond between politics and sport. For the first time, individual athletes had used the medal platform to make an overtly political statement. Prior to their protest, politics entered the Olympics via several methods. Governments and organizing committees had used the Games to improve their national image, as did Nazi Germany and Mexico itself, or as a pawn in diplomatic negotiations, as did South Africa and the Soviet Union. Athletes deemed to have made political statements had always done so simply by their very presence at the Games or by performing well, as Jesse Owens had done in overturning the myth of Nazi superiority in 1936. Both individual athletes and national teams had used boycotts, either threatened or real, to make political statements or encourage policy changes. But never had an athlete taken his protest to the medal stand, a sacred stage of ceremony and, theoretically, a sanctuary devoted to pure athleticism. If athletes were allowed to use the medal stand for such gestures, what would prevent similar displays by Czech athletes opposed to Soviet intervention? Or Vietnamese against the United States? Or Hungarians or Koreans or virtually anyone, for that matter? Smith and Carlos, in the words of one newspaperman, "shook this international sports carnival to its very core."[42] The International Olympic Committee reacted swiftly and authoritatively, for its members must have sensed that such overt political demonstrations had the potential to tear apart the Games. The Olympics were intended to allow athletes from warring nations to challenge each other peacefully on the fields of sport; they were certainly not intended as an alternative venue for such wars to be continued. But the line between the two is very narrow indeed, a lesson the IOC would learn in 1968 and would continue learning in the decades following.

Other Controversies

While the protest of black American athletes was the most visible and memorable, it was hardly the only controversy of the 1968 Olympics. Controversy accompanied these Games from the opening day of the competition, when the Soviet Union faced Czechoslovakia in a women's volleyball match. Only a few weeks before, the Soviet army had rolled into Czechoslovakia, conquering its peaceful neighbor with minimal resistance. After the occupation, which began on 21 August, the Czech organizing committee doubted whether they could even send a team to the Olympics. Communication within the country was disrupted, transportation in some cases was cut off, and sports were temporarily banned by the invading Soviets. By early September, though, some aspects of normality had been restored for the Czech athletes, and the Czech Olympic Committee decided to send a 100-person team to Mexico City, in spite of transportation and organizational hurdles.[43]

Clearly the Olympics offered the Czechs an opportunity to thrive in spite of the occupation of their homeland, and events such as the volleyball match seemed an ideal opportunity for them to seek some retribution, if only in the form of a ball spiked into the face of an opposing player or a charge across the net. The match drew thousands of enthusiastic fans, who were even more excited by the political overtones surrounding it. Many references were made in the press to the similarity of circumstances in the water polo match between the Hungarian and Soviet teams at the Melbourne Olympics, played shortly after the Hungarian uprising of October 1956. That match had deteriorated into a bloody slugfest, with several Hungarian players injured from Soviet blows. Violent though the match was, the Hungarians ultimately prevailed and went on to win the gold medal. One American player speculated on the potential for violence: "If the Czechs have any class, there is going to be some blood tonight."[44] Under heightened security, the match carried on without incident. The Czechs played better than expected, winning a set from the Soviets for the first time in six years, but in the end the Soviets won convincingly. The biggest fanfare came at the press conference after the match, when an agitated press corps eager for headlines misunderstood a statement of the Soviet coach, who commented on the cool attitude of his players under pressure. The statement, after making its way from a Russian to a Spanish to an English interpreter, came out in the press as, "My team is not affected by what the crowd says or to whom. They are professionals."[45] Given the uproar over amateurism, this comment was met with much furor by the press corps, and only after several days of rewrites and the vehement denials of the Soviet coach was the whole affair straightened out. But literally from day one, politics blended with sport at these Olympics.[46]

The amateurism debate surfaced several more times during the Games, most notably when three American track stars were accused of taking cash payments from equipment manufacturers. The rumors, which seemed to swirl perpetually around track and field athletes, intensified midway through the festival, when four American runners turned in $500 cash, apparently left in their shoes by representatives of a shoe company. The four received high marks for scruples, but this incident also renewed discussion of such payments and speculation about other athletes.

An investigation by the USOC revealed more rumors and sketchy details of several athletes living in high style in Mexico, well beyond the means of an amateur. There was talk of two track athletes, "gold medal winners," receiving $7,500 each, and a third accepting 18,000 pesos (about $1,440), but none of the rumors escalated into formal charges or suspensions. Everett "Eppy" Barnes, acting executive director of the USOC, conceded, "We have nothing to substantiate the rumors."[47]

But neither officials nor athletes would let the matter die as the Games wore on. Many officials agreed with Dan Ferris, secretary of the Amateur Athletic Union, who argued that equipment company logos should be eliminated, thus removing their incentive to pay athletes to prominently display their products. This solution hearkened back to the winter Olympics at Grenoble, where Avery Brundage had demanded that ski company logos be painted over. Most athletes agreed with Harold Connolly, a four-time Olympian, who advocated open competition between all athletes, professional or otherwise. "Why don't they make the Olympics an open meet, just like the tennis people did?" he asked. "That would be one way of putting an end to this 'shamateurism' that the Olympic brass claims to deplore."[48] Other athletes urged the IOC to broaden its membership to include former, if not active, athletes, who could better understand their plight. Even as the Games drew to a close, athletes fumed over the IOC decision to limit the number of athletes marching for each team at the Closing Ceremonies, and the clamor for a large-scale restructuring of amateur athletics was louder than ever.[49]

There were other less visible problems during the Olympics as well. The specter of the student massacre never entirely disappeared, and both organizers and participants wondered if the students might protest during the Games. While the students in Mexico City appeared to be thoroughly silenced, those in outlying regions continued to demonstrate. Students at University of Sonora, University of Monterrey, and in Tijuana stopped classes in support of those killed or arrested in the massacre. Those in Tijuana organized several marches, including one of nearly 1,000 people on the eve of the Olympics, and they reiterated the demands of the original student movement. Students in Chihuahua, too, continued to protest, engaging in several marches between the massacre at Tlatelolco and the beginning of the Games. Their protests centered around the disappearance of a student reporter named Sergio Sáenz, who had gone to Mexico City to cover the student movement and had not been seen since the massacre. The unrest in Chihuahua grew so intense that the students were eventually sent on an "Olympic holiday" to prevent further problems during the Games.[50]

Such continued activity was not unnoticed by U.S. government officials, who worried whether these limited incidents might explode under the spotlight of the Olympics. One internal memo expressed such concerns: "The continuing violence raises two concerns for the U.S.: 1) the safety of U.S. athletes and visitors to the games and 2) U.S. participation in scientific and cultural activities associated with the Olympics."[51] Even minor developments, rumors, and speculation heightened U.S. concern. The State Department took note of a leaflet issued by a radical wing of the student movement a week before the Opening Ceremonies, which read, "It will be necessary to mount a major military operation against the government during inaugural ceremonies of [the] Olympic Games."[52] Given such activity, the U.S. ambassador to Mexico speculated: "The Olympic Games will be held, although marred by sporadic violence. Students are not likely to attract significant support from other important sectors and will not threaten the stability of the Government in the short run."[53]

The State Department need not have worried much about the prospect of student unrest. Not only were the students in Mexico City terrified into submission but also the Mexican police and Olympic security were constantly on the lookout for troublemakers and kept the U.S. government abreast of developments. Rumors of the possibility of sabotage of Olympic facilities or even kidnapping of athletes proved unfounded. The Games were not without student unrest, though. A State Department memo cited one incident in which a student named Ramón Hernández Vallejo was hired by a group of Cubans to kill an American athlete. Hernández Vallejo had second thoughts and failed to carry out the attack and was then himself attacked by a group of Cubans, nearly killing him. In another incident, a student attempted to incinerate an Olympic bus, but all athletes and passengers escaped without harm. In yet another, "A Mexican spectator shot himself at the start of a cycling team trial . . . in protest of the Mexican government's treatment of students."[54] Aside from these incidents and a few small student gatherings, all of which were peaceful and relatively quiet, there were no serious protests during the Games. The city was consumed with the Olympic spirit, and those students who were not incarcerated either joined in the celebration of the Games or kept quiet, not wanting to revive the ire of the government.[55]

Still other controversies flared up during the Games. The Olympics in Mexico City were the first to implement widespread drug testing, combating another issue that had plagued amateur athletics in the mid-1960s. The testing was also instituted to ensure the safety of athletes exerting themselves at high altitude. Athletes were subject to random drug tests, as each day the Olympic Medical Committee tested ten athletes from one sport, all chosen at random. For team sports, two members of every participating team were tested. As many still do today, athletes questioned the logic of the substances listed as banned versus those that were permitted. One magazine noted, "The sprinter who fancies a double scotch to steel himself for the big occasion must not imbibe, though he can pep himself up with caffeine from a cup of strong black coffee."[56]

In spite of repeated warnings and lengthy lists explaining the forbidden substances, there were several transgressions, some influencing medals awarded. In one case, middleweight boxer Chris Finnegan refused to take a blood test after his match, saying, "standing at those long urinals . . . with all the other blokes" made him uneasy. Eventually he was cleared of any wrongdoing and awarded the gold medal, but his actions certainly aroused suspicion among other competitors, fans, and the media. While Finnegan kept his medal, the Swedish modern pentathlon team was forced to surrender its bronze medal after one of its members, Hans-Gunnar Liljenvall, was found to have an illegally high alcohol content in his blood. Similarly, Bulgarian Greco-Roman wrestler Hristo Traikov was banned from the Olympics when it was discovered that his trainer had administered ammonia, an illegal substance, to him during a match with David Hazewinkel of the U.S.[57]

The 1968 Olympics also saw the first examinations of females to verify gender. Female athletes, especially those whose muscularity and performance approached that of men, had always fallen under special scrutiny. Stella Walsh, a top female athlete of the 1920s, and Babe Didrikson, among many others, were often called lesbians and were sometimes even accused of being male. Walsh ultimately was revealed to possess sexual organs of both sexes after her death in 1980. Such suspicions were further aroused beginning in the early 1960s, when female athletes from Eastern bloc suddenly began to break world records and crush the competition from other nations. As such, in 1966 the IOC announced that it would perform gender tests at the 1968 Olympics. While no athletes failed the tests in Mexico City, several prominent athletes either withdrew from qualifying tournaments or retired at the announcement that they would be tested. It has since been revealed that female athletes from East Germany, Russia, and elsewhere were routinely forced to take steroids and male hormones, with tragic consequences for many such athletes later in life.[58]

One controversy that never attracted the attention of the media involved the German flag. It appeared for a time that East and West Germany might be represented separately in Mexico City for the first time, and Olympic organizers were torn as to how they should handle this obvious intrusion of politics into the world of sport. Brundage and the IOC decided that East and West Germany should march together under one flag at the Opening and Closing Ceremonies and that the national anthem would be Beethoven's Ninth Symphony. The East Germans lobbied vigorously for their own flag and anthem, and for nearly two weeks they engaged the Mexicans in an often humorous cat-and-mouse game to secure their own symbols. The East Germans wanted their own anthem; the Mexicans explained that their band could not learn a new song on such short notice. The East Germans found a different band, which said they could play the song; Ramírez Vázquez told them, "They are Mexicans. If you asked them to play Beethoven's Eleventh Symphony, they would tell you they could do it."[59] The East Germans hired another band and trained them to play their anthem; the Mexicans sent that band on a fool's errand to Guadalajara on the day of the Closing Ceremonies to avoid any embarrassing incidents.[60]

The two camps engaged in similar machinations over an individual flag for East Germany. The Mexicans explained that they had only one flag for Germany. The East German contingent worked feverishly over several days to produce an East German flag. On the morning of the Closing Ceremonies, they handed the flag to Ramírez Vázquez, who unfolded it only to realize that it was bigger than both the Mexican and the Olympic flags. "If I put out a flag like that, the Mexican army will shoot me!" he told the Germans, expecting the affair to be settled.[61] The Germans were more stubborn than anyone expected, though, and in the few hours before the Closing Ceremonies, the ambassadors and their wives put together still another flag, which they brought to the Mexicans only moments before the ceremony was to begin. Avery Brundage was there, and everyone present recognized not only that the group had put great effort into making the flag but also that the new flag was more expertly crafted than many of the other flags flying at the Olympic stadium. They relented. Willie Daume and the East German contingent celebrated, and so it was that East and West Germany flew separate flags at the Closing Ceremony of the 1968 Olympics for the first time.[62]

After weeks of scandal and controversy—and stunningly successful athletic contests—the Olympics came to a close. The final events of the Games were held on Sunday afternoon, 27 October, and afterward all the athletes and supporting staff made their way to the Olympic stadium for the Closing Ceremonies. As they waited for the ceremonies to begin, the athletes did their best to entertain the fans, putting on impromptu gymnastics displays and waving to the crowd. At last, Avery Brundage got the ceremony under way by declaring the Games of the Nineteenth Olympiad closed and calling for the teams to reconvene four years later in Munich. The stadium descended into darkness before the scoreboard reading "Mexico '68" flickered for a moment then switched to "Munich '72." A tremendous fireworks display followed, lighting up the night sky for ten minutes. As the fireworks crackled to a conclusion, some 800 mariachi bands entered the stadium and circled the track, playing several traditional Mexican tunes. They concluded with "Las Golondrinas," a song about swallows migrating south for the winter but always returning the following year. It was a fitting tribute to the athletes who, like the swallows, were preparing to leave the spotlight until the next Olympics four years later. It was a beautiful, moving ceremony.[63]

But even the Closing Ceremony was not entirely without controversy. The Closing Ceremonies had always been something of an enigma for

Olympic organizers, clearly an anticlimax after the exhilarating Opening Ceremonies followed by weeks of heated competition. At the Tokyo Games in 1964, the IOC tried a little something different to maintain interest. Heeding a suggestion from a twelve-year-old Japanese boy, the IOC decided to allow the athletes at the Closing Ceremony to march in whatever groups they wanted, rather than the strict national groups as in the Opening Ceremony. It was hoped that such a change would lend an informal air to the Closing Ceremony and also encourage goodwill and brotherhood between nationalities. The plan worked but perhaps too well. The athletes danced and paraded their way around the track as a joyous mob, led by the New Zealand contingent, who bowed, waved, and blew kisses at the Japanese emperor. The emperor seemed to enjoy the gesture, however irreverent it may have been, and he laughed and waved in response. IOC members, though, were appalled at the informality and feared that a similar display at future Games might set off a riot.[64]

Hoping to prevent such chaos in Mexico, the IOC ruled that only seven members of each national team would be allowed to march in the Closing Ceremonies, and the remaining athletes would have to sit in the stands. The new rules seemed to have worked, as the athletes entered the stadium in well-ordered fashion. Not long into the ceremony, though, an American athlete from the stands hopped over the wall and onto the track, joining the other athletes. He was followed at first by a handful of athletes, then dozens and hundreds, and before it was over virtually all of the athletes, and many spectators, had filed from the stands onto the field. They danced around the track while the mariachi bands played, smiling and whooping it up. Athletes borrowed sombreros from Mexicans in the bands and on the field, and a Mexican gold-medal winner was carried around on the shoulders of his countrymen. The jubilation carried on for half an hour as the Mexicans and athletes alike milked all they could from the experience.[65]

Even amidst such joy and spontaneity, though, reminders of the tension that had surrounded the Games' beginning still surfaced. Military police wearing jackets and white helmets stood guard in the stands and around the field, and plainclothes police mingled among the spectators. Díaz Ordaz kept a watchful, though not unhappy, eye on the proceedings from his presidential box, and an occasional helicopter swooped around the stadium. As the celebration drew to its close and jubilant fans wandered out into the night chanting "May-hee-co," the military and the plainclothes police followed closely behind.[66]

Settling the Score

six

The day after the Closing Ceremonies, Willie Daume walked through the Olympic Village with a particular glow about him. As the president of the German Olympic Committee, Daume would supervise the organizational efforts for the 1972 Olympics in Munich. It would be an enormous task, but he was excited and eager to try to match the show put on by the Mexicans. He found Pedro Ramírez Vázquez and Eduardo Hay chatting and reminiscing with Avery Brundage. "Willie," Brundage called, beaming. "It's a tough thing for you, eh? Have you seen these Games? It will be tough for you to do better than this."

Daume shook his hand and replied, "Look, I will do my best. But I can't do a Mexican miracle."

They all laughed, and Hay asked, "Willie, what do you mean by a Mexican miracle?"

"When I arrived in Mexico," Daume said, "we saw the workers and the painters and construction men coming out of the city, and we were coming in at the same time! So it was finishing up just as we arrived. And this is the miracle. I will try to do my best, but we can't do the miracle."[1]

Mexico garnered much praise for staging a successful Olympics, but over the ensuing months and years, the lasting impact of the Olympics in Mexico grew more dubious. The financial balance sheet of these

Games is complex, but even if they may have been profitable in the short run, they demonstrated a fiscal irresponsibility on the part of a government confronted with much more pressing issues than hosting an athletic festival. There were dark times ahead for the Mexican economy, and the Olympics and the spending policies associated with the Games probably contributed to them.

There were other issues to consider after the Games. The athletic results seemed to favor the United States, a worrisome result for the Soviet Union, which placed so much significance on athletic success. The mediocre showing led to wholesale changes in the structure of Soviet athletics. Black American athletes and Mexican student-activists also took the measure of their place after the Olympics. Both felt the scars of 1968 for years to come. For the athletes who had participated in protest at the Games, there were many challenges in finding employment commensurate with their talents. And for black athletes in general, there were still decades of marginalization ahead before the athletic system finally grew more egalitarian in the late 1980s, a process still in motion today. Mexican students, too, faced a long struggle before their demands were met. The tattered student movement never completely reformed, and the students retreated into their personal lives, becoming part of a generation of Mexicans dissatisfied with their government. The government did gradually become more "open" in ensuing decades, and the most recent elections in 2000 and 2006 indicate that true democracy in Mexico may be achieved, but questions about the electoral process still remain.

Finally, the Olympics themselves changed dramatically in 1968. The Mexico City Olympics were a portent of many things to come in international sports, from the gigantism and expense of the Games to the bidding scandals that rocked the Olympics in the new millennium. The student movement that was thought to threaten the Games initiated enhanced security measures to prevent terrorism, a process expedited after the tragedy at the 1972 Munich Olympics. And concern over doping and drug use that led to the implementation of drug testing in Mexico City only presaged the drug scandals that have marred so many Olympics since then. The echoes of 1968 still reverberate today.

While work on some venues was not completed until the eve of the Opening Ceremonies, few organizational glitches occurred, and the casual observer would never guess that there had been a frenzied rush to finalize preparations in the weeks before the Games. No one wanted to discuss any of the troubles or controversies surrounding the Games in the immediate aftermath. Official announcements by Ramírez Vázquez and others declared that the protest of Smith and Carlos did not diminish the event at all; the student protests went all but unmentioned except for a handful of editorials. Praise came from all quarters. Over the following days, organizers and political officials gathered at parties and reunions, where congratulations abounded. Committee members congratulated each other. IOC members congratulated the Mexicans. Organizers congratulated athletes, and athletes congratulated organizers. Josué Sáenz, president of the Mexican Olympic Committee, made several speeches thanking Díaz Ordaz, and legislators congratulated him for his unfailing support of the endeavor. Pope Paul VI praised the Games as "a forum of universal brotherhood."[2] French President Charles DeGaulle sent a letter praising the Mexican government and Olympic committee for a well-prepared and -organized Games, and U.S. President Johnson sent his congratulations as well. A Peruvian news program called the Mexico City Olympics "the most brilliant and astonishing in the history of the sports world."[3] U.S. President-elect Richard M. Nixon chimed in, proclaiming that the Olympics signaled that Mexico was ready to join the ranks of the most advanced nations and that the Games had formed, "a bridge of international understanding and a contribution to the cause of peace."[4]

The Mexico City Olympics set many precedents that future Olympics would struggle to match. The Cultural Olympics was a great success and would become a mainstay. More athletes representing more nations competed in Mexico City than ever before, including representatives from more than twenty African nations as well as the Vatican. It was the first Olympics to be transmitted globally on color television, and the official film of the Olympics was nominated for an Oscar. Much of the technology associated with the Games was revolutionary, including the Tartan track and the timing pads in the swimming pool. The Mexico City Olympics featured a number of firsts: for the first time, a woman lit the Olympic flame, and for the first time drug and gender testing were conducted at the Olympic Games. Mexico also won praise for achieving all this as the first "developing" nation to host the Olympics as well as being the first Spanish-speaking and Latin American country to do so. Adding to Mexican pride was the fact that Mexico won more medals than it ever had before, including three golds. If, as Joseph Arbena has written, "The objective was to show Mexico at its best, both to enhance image and pride as an end in itself, but clearly also to open channels for more trade, investment, and tourism," then in the short term at least, it seemed they had succeeded.[5]

Economic Impact of the Olympics

The initial flush of success lingered for several months as Mexicans anticipated that the benefits of the Olympics would far outweigh the expenses of staging them. Alfredo Santos, president of the Mexico City Chamber of Commerce, described the Olympics as "a seed planted, that if well-fertilized would produce abundant fruits, such as having other events of world importance in the future, like the 1970 World Championship of

Soccer."[6] He, along with many other analysts at the time, dismissed the notion that the expense had not been worthwhile. After all, the economy enjoyed a great boost from tourists visiting during the Olympics, many of whom enjoyed their experience and would return later, hopefully with friends. He estimated that tourists spent about 300 million pesos beyond expectations, largely offsetting the cost of the Olympics themselves.[7]

But financial analysis of the Games is not quite so simple. The expenses of the Olympics were one of the most glaring symbols of a government that spent lavishly on luxuries while neglecting obvious areas of need, a country engaged in a dangerous game of "keeping up with the Joneses" that left the majority of the populace impoverished. Mexico would never again approach the financial heights of the "Miracle" of the 1950s and early 1960s. One might argue that the Mexican economy was past its peak anyway and would have suffered during the oil crisis of the 1970s regardless of policy, but in hindsight many Mexicans were right to question the prudence of staging a massive sports festival when there were so many other problems to be dealt with. In any case, the ledger reveals this: $153.2 million spent in total, of which $92.5 million was paid for by income from ticket sales, advertising, television rights, and other sources. The Mexican people paid for the remaining $60.7 million.[8]

But the balance sheet extends far beyond these numbers, for the total spending does not incorporate the construction of roads and subways, many improvements to hotels, and the like. Such expenditures stretched the Mexican budget even further. At the same time, the Olympics brought residual benefits. Television sales boomed throughout 1968, as many Mexicans bought their first television to be able to watch the Olympics. The construction sector of the economy jumped by 11 percent during 1968, with many projects devoted to Olympic preparations. The airline industry flourished, and tourism brought other benefits to the economy as visitors stocked up on souvenirs and trinkets and boosted the restaurant business as well.[9]

What can be made of such figures? First, it would be easy to exaggerate the impact of the Olympics on the economy. It is important to remember that virtually all of the economic impact of the Olympics, both positive and negative, concentrated on Mexico City. Aside from a limited program of improvements along the U.S./Mexican border and expansion of the major highways leading into Mexico City, few of the improvements and expenditures and very little tourism and tourism-generated income reached into the Mexican countryside. Many Mexicans reaped no material benefit from the Olympics at all. Second, the overall Mexican economy for 1968 was not substantially different from that of the years just prior to or following. The GNP grew by 7.1 percent, which was precisely the average growth rate over the years 1963–1967. While there was much excitement generated over the Olympics, it seems that the expenses and income balanced each other out. Most important, though, the Olympics represent the vision of a government determined to emulate Western economies, especially that of the United States, and determined to join the ranks of "modern" nations. Such policy involved a host of issues—all of which ultimately debilitated the economy—including dependence on oil rather than a diverse economy; a growing trade deficit; inflation; high interest rates; low savings rates among Mexican citizens; tax benefits to foreign investors and companies; concentration on urban development while neglecting rural areas; and high superficial expenditures, including such luxuries as the Olympic Games. Even in the late 1960s, as the Mexican economy chugged along, experts worried that these policies could not be sustained indefinitely and that without wholesale changes in philosophy the Mexican economy would crumble. At least one article, published in *The Economist* in August 1968, suggested that one key to Mexican economic survival would be "austerity" in consumption. Cutting back on unnecessary expenses and superficial projects could save the Mexican economy. While we can only speculate in hindsight, it seems clear that spending on projects such as the Olympics contributed to the economic woes of the 1970s and '80s.[10]

Problems during the Olympic era foreshadowed far more crippling difficulties to come, many of which still afflict Mexico today. Following Díaz Ordaz as president was Luis Echeverría, who had been secretary of the interior under Díaz Ordaz and "the non-military official most closely associated in the public mind with the policy of repression of the students in 1968."[11] He was humorless, unimaginative, and tactless and endured dozens of protests against his regime. Problems such as malnourishment, illiteracy, unemployment, poverty, and poor health approached epidemic proportions, exacerbated by soaring population growth and a steady urban migration. Mexico City, which had put on its best face during the Olympics, became a filthy city, filled with slums and beggars, choked with smog and pollution, and slowed by endless construction and traffic jams. Echeverría poured money into public works projects and subsidized dozens of industries, many of which floundered or produced inferior products. His administration was also rife with corruption, and bribes and kickbacks siphoned off untold millions from the national budget. Increasingly dependent on loans from the United States and foreign investment to fund such projects, the Mexican economy suffered even more as the U.S. economy sagged in the mid-1970s. Coupled with staggering inflation and careless monetary policy, this debt had caused a virtual collapse of the Mexican economy by 1976. The prosperity that had been so crucial in winning the Olympic bid was a distant memory, and Mexico still struggles to lift itself from economic depression. While it is folly to suggest that the Olympics caused this economic crisis, the Games are a fitting symbol of an economic policy that steered the nation into such crisis.[12]

Settling the Score—Cold War Competitions

While economists would debate the financial significance of the Olympics for many years, other experts attempted to settle the score by examining the athletic competitions. Had the Olympics truly been an exhibition of friendly competition, victories and defeats would be of no import. While there is no official measure of team success in the Olympics, writers, observers, and participants alike have found the urge to tally up the final results by nation irresistible. The most common means of comparison are a total medal count for each team and a total "score" weighing the quality as well as quantity of medals, in which three points are awarded for each gold medal, two for silver, and one for bronze. Experts were quick to point out that the United States had "won" the Mexico City Olympics on both counts and fairly comfortably at that. By such measure, the United States finished with 107 total medals and 225 points; the Soviet Union was second with 91 total medals and 181 points. The two were far and away the top performers, as the next highest finisher, Hungary, tallied only 32 total medals. Both should have been pleased with their totals; however, representatives from the United States trumpeted the superiority of their system in winning so many medals, and those from the Soviet Union were clearly disappointed and more than a little surprised that they had fared so "poorly."[13]

In the weeks after the Olympics, considerable finger-pointing occurred in the Soviet press, and a number of athletes were singled out for their failures. Valery Brumel, once the world-record holder in the high jump, wrote: "some of our sportsmen, especially the younger ones, were unable to overcome a lack of confidence, a subconscious awe of the great names."[14] Other writers, too, pointed to "fear" or "nerves" as a cause of poor performances. There was no shortage of explanations for poor performances, from the altitude to lack of experience running on Tartan tracks to stomach problems to poor coaching. The Soviet Union, "smarting from a mediocre Olympic Games record," reorganized its sports establishment in the wake of the Olympics. It announced the formation of the Union Republican Committee on Physical Culture of Sports, whose leader would be Sergei Pavlov. It was hoped that such a committee could address some of the failings that had afflicted the team in Mexico City.[15]

In general, though, the Soviets attempted to spin the Olympic venture as a success, either by downplaying their failures or by slighting American achievements. Press coverage concentrated on Soviet victories or medalists, while those athletes who had failed to live up to expectations were relegated to the back pages. The papers avoided listing the total medal counts so common in American papers, instead focusing on events in which the Soviets bested the Americans head-to-head. In events where no Soviet athlete excelled, the papers often wrote about other socialist athletes rather than Americans. The exception to this rule was the African American athletes, who received ample attention in the Soviet press. Not only did black athletes carry the American team, but they also openly criticized the United States, a point not unnoticed by the Soviet papers. The Soviet media leaped at the protest of Smith and Carlos, speculating about racism within the United States and racial tensions on the U.S. team. Television coverage, including two hour-long programs and several other fifteen-minute news clips each day, was more comprehensive as the achievements on the screen were less easily manipulated. Special reports and praise concentrated on Soviet athletes.[16]

The United States played the same kinds of games, praising American accomplishments and downplaying their failures. While coverage in the major newspapers was reasonably even-handed throughout the competition, all the talk after the Games was of the poor Soviet showing. Arthur Daley, Olympic correspondent for the *New York Times,* wrote of the Soviet performance in track and field, "The most red-faced country, properly enough, was the Soviet Union, with only three gold medals in men's and nary one in the women's competition, a phase that the Russians once used to dominate."[17] If there were political motivations for such commentary, the fact remains that the 1968 Olympics were the only Summer Olympics from 1952 to 1996 that the Soviets did not "win" according to medal count. Still, both nations continued to try to promote the efficacy of their social systems by engaging in sports matches and exhibitions. In 1969 the United States Olympic Committee sent its boxers on a global tour, including matches in the Soviet Union, Poland, England, Mexico, and other countries. Perhaps hoping to avenge the disappointments of 1968, Soviet track coach Gabriel Korobkov also cleared the way for a pair of track-and-field meets between the United States and the Soviet Union, a tradition that continued until the Olympic boycotts of the 1980s.[18]

It is possible that such victories in the field of sport might have convinced some members of the international community that the American social system was superior to that of the Soviets. Whatever diplomatic gains might have been won, however, they were overwhelmed by the image of Tommie Smith and John Carlos on the medal stand. The protest had a profound impact on international observers, who remember it above all else from those Olympics. Here were two Americans, in what should have been their proudest moment, announcing to the world that they were dissatisfied with their own nation. While the United States may have prevailed according to the medal count, it was a hollow victory.

The Black Athletes Revisited

For the black athletes, the 1968 Olympics were a great success on the field. Black Americans won gold medals in seven events in track and field, including two four-member relay teams, and they took sixteen total medals—and that was just the men. The women added gold medals in three events, most notably Wyomia Tyus's repeat of her gold-medal performance in the 100 meter sprint. Black athletes added two gold medals in boxing, and they anchored the gold-medal winning basketball team. Bob Beamon's leap was unforgettable, and the parade of world and Olympic records broken by the group was unprecedented.[19]

In terms of their broader social protest, though, the '68 Olympics can best be considered a distant precursor to changes that only came many years later. For Smith and Carlos, the protest would remain an albatross to bear for decades. The pair were swamped with letters and comments for months, many threatening, most negative, and a few supportive. According to Carlos, "We got letters saying 'You set us back a hundred years,' and others saying, 'You freed us.'"[20] Response from the black community was generally supportive. Smith recalls returning to his hometown and finding acceptance from his father, who had always been cold and distant. The protest brought the two men together.[21]

The Mexicans themselves generally supported the men, for a number of reasons. Both Smith and Carlos were sympathetic to the plight of many Mexican people and had made statements in support of them prior to the Olympics, increasing their popularity. Their popularity ran deeper than such a superficial quid pro quo, however. First, black athletes were making a protest against the United States, a nation often resented by Mexicans for its supremacy in the region and, some would say, bullying style of diplomacy. Such resentment had accrued from the injustice of the Mexican War and even earlier. Any protest against the American government was one worth supporting. Second, the Black Power protest came during a time of significant unrest within Mexico itself. While the student movement was the most visible in the immediate sense, vast numbers of Mexicans, including farmers, laborers, teachers, and others, struggled for social gains. Although those in power cringed at such protest, rank-and-file Mexicans largely applauded them. Finally, the hope of racial equality struck a chord with many Mexicans. The Mexican people are descended from centuries of mixing indigenous peoples with those of European, Indian, and African heritage. While Mexico is not without its racial tensions (the selection of Enriqueta Basilio as the torch bearer was intended, in some degree, to ease such tensions), even Mexicans within the power structure respected the black athletes' call for racial equality—so long as their protest did not interfere with the Olympics themselves.[22]

Not everyone was so quick to support black athletes. Tommie Smith set out to build a career after returning from the Games and found obstacles put before him at every turn. The ROTC back at San Jose State would not have him. Banned by the USOC, his amateur track career was finished. He also found NFL teams uninterested in signing him, a surprising development for a world-class sprinter who had played high school ball and had been wooed by several teams before the Olympics. Finally, Bill Walsh, then an assistant coach for the Cincinnati Bengals, offered Smith $300 a week to play on the practice squad, a position he held for three years. Three years of meager earnings, often separated from his wife and young child, ultimately proved too much for his marriage to bear. Released by the Bengals, with no job and few prospects, he suffered through a divorce. Eventually Smith entered a stormy career as the track coach at Oberlin College. He represented a young, black, militant group that clashed with the older guard of the administration, and his position was never secure. Denied tenure in 1978, he hit the low point in his life. Turned down as "too good" for several coaching positions, he moved around the country, borrowed money from family and friends, and considered positions as insurance salesman, policeman, or garbage collector. He gained nearly fifty pounds over his racing weight of 190. Finally, he took a position coaching track at Santa Monica College. In his autobiography Smith blames reaction to the "silent gesture" on the medal stand in Mexico City for virtually all of the suffering of his life from that point on.[23]

Carlos took a slightly different path but also found himself in the NFL within two years. After the Olympics, he continued to run on the track circuit, a star sprinter at his peak. He was the best in the world at the 100 and 200 meters and dominated track meets around the world throughout 1969. He won the NCAA championships and the AAU meet, but his crowning moment came at the 1969 Fresno Relays. In the 100 yard dash at that meet, Carlos had his greatest race. Watches in the stands showed different times, from 8.7 to 9.0 seconds. After a wait of several minutes, the official timer flashed 9.1 seconds on the board, merely tying the world record. Carlos, convinced he had run 8.8 at worst, left the meet feeling cheated again. Still, he dominated every meet in which he competed, and after that season he felt he had no other worlds to conquer in track. He turned to football, but like Smith he could not translate his raw speed into success on the football field. He was out of the NFL by 1972 and attended the Munich Olympics not as a competitor but as a representative with the Puma shoe company. After making his appearance in Munich, Carlos found his career in a tailspin. Without a college degree, he worked odd jobs, took on speaking engagements when he could find them, and finally established a children's foundation in Los Angeles in 1977. Unsure where her next meal would come from and shaken by years of uncertainty, Carlos's wife committed suicide shortly thereafter. He turned to drugs and was arrested in December 1986 for possession of co-caine. In 1988 he was hired as an assistant on the Palm Desert High track team and in 1990 became head track coach at Palm Springs High.[24]

For both Smith and Carlos, the road to peace, success, and security was long and difficult as they toiled to overcome the memory of their protest. Both men still show signs of bitterness over the consequences of their actions of almost forty years ago. Smith, who once claimed that the Olympic gold medal "meant everything" to him, as recently as the year 2000 put the medal up for sale on his Web site. He eventually took it down after receiving no offers at his asking price of $500,000. His autobiography, *Silent Gesture,* describes a life filled with rejection, anger, torment —most as a result of the protest on the medal stand. Carlos finally explained his side of the story in his 2002 biography, entitled *Why?* He is as defiant as ever in these pages, still convinced he was cheated out of world records at the Lake Tahoe Olympic Trials and at the 1969 Fresno Relays. The demons of 1968 still haunt both men.[25]

Other black athletes were dragged down by association with Smith and Carlos. Jim Hines, who won the gold medal in the 100 meter dash, found his once promising endorsement prospects on shaky ground after returning from Mexico City. Adidas withdrew offers of a lifetime contract. Hines hung on in professional football for five years, usually coming off the bench or on the practice squad. He believed NFL teams did not give him a fair chance. With only a little bitterness, Hines says, "The gesture cost me a total of $2 million."[26]

Larry James, silver medallist in the 400 meters, also felt the weight of the protest. He returned to a place on the Villanova track team, but after receiving hundreds of letters and countless comments challenging his actions, he lost focus and withdrew from social activity. For two years, he questioned himself before finally joining the Marines in 1972 and finding a sense of purpose again. James has gone on to a career in teaching and coaching, like many of the black athletes from the '68 team who found solace teaching in Africa or the Caribbean.[27]

Was it worth it? To the men who sacrificed countless dollars, stable careers, and adoration by millions, did the gains outweigh the cost? Early financial struggles subsided with the passing years, and all the key actors in the 1968 drama eventually found employment, even if not as professional athletes. The stigma associated with their protest is virtually gone, and the moment on the medal stand now signifies a defining event in the Civil Rights Movement of the late 1960s. No longer villains, Smith and Carlos are revered by many, respected by all but the most ardent racists. They had the courage and will to use their brief time in the public eye not for personal gain but in an effort to make profound change in our society. In the words of Steve Holman, an Olympic miler in 1992, "At great personal cost, against negative public opinion and an antagonistic media, in spite of numerous death threats, they still had the courage to stand up for what they believed."[28]

If their reputations have been vindicated, then can we say that their protest was an unmitigated success? The protest did attract a great deal of attention, both in the United States and abroad. And while such attention was the immediate goal of their gesture, the changes they sought were not so easy to achieve. It would be many years before black athletes began to attain the equality and respect that Smith, Carlos, and the others fought for. In his 1992 book *Necessities*, Phillip Hoose explained that the situation for black athletes in the early 1990s was scarcely better than it had been twenty years before. At that time, there was only one black head coach in all of professional sports. On college campuses, black athletes endured the same kinds of social limitations, though with more blacks on campuses there were more activities to be involved in. Athletes still complained of "stacking," racism, and opportunity in only a few sports. And, too, the road to athletic stardom was increasingly littered with the sad tales of thousands of black youths who dedicated their lives to sport only to find their careers cut short after college or even sooner. A roundtable discussion of top black athletes in 1991 reached similar conclusions, although it noted the important improvement in the salaries of black athletes. No longer did they toil at menial wages; salaries of the best black athletes, such as Eric Dickerson and Bo Jackson in football, Magic Johnson and Michael Jordan in basketball, and Dwight Gooden in baseball, were equal to those of white athletes.[29]

The ensuing decade has brought great change to the sports landscape. Black head coaches, while still a minority at the professional level, at least equal their percentage of the overall population. Black athletes now have a significant presence in all the major professional team sports, with the exception of hockey, and they thrive at all positions, including quarterbacks in football and pitchers in baseball, positions once denied to blacks as they had too much control of the game. They have achieved great successes in traditionally white-dominated sports such as tennis and golf, including one of the world's most recognizable athletes, Tiger Woods, and two of the top women's tennis players, Serena and Venus Williams. Blacks have begun to crack into ownership in professional sports as well, often after successful playing careers; among their ranks are Joe Dumars, Michael Jordan, and Isaiah Thomas, who are partial owners of NBA franchises. The changes sought by the black athletes of '68 have largely been achieved; at the least, situations continue to improve. Still, writers such as William C. Rhoden lament that even the most successful black athletes often endure a youth and upbringing in which they are torn away from their peers and made to perform on teams or in leagues distant from their true roots. Those successful black athletes leave behind them a wake of poorly educated and physically and emotionally debilitated failed black athletes. Most damning in Rhoden's view is the successful black athlete, showered in riches, who overlooks the hardships confronting the masses of black Americans, neglecting their "responsibility to the community."[30]

The Student Movement Revisited

Like black athletes, Mexican students had to wait many years before their efforts paid dividends. The slaughter in Tlatelolco had stunned the students into silence, and the Olympics further slowed the movement. All eyes, including those of the students, were diverted to the athletic competition, and the heightened attention that the Games had brought to the student movement evaporated quickly as the athletic events got under way. Also, a genuine aura of goodwill surrounded the Olympics, and neither the students nor the government wanted to spoil it with further violence. Díaz Ordaz may have sidetracked student efforts by freeing many of the imprisoned students and continuing to negotiate for the release of all of them. He also withdrew all military forces from campuses throughout the city. For the duration of the Olympics, the students remained quiet, and the government did its best to keep them that way.[31]

After the Olympics, the tattered remnants of the student movement attempted to reorganize but found that only a few thousand courageous protesters remained. A well-publicized "unity meeting" on 31 October attracted only 3,000 students, which the government interpreted as a sign that support for the movement was waning. After Tlatelolco, the movement was divided and disorganized, and most of the frightened students returned to school. Others wanted to continue the strike, fearing abandonment of both their cause and their imprisoned comrades. While much quieter than before the massacre, talk of further protest, even revolution, meant continued attention from the government. Díaz Ordaz secretly promised representatives of the Mexican Communist Party official recognition and four seats in the legislature if they would help halt the student strike. On 27 November he announced the seizure of more than 100 tons of subversive propaganda from Communist China, USSR, and Cuba, a sign that dissidents were still being watched and controlled. By the end of November, some 60 percent of the student body at the National University was back in classes. By early December, only a handful of student holdouts remained, and the strike was officially called off. The movement declined even further over the holidays, as most students focused on their exams and then took a break for Christmas. The holiday season ended on an ominous note, as Díaz Ordaz announced that the Department of the Federal District had purchased twenty anti-riot tanks from France. After 2 October, such an announcement could not be simply dismissed as an idle threat.[32]

The feeling of goodwill surrounding the Olympics had faded by the New Year, and the most radical elements of the student movement settled in for a bitter and difficult fight, their efforts concentrated on securing the freedom of the eighty-seven students who remained imprisoned. In January they organized a series of one-day strikes among the students, which were well attended. School officials estimated that only a small minority of the students were active protesters, and the majority simply wanted a free day off from school. Slogans and symbols degrading Díaz Ordaz reappeared, and it seemed the movement was regaining some momentum, though never with the nearly unanimous support it had enjoyed the previous summer. By the end of that spring semester, the student movement was no more; the students were back in class, their chants no longer heard in the streets.[33]

The movement had been effectively silenced, though not without winning a few concessions. Within three years, all the student prisoners were freed. The hated law against "social dissolution" was repealed. The chief of police was fired, though not until June 1971 after several more complaints of brutality were lodged against him. The student movement had its most lasting impact in inspiring political change. The unrest of the Díaz Ordaz regime never entirely died out, and the protests of the students lived on in the efforts of teachers, intellectuals, Sonoran farmers, women, various minority parties, and many other groups who continued to agitate for broader representation in the years and decades after 1968. In overcoming his political enemies, Echeverría found it most expedient to broaden representation within the Institutional Revolutionary Party (PRI), and thus he appointed students, intellectuals, and some laborers to positions within his government. More concessions came in 1976, when Echeverría's successor, Jose Lopez Portillo, ascended to the presidency with Mexico on the verge of social and economic collapse. He opened the political process slightly, allowing for several representatives of minority parties to win seats in the legislature. This gesture, while it served at first only to divide the other parties even further as they fought furiously for their few seats, was an initial wedge that ultimately pried open the door for truer democracy. This development was consummated in 2000 with the election of Vicente Fox, a non-PRI candidate, to the presidency. While the electoral process remains far from perfect, Fox's election over thirty years after the slaughter at Tlatelolco would not have been possible if not for the efforts at reform instigated in part by the students in '68.[34]

The United States took a keen interest in the student movement and the political changes following it. Deep in the throes of the Cold War, the U.S. government was on the lookout for communism, and it paid particularly close attention to the student movement in 1968. It was not the first time that the United States observed communism infiltrating the Mexican educational system. In 1962 the State Department heightened surveillance of Dr. Juan M. Capallera, rector of the Preparatory School of Veracruz, after he allegedly circulated communist materials while discussing Russian films in a seminar. In 1964 it watched closely as three Mexican students were expelled from the Seminar for Central American University Student Leaders for distributing pro-Castro propaganda. The United States kept careful count of the number of registered communists in Mexico and enlisted informants to keep them abreast of developments within the party. It kept a list of bookstores suspected of distributing communist propaganda and detailed records of the owners and patrons of such stores. Recognizing the communist influence within student movements elsewhere in the world, the State Department expected communist infiltration of the Mexican student movement and feared a broader communist influence. "Communists have doubtless attempted to influence and manipulate [the] movement, and several points in [the] student demands have been communist slogans for years," one memo claimed.[35] The full extent of communist involvement in the student movement is impossible to gauge, though it is clear that at the core of the movement was a dedicated group of students, perhaps a few hundred, who were largely communist. The rank and file, though, were mostly middle- to upper-class youth excited to be involved in a new sort of activity.[36]

The U.S. government feared that the student movement in Mexico might explode into a broader-based revolution, as had the movement in France, where massive student protests won the admiration and support of workers, who joined in the protests. Students in Mexico, though, never achieved such broad-based support, due in part to a class disparity between students and workers. And, too, the most important labor unions and organizing bodies among the workers had been incorporated into the PRI. They already had a voice in government, and to join the student protest would have meant the possibility of sacrificing gains already won. The Mexican students simply had no chance to win great support from the workers, whatever grievances they may have had with the government.[37]

U.S. interest in Mexico went beyond the student movement. U.S. diplomacy in Mexico throughout the years leading up to the '68 Olympics concentrated on two themes: building neighborly relations and combating communism. On the one hand, it promoted cultural exchange and assistance programs across the U.S.-Mexican border. In 1966, the two nations formed the United States–Mexico Commission for Border Development and Friendship, partly in connection with the Olympics. Among many programs created by this commission was an exchange of athletes and coaches to help both nations prepare for the Olympics, and a scrimmage took place between the Mexican basketball team and the Texas Western All-Stars, dubbed the "Olympic Friendship Basketball Game." In addition, students from the Texas A&M School of Architecture visited Mexico City to study some of the architectural plans for the new Olympic facilities.

The two nations engaged in many other friendly exchanges, not all so closely linked to the Olympics. Among dozens of such programs were a student exchange program; various ecological and biological studies of the border region; recovery of space fragments; and participation in numerous fairs and cultural activities across the border. The presidents of Mexico and the United States met three times in 1966 and 1967, and exchanges of letters between them were always friendly. So positive were relations between the two nations that Díaz Ordaz, entering the year of the Olympics, described them as "exceedingly cordial and based on an absolute reciprocity of respect and show of friendship and truth."[38]

On the other hand, State Department documents during this period were filled with references to communism in Mexico, possible communist agitators, and the threat of Soviet influence. While some contacts between Mexico and the Soviet Union were denied, others were accepted and were viewed with some suspicion by members of the U.S. State Department. In June 1968, alone, former Mexican president Miguel Alemán traveled to Poland, the USSR, and Yugoslavia; the Mexicans received a commercial mission from Czechoslovakia, and Mexico and Yugoslavia signed a trade agreement. Might such cordial relations mean that Mexico was opening itself to infiltration by communism? The period of goodwill associated with the Olympics also inspired some Mexican-Soviet talks, though little of substance was accomplished. In May, the two nations announced a program of cultural and scientific exchange associated with the Mexican Cultural Olympics. Some in the State Department feared that such cultural exchanges would ease the entry of Soviet students into Mexico, where they might stir up trouble on the campuses. During the same talks, though, the Soviets flatly refused to sign Mexico's Treaty of Tlatelolco, the Latin-American Nuclear-Free Zone agreement. Olympic goodwill only went so far.[39]

The United States took note of several developments that seemed to weaken the Mexican communist party, including the Soviet invasion of Czechoslovakia and the massacre at Tlatelolco. Communists in Mexico were torn by the invasion of Czechoslovakia, as even staunch supporters of the Soviet Union found it difficult to defend. The party was divided all the more as Fidel Castro announced his support of the Soviet action; many Mexican communists, who typically followed Castro's lead, could not agree with him on this matter. Finally, Díaz Ordaz condemned the Soviet action, indicating tacit agreement with the United States.[40]

The movement was weakened further by the massacre at Tlatelolco, in which several communist student leaders were either killed or arrested. Some student communists announced their break with the party, which some felt had provoked the attack in Tlatelolco. It must be noted that such announcements, prominently placed in the Mexican newspapers, may have been planted by the government to further weaken the communist party. Such a tactic would be in line with Díaz Ordaz's approach to leftist groups in the early portions of his presidency, which was not supportive. Unlike the friendly exchange with the United States, cultural exchange with the Soviet Union was "polite but constrained," according to one State Department memo. The Mexican government declined a request by the Soviet Union to establish a tourist office in Mexico City, and it denied visas to the Russian Circus, which had been scheduled to tour Mexico in 1966. While such developments did not warrant an international scandal, they did indicate that Díaz Ordaz was not warm in his reception of leftist groups or ideas. The United States took some solace in the fact that communism in Mexico was on the wane, and the tone of most State Department memos of this period indicates that they were satisfied that U.S. support in Mexico far outweighed that of the Soviet Union.[41]

These worries over losing Mexico to the communists inspired the U.S. government to support Díaz Ordaz even as he encouraged the repression, and ultimately the destruction, of the student movement. CIA operatives and others in the U.S. government observed the Mexican handling of the student uprising with a critical eye but insisted that the United States continue to support Díaz Ordaz. Immediately after the Tlatelolco massacre, one source speculated that the attack would greatly damage the reputation of Díaz Ordaz, and perhaps that of the Olympics, but the United States must not give the impression that it lacked confidence in Díaz Ordaz. Throughout the summer, the United States sent supplies, riot gear, and weapons to Mexico, much of it intended to contain the students. None of the criticisms leveled in confidential government circles are believed to have reached the ears of Díaz Ordaz, who continued to receive support and encouragement from the United States.[42]

At the same time, though, the Mexican government showed some signs of inching to the left, a trend that accelerated after the student massacre. In May 1968, Díaz Ordaz hosted a "broad meeting" with top leaders of the Mexican Communist Party, the PCM. State Department officials interpreted the meeting in two different ways. As one memo read, "This is [the] first time, at least in this administration, that [the] president has formally received PCM leaders and will probably be used by [the] latter to further [an] effort for recognition as [a] legitimate political party." The meeting was also in keeping with a "general effort to build [a] spirit of harmony for [the] Olympics."[43] It is also likely that opening the door, however slightly, to the Communist Party was an initial maneuver to begin co-opting communist leaders into the PRI. Whatever the reasoning, such recognition was not as warmly received by observers within the State Department, always wary of communist infiltration. This move to the left contributed to a decline in U.S.-Mexican relations that marked the Echeverría tenure. Echeverría's ineptitude in handling protest, poorly conceived economic policy, and lack of personal friendship with U.S. presidents contributed to this decline, but the prospect of communist infiltration was the chief concern. So the positive atmosphere surrounding the Olympics also marked a high point in U.S.-Mexican relations.

Impact on the Olympic Games

The year 1968 was a watershed year in Olympic history. Many of the problems and challenges experienced by the Olympics in the ensuing decades either began or underwent a critical change at the Mexico City Olympics, including the growth and expansion of the Olympic movement and the Games themselves, the infusion of politics, the corruption of the bidding process, the threat of terrorism, the challenge of drug testing and the continued use of performance-enhancing agents by athletes, the erosion of the amateur ideal, and the manipulation of the medal stand and the Olympics in general as a forum for protest.

The expansion of the Games has placed enormous pressures upon each city to produce a spectacle larger and more grandiose than the last, a trend that has escalated the cost of staging the Games with each passing Olympiad. In recent years, the costs for each host nation have been astronomical, and for a developing nation, or one suffering particular hardships, they have been crushing. Mexico City was certainly not the first host city to undertake vast and expensive preparations and construction for the Olympics. The trend since 1932 in Los Angeles and 1936 in Berlin had been for each Olympics to be more spectacular than the last. But organizers of the Mexico City Olympics had an opportunity to pare down the size of the Games, to appeal to the humble nature of the Mexican citizenry, to stage a sports festival with a rustic, unpolished feel. Instead, under the leadership of López Mateos, they embarked on an ambitious construction plan, including not only the Olympic Village and dozens of athletic facilities but also roads, highways, and a vast subway system, which did not reach completion until 1974. While Pedro Ramírez Vázquez reined in expenses considerably after taking control of the Organizing Committee in 1966, much of the groundwork had literally been laid. Gustavo Díaz Ordaz and his team of planners simply could not sacrifice the one opportunity to prove that Mexico was indeed a modern nation with the most modern facilities available. While far less costly than the Tokyo Olympics of 1964, the Mexico City Games were hardly humble and still extravagant.[44]

Since 1968 the trend toward gigantism in the Olympics has only worsened. Thus far, each host city has managed to complete the necessary preparations and stage a successful competition. But there have been close calls, and in a number of instances the cost of staging the Olympics has nearly crippled the host nation. The most famous example is Canada, which hosted the 1976 Summer Olympics at Montreal. Montreal's Mayor, Jean Drapeau, had promised a smaller, humble affair when Montreal made its bid for the Games in 1970. His operating budget of $125 million indeed appeared to demonstrate a commitment to stopping the trend of the gigantism of the Olympics. But Drapeau and his organizers went on a wild spending spree in preparing for the Games, blowing out the original budget in spending over $350 million on a new stadium alone. All told, the cost of the Games approached $2 billion, a crushing blow to the national economy that left the province of Quebec indebted for years. More recently, in 2004, Greece struggled mightily to finance the enormously expensive Athens Olympics. Successfully making such preparations forced Athens well over its original budget and put the nation of Greece deep into debt. The struggles of Mexico City, Montreal, Athens, and others demonstrate that the Olympics are dangerously close to outgrowing their own feasibility and are realistically beyond the grasp of all but the largest and wealthiest cities in the world.[45]

In spite of the escalating costs and prohibitive challenges presented by hosting the Games, there is still a bevy of nations clamoring for the honor of hosting. While calculating the balance sheet after the Olympics is nearly an impossible task, on the whole economists agree that the collective boon from ticket sales, television rights, tourism, and ancillary benefits makes the Olympics a profitable venture. And, as Mexico City amply demonstrates, the Olympics are equally important as a public relations vehicle, a mechanism for proving the legitimacy, vitality, and soundness of the host nation and its government. Such benefits have made the Olympics an international prize of great renown, and nations fight with vigor for the right to host the Games.[46]

This super-competitive bidding atmosphere created the most severe crisis in Olympic history, as revealed in the bidding scandals between 1998 and 2000. The scandals, well documented in books by Andrew Jennings and elsewhere, demonstrate shocking dishonesty, conceit, and even illegal behavior by many members of the IOC, who routinely bartered their votes in the bidding war for all manner of financial compensation—from airline tickets to posh meals and housing to gifts and shopping sprees to scholarships for their children. The offenses were in some cases illegal, as in many instances of fraud, racketeering, and bribery, and in others morally reprehensible, as in the occasional exchange of sexual favors for votes.[47]

Some level of dishonesty has always been present in the bidding process. It is simply too easy to sway a voter, or a number of voters, with bribes and gifts rather than the true merits of a bidding city. While it is impossible to know the full extent of such behavior, as any records of such things are inevitably destroyed, it is clear that the heated contest of 1963 was not free of such illegalities. Even within one nation, the United States, the cities of Los Angeles and Detroit engaged in a bitter struggle simply for the right to make a bid for the Olympics, and allegations of bribery and political favors broke in the national press.[48]

The Mexican bidding group, too, learned the artistic and cultural preferences of the IOC's voting members as best it could and made every effort to please those members before the vote. Other contesting nations may well have done the same thing. In any case, the transgressions are relatively minor compared to the widespread corruption plaguing the IOC by the 1990s. Soaring television and sponsorship contracts—and increased visibility as coverage of the Games reaches even the most remote locations—have raised the stakes in the bidding game. From Baden-Baden to today, increased pressure to win the bid has compelled national committees to go after the voting members by all methods at their disposal, legal and illegal. A report issued by the United States Olympic Committee in 1999 estimated that for the previous fifteen years, the true merits of a nation bidding for the Olympics had not been the decisive factor; rather, its ability to bribe and coerce IOC members was. Incidentally, the defeated team from Lyon leveled similar accusations after Mexico had won the bid in 1963.[49]

As the size, scope, and financial importance of the Games have all skyrocketed, so has the accompanying threat of activism and terrorism. Here, too, the 1968 Olympics were a benchmark; for the first time, the host nation was legitimately frightened at the prospect of terrorism during the Games, in this case via the student movement. Prior to 1968, security concerns around the Olympics had roughly paralleled such concerns at other major sporting events, but the thought of a terrorist strike rarely entered the minds of Olympic organizers. Bringing the Olympics to Mexico City, though, introduced the possibility of chaos and lawlessness, and the rising student movement offered a potential source of disruption. Planners of the Mexico City Games spent more money, time, and effort on the issue of security than had any previous Olympics. They recruited and trained a special police force solely for the protection of the Games, and there was a heavy military presence in Mexico City during the Games; the events played out under the shadow of armed sentries. The increasingly militant approach of the government helped spark the slaughter at Tlatelolco and, it should be noted, was successful in discouraging terrorist activity during the Games. After Mexico City, though, every host city had to seriously consider the possibility of terrorism, and the disaster in Munich in 1972 only served to reinforce the reality of the threat. The years since have witnessed the bombing in Atlanta in 1996 and the extremely tense security conditions surrounding the Athens Games in 2004, and the possibility of terrorist attacks will no doubt loom as a chief concern for Olympic organizers in the future.[50]

Ranking only behind the possibility of terrorism in the minds of Athens organizers was the doping issue. Here again, 1968 marked a turning point in Olympic history, when drug testing was carried out at the

Olympics for the first time. Doping was not considered a major concern until the 1950s and 1960s, as scientists gained a clearer understanding of the effects of steroids on the human body and as allegations of extensive and systematic doping in the Soviet Union and Eastern bloc countries multiplied. The IOC issued a resolution against doping in 1962 and in 1967 established the IOC Medical Commission to study and combat doping, which carried out its first tests in Grenoble and Mexico City. This commission quickly came to be regarded as the international standard, and its work in listing banned substances, developing tests, and establishing punishment was admired and mimicked by sporting bodies all over the globe. But athletes seemed to be one step ahead of the authorities until the dramatic positive steroid test of Ben Johnson, winner of the 100 meter sprint at the 1988 Seoul Olympics who was stripped of his medal in shame a few days later. The fall from grace of the "world's fastest human" inspired more extensive and strict anti-doping measures from the IOC and other sporting bodies.[51]

Finally, the Mexico City Games contributed to the politicization of the Olympics. Politics and sport had always been intertwined in the Olympics, but never before had politics mingled with sport on so many levels and quite so overtly as at the Mexico City Olympics. Several nations had threatened a boycott of the 1936 Olympics after Hitler took power in Germany, but that movement had fizzled out. Recognition of various nations for Olympic participation had been wielded as a carrot in the past, but never had it created quite such a stir as the South African question did in 1968. Perhaps most troubling of all, the deepening rift between East and West had begun to erode the Olympic spirit. Intended to bring together athletes from different ideological and political backgrounds by providing them with a peaceful forum for competition, instead the Olympics began to reflect those very differences by enhancing the distance between nations. They had become a fiercely competitive extension of the Cold War, in which contestants would lie and cheat in order to win and in which both sides flung accusations and insults in hopes of bringing the other down. While most of the athletes looked upon one another as friendly rivals, organizers never knew when national differences would supersede good sportsmanship. Representatives of rival nations were closely watched and separated from one another as often as possible. In Mexico City, for the first time national teams were designated separate sections in the dining hall at the Olympic Village. The Soviets and the East Germans ate in one section; Austrians, Czechoslovakians, Hungarians, Poles, Rumanians, and Yugoslavians ate in another.[52]

In the years after 1968, the Olympics became less a simple sports competition and more a political and diplomatic tool. This development was visible most starkly in the 1980s, when the United States and Russia engaged in "dueling boycotts." President Jimmy Carter withheld the U.S.

Olympic team from competition at the 1980 Summer Olympics in Moscow. Similarly, the Soviet bloc refused to attend the 1984 Games in Los Angeles, afterward held up as a great triumph for the U.S. team, who dominated in the absence of their most capable opponents.

But the infusion of politics into the Olympics reached its most terrifying extremes four years after Mexico City at the Munich Olympics. In Munich, just before dawn on 15 September, eight Palestinian terrorists made their way into the building housing the Israeli Olympic team, and in a matter of fifteen minutes killed two Israelis and took nine more as hostages. Over the next nineteen hours, terrorists, national leaders, police, and Olympic officials engaged in fruitless negotiation, ending with a two-hour firefight at a German air base in which all nine hostages, five of the terrorists, and one policeman were killed. In the midst of it all, while the Israeli athletes were shuttled to their deaths, athletes from other parts of the world continued to compete in volleyball, boxing, and canoeing. Eventually, the sporting events were suspended, though they resumed again only hours after the tragedy's conclusion.[53]

The friendly and open atmosphere of the Olympics was largely to blame for the tragedy. Hoping to avoid the militaristic images of Mexico City, few armed guards surrounded the Olympic Village in Munich, and the Israeli athletes received no special security in spite of the ongoing conflict in the Middle East. The terrorists achieved their attack by simply donning sweat suits and hopping a fence, mimicking many of the athletes who had taken to sneaking out of the Olympic Village for late-night carousing. Were it not for the air of peace and harmony that surrounded the Olympics, the tragedy might have been avoided. As one Israeli student said after the attack, "We have learned to be on guard for this kind of thing almost all the time. But not here—not with all the nations gathered in peace, with all the talk about sportsmanship and freedom."[54]

Avery Brundage, in one of the final acts of his long tenure as president of the IOC, stood before a crowd of 80,000 somber fans at the memorial service for the slain Israelis and announced, "The Games must go on!" He rejected the possibility that the Games be discontinued out of respect for the dead and the chance of further violence and begrudgingly called for only a twenty-four-hour mourning period—beginning retroactively from the moment the Games had first been suspended. Sport must not become the bargaining chip for political fanatics, he argued. But had it not already been so transformed? "What Brundage failed to recognize," according to historian Richard Espy, "was that sport was in fact a terrific stick for achieving political objectives."[55] The weight of this realization had finally settled on Brundage, who was wearied after a lifetime of fending off political intrusion into the Olympics. In the week prior to the Olympics, he had decided not to seek reelection to the presidency of the IOC; as his final action as president, he had the unfortunate privilege of overseeing one of the most difficult weeks in the history of sport. With the end of Brundage's tenure, a powerful advocate of amateurism and purity in sport was removed. Though he frustrated many in the Olympic community with his stubbornness and strict adherence to policy, Brundage was sincere in his mission to separate politics from sport. With Brundage gone, no one picked up the mantle of that mission. The influence of politics, so profound in '68, came to dominate the Olympics in the post-Brundage era.[56]

Picking Up the Pieces—Mexican Self-Image since 1968

Mexico had won the right to host the Olympics in part by projecting the image of a modern and peaceful nation, and the organizing committee, and especially president Gustavo Díaz Ordaz, hoped that the Olympics themselves would only enhance that image. And yet despite a riveting athletic contest, the lasting impression and most memorable moments of the '68 Olympics ultimately proved to be the protest of Smith and Carlos and, for Mexicans, the massacre at Tlatelolco. After the massacre of 2 October and during the Olympic Games, it seemed that one could not mention the massacre without mentioning the Olympics and vice versa. As *Sports Illustrated* aptly predicted, "When the big show moves into the stadium on Opening Day, there will be almost as large a crowd of soldiers outside the place—guarding it." The soldiers were a constant reminder of the massacre of a few weeks before, and both Mexican and American newspapers greeted the ceremonies with a mixture of joy and sadness. One of the most telling images appeared in the 13 October *New York Times*: the United States Committee for Justice to Latin American Political Prisoners took out a quarter-page ad depicting the Olympic torch accompanied by the quote, "Mexico's Students Uphold Freedom's Torch." The marriage of the two movements was complete.[57]

The students joined doctors and railroad workers as groups whose movements were crushed by the government. But this ending was unique and changed the course of Mexican history. The massacre was so brutal and senseless—hundreds of fully armed and professionally trained soldiers leveling all their resources at a crowd of unarmed students—that the rest of the population simply *had* to question the actions of their government. Editorials following the massacre were angry, at times despondent, and spoke of a people whose confidence in the government was shaken, perhaps even destroyed. Citizens were further angered as government spokesmen either refused to answer questions or issued vague and misleading answers—and even blamed the parents of the students for the attack, saying they had lost control of their children. Observers in the U.S. government wondered what effect the massacre might have on the Díaz Ordaz administration and on the credibility of the government as a whole, speculating that the administration and its reputation was severely damaged by the incident. Octavio Paz, winner of the Nobel Prize for Literature, became a vocal critic of the government. Only democratization and an opening of the government to criticism could solve the deep-seated problems in Mexico, he argued. Racked with anger and disappointment after the massacre, he immediately resigned his post as ambassador to India. He then authored a scathing poem for submission to the Cultural Olympics, condemning the actions of the government. Paz was joined by the popular historian Daniel Cosío Villegas, who wrote many works criticizing then President Luis Echeverría in the 1970s.[58]

In addition to Paz's works, the massacre inspired an entire genre known as "Tlatelolco literature," which included critical essays, documentaries, novels, short stories, and poetry—all of which galvanized the night of 2 October 1968 as a crucial and tragic memory in the Mexican conscience. Finally, the massacre helped change the direction of Mexican historiography, as many historians rejected the "official mythology" that had been advanced by the revolutionary state. Official history, as might be expected, glorified the Revolution and all of its accomplishments. Post-Tlatelolco history has tended to be more skeptical of the achievements of the Revolution, with many historians even questioning the contributions of Lázaro Cárdenas.[59]

The massacre had profound implications for the Mexican self-image, as well as its image within the international community. In one night, the perception of Mexico as a peace-loving moderator between the two superpowers was shattered. Reflecting this sudden change in perception are the thoughts of one student, Luis González de Alba: "I'm not the same now; we're all different. There was one Mexico before the student movement, and a different one after 1968. Tlatelolco is the dividing point between these two Mexicos."[60] A populace that had been raised on an idealized vision of the Mexican Revolution was forced to question the validity of its policies. The dream that Mexico might become a modern nation by allowing a privileged few to partake of the benefits of modernization was crushed. The argument advanced by intellectuals such as Paz, that only through democratization could a nation be truly modern, became more apparent even to those in power.[61]

Criticism from outside the government was compounded by criticism from within. Even politicians who had been groomed under the PRI were shocked and appalled at the handling of the student protest, and many recognized that changes had to be made. Such critics might have noted hypocrisy in their president, who two years prior to the massacre had announced in his annual presidential address: "We shall not fall into the trap of the trouble makers. Faced with irresponsible violence, we shall not resort to arbitrary counterviolence."[62] Clearly, Díaz Ordaz had broken this promise, and his credibility was destroyed. The massacre signaled the beginning of a long, slow erosion of the party, an erosion still in progress today.[63]

Recognizing the irreparable damage done to the national image by this act, one considers what Díaz Ordaz might have been thinking in authorizing, or at least allowing, such an attack. It should be remembered that just as the students drew inspiration from student uprisings in other nations so too did government officials witness the global tumult and considered the fate of their own nations in this international context. As Jeremi Suri has written, in 1968 it appeared to many heads of state that "their world was crumbling around them," and they faced enormous pressures to preserve their governments and their nations, as well as their reputations and national images. And while many other international leaders faced crises during 1968, few encountered such an unyielding deadline as Díaz Ordaz with the beginning of the Olympic Games. The closest comparison might be Chicago Mayor Richard Daley, who attempted to preserve order during the Democratic National Convention that August by unleashing the police department, National Guard, and unknown numbers of federal agents to crush the youth protest around the convention. Daley, it is now known, directly ordered the arrests and vicious attacks and did so with profanity-ridden invective; he has also been condemned by historians for such acts. Charles DeGaulle, who faced no specific deadline in France but who came perilously close to losing all control over his government during the student rebellion that May, also found that it was only in clamping down forcefully on the protesters that he was able to restore control. Perhaps, then, based on these precedents, Díaz Ordaz believed that it was only with a brutal strike that he could prevent the "crumbling" of his government.[64]

There are differences, of course. In Chicago, while the sight of policemen ruthlessly bludgeoning American citizens without cause was shocking, the onslaught never deteriorated into an outright massacre. While the victims came away in many cases bloodied, bruised, and incarcerated, none of them wound up dead. And, while there is no justification for the attacks, even participants have noted in hindsight that it was perhaps foolhardy to proceed to a heavily guarded location, day after day after repeated warnings, and provoke the authorities with verbal taunts and mild attacks such as throwing bags of feces. In France, the parallels between its student movement and the one in Mexico are considerable. Both movements were sparked in response to police brutality and fueled by breaches of university autonomy. Both movements failed after repeated efforts at good-faith negotiation with government officials; however, the student movement in Mexico never resonated with the populace at large as it did in France, where student marches combined with labor strikes to nearly shut down the country at the movement's peak. DeGaulle's government was in grave trouble, and some extreme action was necessary.

And, as in Chicago, while the students in France might not have fired the first salvo in the worst of the combat, they did invite some retaliation by constructing barricades in the streets and gathering stockpiles of rocks, chunks of concrete, and Molotov cocktails. In Mexico, even as the opening of the Olympic Games approached, the student movement had grown relatively quiet and was wholly peaceful in the days prior to the attack at Tlatelolco.[65]

The massacre contributed to the political changes that followed in the 1970s and 1980s, culminating in the election of Vicente Fox in 2000. In the following years, during the presidency of Luis Echeverría, politics in Mexico underwent an "opening of the left." At least partly in an effort to reestablish the credibility of the government, Echeverría allowed the release of many political prisoners and incorporated outspoken proponents of leftist policies into the system. In addition, the government conceded additional seats in the Chamber of Deputies and more truly democratic elections, although even today election fraud remains a problem. The number of opposition candidates winning seats in the Chamber, while always a minority to the majority PRI seats, steadily increased throughout the 1970s and '80s. Beginning in the late 1980s under President Carlos Salinas, the PRI settled for only "small majority" victories in elections, rather than grossly lopsided ones.[66]

The events of 1968 also had effects within the military. Tensions between civilian leaders and career military officers may have triggered some of the atrocities in the square. The historian Roderic Camp describes an atmosphere of distrust and disdain between the civilian leaders of the country and General García Barragán, the military leader of the operation in Tlatelolco. He suggests that the incident only worsened already deteriorating relations between the two sides and that considerable effort in the wake of the massacre has been invested in reshaping military leadership to be more compatible with civilian goals. Several generals fell out of favor with Díaz Ordaz and top military officials, as they assumed the blame for escalating the attack on the students, which was intended to contain and intimidate the students, not slaughter them. The government has also invested in programs to improve training and equipment within the military, making it more efficient and responsive to potential problems, thereby removing the need for gross overreactions such as that in Tlatelolco. Finally, younger officers were promoted while older ones were phased out, in hopes that younger leadership might react less offensively to the demands of a younger populace.[67]

Barring an unexpected confession from one of the central figures, the full extent of a government and military conspiracy may never be known. The complete results of a government investigation launched in 1997 are still forthcoming, but preliminary findings indicate that the military initiated the attack, and high-ranking government officials either coordinated or at least knew the attack was coming. A special investigator appointed by President Vicente Fox in 2001 has still yielded little new evidence, but it is clear that the planners of the attack put a great deal of thought into their efforts. Long-secret files, recently opened, have revealed graphic pictures of soldiers abusing near-naked students, beating and bloodying them, and lining them up for arrest. Such pictures contribute to the ongoing revision of Mexico's image from that period, no longer the modern, progressive, peace-making nation. For historians of this era, images of the Olympics are often overlooked; the defining images are those of the tattered, frightened, and beaten students.[68]

Notes

Introduction

1. Roger D. Hansen, *The Politics of Mexican Development* (Baltimore: Johns Hopkins University Press, 1974), 35.

2. Alan Tomlinson, "Olympic Survivals," in Lincoln Allison, ed., *The Global Politics of Sport: The Role of Global Institutions in Sport* (New York: Routledge, 2005), 46.

3. Arthur Daley and John Kiernan, *The Story of the Olympic Games, 776 B.C. to 1968* (New York: J.B. Lippincott Co., 1969), 420.

4. Dave Zirin, *What's My Name, Fool? Sport and Resistance in the United States* (Chicago: Haymarket Books, 2005); Amy Bass, *Not the Triumph but the Struggle: The 1968 Olympics and the Making of the Black Athlete* (Minneapolis: University of Minnesota Press, 2002); William C. Rhoden, *Forty Million Dollar Slaves: The Rise, Fall, and Redemption of the Black Athlete* (New York: Crown Publishers, 2006); *Fields of Fire: Sports in the 60s*, HBO Films, 1995.

5. Richard Espy, *The Politics of the Olympic Games* (Berkeley: University of California Press, 1979), 17–18.

6. Daley and Kiernan, *Story of the Olympic Games*, 405.

7. Debbie J. Denbeck, "A Comparison of United States Olympic Athletes Concerning Political Involvement in the Olympic Games," in Gerald Redmond, ed., *Sport and Politics* (Champaign, IL: Human Kinetics Publishers, Inc., 1986), 179–84.

8. "Felicitan por la Olympiada los Legisladores, al Lic. Diaz Ordaz," *Excelsior,* 1 Nov. 1968, 1.

9. Mauricio Tenorio-Trillo, *Mexico at the World's Fairs: Crafting a Modern Nation* (Berkeley: University of California Press, 1996); Arthur Schmidt, "Making It Real Compared to What? Reconceptualizing Mexican History since 1940," in Joseph et al., eds., *Fragments of a Golden Age: The Politics of Culture in Mexico since 1940* (Durham: Duke University Press, 2001), 23–68; Alex Saragoza, "The Selling of Mexico: Tourism and the State, 1929–1952," in Joseph et al., eds., *Fragments,* 91–115; Seth Fein, "Myths of Cultural Imperialism and Nationalism in Golden Age Mexican Cinema," in Joseph et al., eds., *Fragments,* 159–98; Eric Zolov, "Discovering a Land 'Mysterious and Obvious': The Renarrativizing of Postrevolutionary Mexico," in Joseph et al., eds., *Fragments,* 234–72; Elena Poniatowska, "The Student Movement of 1968," in Gilbert M. Joseph and Timothy J. Henderson, eds., *The Mexico Reader: History, Culture, Politics* (Durham: Duke University Press, 2002), 560–62.

10. Lincoln Allison and Terry Monnington, "Sport, Prestige, and International Relations," in Lincoln Allison, ed., *The Global Politics of Sport: The Role of Global Institutions in Sport* (New York: Routledge, 2005), 5–6.

11. Eric Zolov, "Showcasing the 'Land of Tomorrow': Mexico and the 1968 Olympics," *The Americas* 61:2 (Oct. 2004): 159–88.

1—How the Olympics Came to Mexico

1. "Calles Inaugurates Meet in Mexico City," *New York Times,* 13 Oct. 1926, 31; "Recibimos Ayer a Los Atletas de Guatemala en Nuestra Redaccion," *Excelsior,* 12 Oct. 1926, 2:1.

2. "Recibimos Ayer," *Excelsior,* 12 Oct. 1926, 2:1; "México y Cuba se Disputaran los Honores en las Pruebas de Tiro de los Juegas Centroamericanos, Inaugurandose Mañana," *Excelsior,* 11 Oct. 1926, 2.

3. The Mexican team consisted of 228 athletes; the Cubans brought 145, and Guatemala 50. See "Una Ceremonia Solemne en el Magno Estadio," *Excelsior,* 12 Oct. 1926, 2:1.

4. "Enemigo en el Primer Juego del Torneo de Baseball," *Excelsior,* 15 Oct. 1926, 2:1, 8.

5. For some examples of the sporting events themselves, see "Cuba Gano la Serie Olímpica de Base-ball Derrotando al México en un Notable Juego," *Excelsior,* 17 Oct. 1926, 2:1; "Mexico se Apunto Ayer una Gran Victoria en Basket Sobre Cuba," *Excelsior,* 18 Oct. 1926, 2:2; "Cuba Gano en el Torneo de Armas Nobles," *Excelsior,* 19 Oct. 1926, 2:1; dozens of other articles in *Excelsior* describe the athletic contests, 14–29 Oct. 1926.

6. "Se Iniciara hoy la Competencia," *Excelsior,* 13 Oct. 1968, 2:1; "Al Aparecer las Enseñas de Cuba y Guatemala la Multitud Estalló en un Aplauso Cálido y Sincero," *Excelsior,* 13 Oct. 1926, 2:1; "El Presidente Recibio Ayer a los Atletas," *Excelsior,* 17 Oct. 1926, 1.

7. Richard McGehee, "The Origins of Olympism in Mexico: The Central American Games of 1926," *International Journal of the History of Sport* 10:3 (Dec. 1993): 319–23. In spite of its limited scope, the event was front-page news in Mexico City and filled the sports pages for over two weeks. See, for instance, "Una Encantadora Kermesse En Honor de los Atletas," *Excelsior,* 11 Oct. 1926, 3; "Tres Paises de la America van hoy a la Lucha," *Excelsior,* 12 Oct. 1926, 2:1.

8. Tenorio-Trillo, *World's Fairs,* 18–19.

9. Ibid., 32.

10. Ibid., xi–63.

11. Ibid., 158–253.

12. David Brooks, "Mexico: Whose Crisis, Whose Future," *NACLA Report on the Americas* XXI: 5–6 (Sept./Dec. 1987): 14–29; James W. Wilkie, *The Mexican Revolution: Federal Expenditure and Social Change since 1910* (Berkeley: University of California Press, 1970), xxii–xxiii.

13. Daniel Levy and Gabriel Szekely, *Mexico: Paradoxes of Stability and Change* (Boulder: Westview Press, 1987), 32–33; Colin M. Maclachlan and William H. Beezley, *El Gran Pueblo: A History of Greater Mexico* (Upper Saddle River, NJ: Prentice Hall, 1999), 349–56.

14. Michael C. Meyer, "Introduction," *Essays on the Mexican Revolution: Revisionist Views of the Leaders* (Austin: University of Texas Press, 1979), xvi–xvii.

15. Alan Knight, "Cardenismo: Juggernaut or Jalopy?," *Journal of Latin American Studies* 26:1 (Feb. 1994): 73–107; Wilkie, *The Mexican Revolution,* xxiii; Arturo Anguiano, "Cardenas and the Masses," in Joseph and Henderson, eds., *The Mexico Reader,* 457.

16. Maclachlan and Beezley, *El Gran Pueblo,* 385–87; Roger D. Hansen, *Mexican Economic Development: The Roots of Rapid Growth* (Washington: National Planning Association, 1971), 45.

17. Hansen, *Mexican Economic Development,* 41; W. Dirk Raat, *Mexico and the United States: Ambivalent Vistas* (Athens, GA: University of Georgia Press, 1992), 152–55.

18. Joseph and Henderson, eds., *The Mexico Reader,* 461–63; Joseph et al., eds., *Fragments.*

19. Schmidt, "Making It Real," 23–68.

20. Saragoza, "The Selling of Mexico," 94–95, 101; Fein, "Myths of Cultural Imperialism," 159–98.

21. Zolov, "Discovering a Land 'Mysterious and Obvious,'" 234–72.

22. Jorge Castañeda, *Perpetuating Power: How Mexican Presidents Were Chosen* (New York: The New Press, 2000), x–xiv.

23. Ibid.; Barry Carr, *Marxism and Communism in Twentieth-Century Mexico* (Lincoln: University of Nebraska Press, 1992); Alan Knight, "The Peculiarities of Mexican History: Mexico Compared to Latin America, 1821–1992," *Journal of Latin American Studies* 24 (Quincentenary Supplement, 1992): 99–144.

24. Enrique Krauze, *Mexico, Biography of Power: A History of Modern Mexico, 1810–1996* (New York: HarperCollins, 1997), 245–403; John J. Johnson, *Political Change in Latin America* (Stanford: Stanford University Press, 1958), 128–52.

25. Samuel Schmidt, *The Deterioration of the Mexican Presidency: The Years of Luis Echeverría*, trans. Dan A. Cothran (Tucson: University of Arizona Press, 1991), 1–30; Maclachlan and Beezley, *El Gran Pueblo*, 387–89.

26. Department of State Airgram, From Amembassy MEXICO to Department of State, 24 Feb. 1967, *National Archives and Records Administration* (hereafter, *NARA*), RG 59, Box 642, folder E 2-2, Mex 1/1/67.

27. Department of State Airgram, From Amembassy MEXICO to Department of State, 29 Aug. 1968, *NARA*, RG 59, Box 642, folder E 2, Mex 6/1/68.

28. U.S. State Department Research Memorandum, 12 June 1968, *NARA*, RG 59, Box 643, folder E 12, Mex 1/1/67.

29. William H. Beezley, *Judas at the Jockey Club and Other Episodes of Porfirian Mexico* (Lincoln: University of Nebraska Press, 1987), 33–52. This adoption of sports imported from European nations was typical of the growth of sport throughout Latin America. Joseph Arbena, among others, has wondered whether this borrowing from the Anglo-American tradition has advanced or hindered the development of nationalism in Mexico and the rest of Latin America. See Joseph Arbena, "Nationalism and Sport in Latin America, 1850–1990: The Paradox of Promoting and Performing 'European' Sports," *The International Journal of the History of Sport* 12:2 (Aug. 1995): 220–38.

30. Beezley, *Judas at the Jockey Club*, 3–26; Colin D. Howell, "Baseball and Borders: The Diffusion of Baseball and Other Sports into Mexican and Canadian-American Borderlands Regions, 1885–1911," presentation at the 116th AHA Annual Meeting in San Francisco, 5 Jan. 2002; Michael M. Oleksak and Mary Adams Oleksak, *Béisbol: Latin Americans and the Grand Old Game* (Grand Rapids: Masters Press, 1991), 47–52.

31. Beezley, *Judas at the Jockey Club*, 52; Maclachlan and Beezley, *El Gran Pueblo*, 144–45; McGehee, "Origins of Olympism," 314; J.M. Leiper, "Political Problems in the Olympic Games," *Olympism* (Champaign, IL: Human Kinetics, 1981), 108.

32. McGehee, "Origins of Olympism," 313–14; Joseph Arbena, "Sport, Development, and Mexican Nationalism, 1920–1970," *Journal of Sport History* 18:3 (Winter 1991): 352–53; Rosario Encinas, "José Vasconcelos," *Prospects* 24:3-4 (1994): 721–23.

33. Veronica Guttierrez Lozoya, "Olympism in Mexico," *Olympic Review* 26 (Oct.–Nov. 1996): 24–25; McGehee, "Origins of Olympism," 313.

34. For examples of such developments, see "Se Entrenan Para las Exhibiciones Atleticas de Septiembre," *El Universal*, 11 July 1924, 2:3; "Fiesta de Aniversario del 'Deportivo Internacional,'" *El Universal*, 14 July 1924, 8; "Festival Deportivo en el Hipodromo de la Condesa a Beneficio de la Casa de Salud dei Periodista," *El Universal*, 5 Sept. 1924, 5; "Two Thousand Magnificent World Athletes at Olympic Games," *El Universal*, 6 July 1924, 6; McGehee, "Origins of Olympism," 314–17.

35. "Contreras Injured," *El Universal*, 9 July 1924, 2; McGehee, "Origins of Olympism," 314–17.

36. *El Universal*, 8 Oct. 1926; McGehee, "Origins of Olympism," 318–23; Major

Sylvio de Magalhaes Padilha, "The Olympic Movement in the Americas," *Olympic Review* 78:78 (1974): 196–97.

37. McGehee, "Origins of Olympism," 326.

38. For background on the workers' sport movement, see David A. Steinberg, "The Workers' Sport International, 1920–28," *Journal of Contemporary History* 13 (April 1978): 228–51; Robert F. Wheeler, "Organized Sport and Organized Labour: The Workers' Sports Movement," *Journal of Contemporary History* 13 (April 1978): 188–210; Arnd Kruger and James Riordan, eds., *The Story of Worker Sport* (Champaign, IL: Human Kinetics, 1996); James Riordan, *Sport, Politics, and Communism* (Manchester: Manchester University Press, 1991); J.F. Maldonado Aspe et al., *Confederacion Deportiva Mexicana* (Mexico, D.F.: Partido National Revolucionario, 1932), as cited in Arbena, "Sport, Development, and Mexican Nationalism," 355.

39. Mexico won two medals: Francisco Cabalias, silver medal in the Flyweight boxing division, and Gustavo Huet, silver medal in the Miniature Rifle, 50 meters shooting competition. See Bill Henry, *An Approved History of the Olympic Games* (New York: G.P. Putnam's Sons, 1976): 163–71. McGehee, "Origins of Olympism," 326; Arbena, "Sport, Development, and Mexican Nationalism," 355–57.

40. Arbena, "Sport, Development, and Mexican Nationalism," 357.

41. Ibid.; Maclachlan and Beezley, *El Gran Pueblo,* 335.

42. Arbena, "Sport, Development, and Mexican Nationalism," 357; Harold Rosenthal, "The War with Mexico," *Baseball Digest* 22 (Dec. 1963–Jan. 1964): 53–56; Oleksak and Oleksak, *Béisbol,* 52.

43. "Report from the 48th Session of the International Olympic Committee, Held in Mexico City, 14–18 April 1953," available at the website of the Amateur Athletic Foundation of Los Angeles, <http://www.aafla.org>, accessed 30 Oct. 2004. Avery Brundage, "Report of Commission appointed by the IOC at its meeting in Copenhagen in 1950 to study conditions in Latin America," *Bulletin du Comité International Olympique* 27 (June 1951): 37–39; "Remarks of Welcome by Avery Brundage at dinner given by him to the Ladies and Gentlemen of the I.O.C. attending the Primeros Juegos Deportivos Panamericanos at Buenos Aires, March 3, 1951," *Olympic Review,* 1951, <http://www.aafla.org>, accessed 15 Aug. 2005.

44. "U.S. Athletes Win Four More Titles," *New York Times,* 25 Mar. 1955, 28; "Miranda Defeats Santee in Upset for 1,500 Crown," *New York Times,* 20 Mar. 1955, S1; "Jones of U.S. Lowers World Mark," *New York Times,* 19 Mar. 1955, 19; "Four Records Set for Track Events," *New York Times,* 15 Mar. 1955, 34; "President Starts Games in Mexico," *New York Times,* 13 Mar. 1955, S1. "Pan-American Games," *Bulletin du Comité International Olympique* 41 (Aug. 1953): 22; "Remarks of Welcome by President Avery Brundage," 27–28; Padilha, "The Olympic Movement in the Americas," 196–97; "A History of the Pan-American Games," Amateur Athletic Foundation of Los Angeles website, <http://www.aafla.org>, accessed 30 Oct. 2004.

45. Espy, *Politics,* viii. Mexico had made unsuccessful bids for the Olympics twice before: in 1949, receiving 9 votes for the 1956 Olympics, ultimately awarded to Melbourne; and in 1955, receiving 6 votes for the 1960 Olympics, ultimately awarded to Rome. <http://www.aldaver.com>, accessed 15 Aug. 2005.

46. The five colored rings represent the five regions of the globe: the Americas, Europe, Africa, Australia, and Asia. Africa still has not hosted the Olympics, leading to questions about the "missing black ring" in the logo. Maurice Roche, *Mega-Events and Modernity: Olympics and Expos in the Growth of Global Culture* (New York: Taylor & Francis Group, 2000), 146.

47. For Coubertain's Olympic vision, see among others Anthony T. Bijkerk, "Pierre de Coubertin," in John E. Findling and Kimberly D. Pelle, eds., *Encyclopedia of the Modern Olympic Movement* (Westport, CT: Greenwood Press, 2004), 454–63; John A. Lucas, "The Genesis of the Modern Olympic Games," in Jeffrey Segrave and Donald

Chu, eds., *Olympism* (Champaign, IL: Human Kinetics, 1981), 22–31; ibid., "Genesis," 2–7; Espy, *Politics*, vii–viii.

48. Espy, *Politics*, 25. The elitism of the IOC is an issue that lingers to this day, as many historians have pointed out. As William Johnson has noted, "The favorite sports of the IOC members are yachting, fencing, and equestrian—the high society sports . . . IOC members usually fit one or more of three qualifications—they are men of extreme wealth, of high governmental or social position or of royal birth." If the IOC has come to recognize "common" athletes from largely impoverished nations, its leadership, with rare exception, has not. See William O. Johnson, *All that Glitters Is Not Gold* (New York: Putnam, 1972), 95–96. For a concise summary of each of the Olympiads and other information, see John E. Findling and Kimberly D. Pelle, eds., *Encyclopedia of the Modern Olympic Movement.*

49. Douglas Collins, *Olympic Dreams: 100 Years of Excellence* (New York: Universe Publishing, 1996), 19–62; Karl Lennarz and Stephen Wassong, "Athens 1896," in Findling and Pelle, eds., *Encyclopedia of the Modern Olympic Movement*, 17–26; Johnson, *Glitters*, 107–27; Henry, *Approved History*, 40–62; Andre Drevon, "Paris 1900," in Findling and Pelle, eds., *Encyclopedia of the Modern Olympic Movement*, 27–32; C. Robert Barnett, "St. Louis 1904," in Findling and Pelle, eds., *Encyclopedia of the Modern Olympic Movement*, 33–40.

50. James Coates, "London 1908," in Findling and Pelle, eds., *Encyclopedia of the Modern Olympic Movement*, 51–56; Collins, *Olympic Dreams*, 62–91; Johnson, *Glitters*, 127–38; Henry, *Approved History*, 70–97; Ulf Hamilton, "Stockholm 1912," in Findling and Pelle, eds., *Encyclopedia of the Modern Olympic Movement*, 57–62.

51. Collins, *Olympic Dreams*, 92–101; Johnson, *Glitters*, 140–46; Henry, *Approved History*, 98–113; Roland Renson, "Antwerp 1920," in Findling and Pelle, eds., *Encyclopedia of the Modern Olympic Movement*, 71–78.

52. Women had competed in several other events prior to 1928, including golf, tennis, yachting, and swimming. Collins, *Olympic Dreams*, 102–21; Johnson, *Glitters*, 147–61; Henry, *Approved History*, 114–53; "U.S. Gained Glory in Olympics," *New York Times*, 30 Dec. 1928, 125; "Miss Copeland Sets Mark in Shot-put," *New York Times*, 13 Aug. 1928, 18; "Sports for Women Kept in Olympics," *New York Times*, 8 Aug. 1928, 21; Mark Dyreson, "Paris 1924," and Edward S. Goldstein, "Amsterdam 1928," in Findling and Pelle, eds., *Encyclopedia of the Modern Olympic Movement*, 79–94.

53. Collins, *Olympic Dreams*, 123; Johnson, *Glitters*, 161–72; Henry, *Approved History*, 154–73; Doris Pieroth, "Los Angeles 1932," in Findling and Pelle, eds., *Encyclopedia of the Modern Olympic Movement*, 95–104.

54. Collins, *Olympic Dreams*, 134–37; Johnson, *Glitters*, 172–207; Henry, *Approved History*, 174–94; Duff Hart-Davis, *Hitler's Games* (London: Century, 1986); Bill Baker, *Jesse Owens: An American Life* (New York: Free Press, 1986); Richard Mandell, *The Nazi Olympics* (New York: Macmillan, 1971); Annette Hofmann and Michael Kruger, "Berlin 1936," in Findling and Pelle, eds., *Encyclopedia of the Modern Olympic Movement*, 105–14; David Clay Large, *Nazi Games: The Olympics of 1936* (New York: W.W. Norton & Co., 2007); Jeremy Schaap, *Triumph: The Untold Story of Jesse Owens and Hitler's Olympics* (New York: Houghton Mifflin, 2007); Guy Walters, *Berlin Games: How the Nazis Stole the Olympic Dream* (New York: HarperCollins, 2006); Anton Rippon, *Hitler's Olympics: The Story of the 1936 Nazi Games* (South Yorkshire: Pen and Sword Books Limited, 2006).

55. Allen Guttmann, *The Olympics: A History of the Modern Games* (Champaign: University of Illinois Press, 1992), 97; Vesa Tikander, "Helsinki 1952," in Findling and Pelle, eds., *Encyclopedia of the Modern Olympic Movement*, 135–46.

56. Collins, *Olympic Dreams*, 148–75; Johnson, *Glitters*, 207–35; Henry, *Approved History*, 195–275.

57. Roche, *Mega-Events and Modernity*, 62; J.M. Leiper, "Political Problems in the Olympic Games," *Olympism*, 105.

58. Stephen R. Wenn, "An Olympian Squabble: The Distribution of Olympic Television Revenue, 1960–1966," *Olympika: The International Journal of Olympic Studies* 3 (1994): 27; Stephen R. Wenn, "Appendix C: The Olympic Games and Television," in Findling and Pelle, eds., *Encyclopedia of the Modern Olympic Movement*, 509–20.

59. Allen Guttmann, *The Games Must Go On: Avery Brundage and the Olympic Movement* (New York: Columbia University Press, 1984), 212–19; Roche, *Mega-Events and Modernity*, 162; Harry Edwards, "Crisis in the Modern Olympic Movement," *Olympism* (Champaign, IL: Human Kinetics, 1981), 232; Stephen R. Wenn, "Growing Pains: The Olympic Movement and Television, 1966–1972," *Olympika: The International Journal of Olympic Studies* 4 (1995): 1–22; John Slater, "Changing Partners: The Relationship between the Mass Media and the Olympic Games," *Fourth International Symposium for Olympic Research* (London, Ontario, Canada: University of Western Ontario, 1998), 49–68.

60. Espy, *Politics*, 24.

61. Leiper, "Political Problems," 108–11; Edwards, "Crisis," 233–34.

62. Leiper, "Political Problems," 109; Allison and Monnington, "Sport, Prestige," 10; Mike O'Mahony, *Sport in the U.S.S.R.: Physical Culture—Visual Culture* (London: Reaktion Books, 2006), 151–57.

63. Brundage, *Games Must Go On*, 115–16; Robert K. Barney, "Avery Brundage," in Findling and Pelle, eds., *Encyclopedia of the Modern Olympic Movement*, 471–81.

64. Brundage, *Games Must Go On*, 110–31; Espy, *Politics*, 39.

65. Hernández Shafler interview; Krauze, *Biography of Power*, 625–58; Armando Estrada, "Emocionó la Designación al Presidente," *Excelsior*, 19 Oct. 1963, 1; "'Fiesta de la Victoria,' en Baden Baden," *Excelsior*, 19 Oct. 1963, 27.

66. *Mexico XIX Olympic Games*, Mexican Olympic Committee (1968), located in the Mexican Olympic Committee archives, Mexico D.F., call # 796.48 J44.

67. Ibid.; Zolov, "Showcasing the 'Land of Tomorrow'"; Saragoza, "The Selling of Mexico."

68. *Mexico XIX Olympic Games*, 16.

69. Ibid.

70. Ibid.

71. Ibid.

72. Ibid.

73. Ibid.

74. Ibid., 13; *Mexico '68,* published by the Mexican Olympic Committee, Mexican Olympic Committee Archives, Mexico City. Call # C796.48 M49, vol. 2.

75. Roberto B. Carmona, "Biography of Jose de Jesus Clark Flores: 'Man of Honor,'" Ph.D. diss., Brigham Young University, 1981.

76. "Two Cities Battle to Host the Olympics," *Business Week* (23 Feb. 1963): 36.

77. Ibid.

78. Paul Zimmerman, "L.A. Gets New Chance for Olympic Bid," *Los Angeles Times*, 13 Feb. 1963, III, 1, 4; Paul Zimmerman, "L.A. Gathers Forces for 1968 Games Bid," *Los Angeles Times*, 14 Feb. 1963, III, 1; "L.A. Lobby Gets Bidding Reopened," *Detroit News*, 13 Feb. 1963, 1.

79. Zimmerman, "L.A. Gets New Chance."

80. In 1948, Detroit received only 2 votes against eventual winner Helsinki and a host of other candidates for the 1952 Games. In 1949, for the 1956 Games, Detroit received 4 votes to Melbourne's 21 and Buenos Aires' 20. In 1954, for the 1960 Games, Detroit received 11 votes to 26 for Rome and 21 for Lausanne. In 1959, for the 1964 Games, Detroit received 10 votes to 34 for Tokyo, 10 for Vienna, and 5 for Brussels. All told, these defeats led many to wonder (and rightfully so, in retrospect) whether Detroit could *ever* win the international vote. See Zimmerman, "Financial Nightmare Ruins Detroit's Olympics Dream," *Los Angeles Times*, 10 March 1963, D:2.

See also *Los Angeles Times* articles of 14 Feb. 1963, III:1; 15 Feb. 1963, III:2; 23 Feb. 1963, III:3; 24 Feb. 1963, D:2; 25 Feb. 1963, III:2; 26 Feb. 1963, III:2.

81. Zimmerman, "Financial Nightmare."

82. Al Wolf, "$2–5 Million Surplus Predicted if L.A. Voted 1968 Olympics," *Los Angeles Times*, 26 Feb. 1963, III:2.

83. Paul Zimmerman, "L.A. Strongest Olympic Backer," *Los Angeles Times*, 3 March 1963, D:2.

84. "San Francisco Bid for Olympics Urged," *New York Times*, 15 March 1963, 15; Art Rosenbaum, "Hassle Going On in S.F. over Olympics," *Los Angeles Times*, 5 March 1963, III:7; see also *Los Angeles Times*, 6 March 1963, III:1; 12 March 1963, III:3.

85. "Brown, Yorty, Hollywood Stars Host USOC Brass," *Los Angeles Times*, 17 March 1963, D:2; "13 Named to Olympic Group," *Los Angeles Times*, 27 Feb. 1963, III:3; "L.A. TV Fans to Hear Bid for Olympics," *Los Angeles Times*, 13 March 1963, III:3; "Olympic Group Made Honest 'Goof,'" *Los Angeles Times*, 7 March 1963, III:2; "Detroit Chances Best, Says Wilson," *Los Angeles Times*, 4 March 1963, III:2; Paul Zimmerman, "Detroit NOT In; Wilson Denies Story," *Los Angeles Times*, 5 March 1963, III:2; Don Hoenshell, "Cavanagh, Romney to Lead Olympic Trip," *Detroit News*, 22 Feb. 1963, 2; Hoenshell, "Stars Shine on L.A.'s Bid," *Detroit News*, 18 Mar. 1963, 1.

86. "Michigan Clears Another Hurdle in Olympic Drive," *Los Angeles Times*, 16 March 1963, III:1; Anthony Ripley, "Romney Is Given Go-Ahead," *Detroit News*, 15 March 1963, 1; Paul Zimmerman, "Detroit Awarded U.S. Olympic Bid," *Los Angeles Times*, 19 March 1963, III:4.

87. Damon Stetson, "Motor City Riding High," *New York Times*, 27 March 1963, 6.

88. Quote from Harold Heffernan, "L.A. Ready if Detroit Flops in '68," *Detroit News*, 20 Mar. 1963, 1. Ibid.; Allison Danzig, "Brown Makes Bid for Los Angeles," *New York Times*, 19 March 1963, 16; Don Hoenshell, "Detroit's Chances 'Excellent,'" *Detroit News*, 19 Mar. 1963, 1.

89. The Detroit group lowered the estimated cost of its stadium project from $35 million to $25 million and then to $20 million and also altered its maximum seating capacity as cost became the major obstacle to their bid.

90. Zimmerman, "L.A. Gets New Chance;" "Detroit Chances Best, Says Wilson," *Los Angeles Times*, 4 March 1963, III:2. The only city mounting a truly futile bid was Buenos Aires. The insignificance of the threat posed by Buenos Aires is evident in the official minutes of this meeting. In the section detailing each city's presentation, the other cities responded to serious questions about their bid and clarified key points. (Mexico City, for example, "refuted the arguments concerning the difficulty of athletes adapting themselves to a high altitude.") The Buenes Aires delegation, by contrast, seems only to have "proposed the dates of April/May or September/October" in its closing statement. This hardly seems like the powerful presentation expected for a winning bid. "Minutes of the 60th Session of the International Olympic Committee, Baden-Baden, Kurhaus, Oct. 14–20, 1963," *Bulletin du Comité International Olympique* 85 (Feb. 1964): 68–73. See also Lucien Dania, "Mexico Tiene Todo Para Olimpiada," *Excelsior*, 16 Oct. 1963, 27, which explains that Buenos Aires was judged to have inferior facilities. For more on the failed Buenos Aires bid and its various shortcomings, see "Detroit y Argentina, los Primeros que Expusieron su Petición," *Excelsior*, 19 Oct. 1968, 28.

91. Dr. Eduardo Hay, interview with the author, Mexico City, 17 Nov. 2001.

92. Ibid.

93. "En Baden Baden: Suena Cada ves más el Nombre de la ciudad de México," *Excelsior*, 17 Oct. 1963, 29; "La Battalla Final Sera Entre México y Lyon," *Excelsior*, 18 Oct. 1963, 24.

94. Christian G. Appy, "Eisenhower's Guatemalan Doodle, or: How to Draw, Deny, and Take Credit for a Third World Coup," in Christian G. Appy, ed., *Cold War*

Constructions: The Political Culture of United States Imperialism, 1945–1966 (Amherst: University of Massachusetts Press, 2000); "Mexico: Carrying the Torch in '68," *Time* (25 Oct. 1963): 42; "Battle in Baden-Baden," *Sports Illustrated* (16 Sept. 1963): 6; Hal Higdon, "The Light (Torch Division) that Failed," *Sports Illustrated* (4 Nov. 1963): 47–49.

95. "Lyons Confident on Olympics Bid," *New York Times,* 16 Oct. 1963, 57.

96. "Los Paises de Africa Apoyan a Lyon," *Excelsior,* 17 Oct. 1963, 31; Dania, "México Tiene Todo Para Olimpíada;" Robert Daley, "Lyons to Use Public Relations in Seeking '68 Olympic Games," *New York Times,* 29 Nov. 1962, 50; "Lyons Makes a Lavish Pitch to Be Site for 1968 Olympics," *New York Times,* 17 Oct. 1963, 47.

97. Hay interview; *Official Boletin* 5 (Mexican Olympic Committee: Mexico City, 1968): 2–3; "New Members of the IOC," *Olympic Review* 85–86 (Nov.–Dec. 1974): 592–93; "Mexico and Olympism," *Olympic Review* 95–96 (Sept.–Oct. 1975): 390–402; "Marte R. Gomez fue el Primer Orador de Mexico en Baden Baden," *Excelsior,* 19 Oct. 1968, 27. The role of politics was not lost on the defeated candidates. While the Detroit delegation was gracious in defeat and looked ahead to another bid for the next Olympics, the Lyon group was more bitter and complained that the decision was based on politics rather than on the merits of the candidates. See "El Alcalde de Lyon se Lanza Ahora Contra el COI," *Excelsior,* 20 Oct. 1968, 38.

98. Hay interview; Florenzio Acosta, interview with the author, Mexico City, 16 Nov. 2001; "Mexico City Picked over Detroit, Lyons and Buenos Aires for '68 Olympics," *New York Times,* 19 Oct. 1963, 18.

99. Hay interview.

100. "En un Ultimo Esfuerzo, Detroit 'Presentó' al Presidente Kennedy," *Excelsior,* 19 Oct. 1968, 27; Acosta interview; Carlos Hernandez Schaefler, interview with the author, Mexico City, 15 Nov. 2001.

101. "Brundage, Partidario de que México sea la sede en 1968," *Excelsior,* 17 Oct. 1963, 29; see also "Brundage lamenta la exclusión de Sudáfrica," *El Nacional,* 1 Aug. 1968, 2:3; Hay interview.

102. Hay interview.

103. Ibid.

104. Ibid.; "U.S. Delegation Hurt and Shaken," *New York Times,* 19 Oct. 1963, 18; "Dijo el Lic. Uruchurto en Declaraciones Oficiales, Ayer," *Excelsior,* 19 Oct. 1963, 27.

105. Dania, "México Tiene Todo Para Olimpíada."

106. Felix Belair, "Senate Panel Bars Aid Cut; Approves 4.2 Billion Fund," *New York Times,* 19 Oct. 1963, 1, 6.

107. "U.S. Delegation Hurt and Shaken," 18. See also "Qué Alegra! Exclamó Clark Flores, Emocionado," *Excelsior,* 19 Oct. 1963, 27.

108. Zolov, "Showcasing the 'Land of Tomorrow,'" 163; Espy, *Politics,* 76–82.

109. Hay interview.

110. Dania, "México Tiene Todo Para Olimpíada"; "La Battala Final."

111. Hay interview.

112. Ibid.

113. Manuel Seyde, "Temas del dia," *Excelsior,* 16 Oct. 1963, 2.

114. "U.S. Delegation Hurt and Shaken," 18.

115. Ibid.; "Lyons Makes a Lavish Pitch;" "Mexico Ofrece Construir un Estadio Para 150,000 Personas," *Excelsior,* 18 Oct. 1963, 24. For more on the well-rounded appeal of the Mexican bid, see "'El Deporte de México lo Merece,' Opinó Estopier," *Excelsior,* 19 Oct. 1963, 28.

116. "Romney, Coobernador de Michigan, Presentará la Candidatura de Detroit," *Excelsior,* 18 Oct. 1963, 24; "Qué Alegra," 27; "U.S. Delegation Hurt and Shaken," 18; Hay interview.

117. "Minutes of the 60th Session of the International Olympic Committee, Baden-Baden, Kurhaus, October 14th–20th, 1963," Lausanne, Switzerland: International Olympic Committee, 1963: 69; "Proces-verbal de la 60e Session du Comité International Olympique, Baden-Baden, Kurhaus, du 16 au 20 Octobre 1963," *Bulletin du Comité International Olympique* 85 (Feb. 1965): 23–30; "Clark Transcribió Ayer al Comité Olimpico un Cable que Dirigió al Presidente," *Excelsior,* 19 Oct. 1963, 27.

118. Manuel Seyde, "Temas del dia," 27; "Seleccionada Entre Cuatro por el COI," *Excelsior,* 19 Oct. 1963, 1; "Qué Alegra."

119. Justo Perez, "Reverso de la Política: Negritos de la Olimpiada," *Excelsior,* 31 Oct. 1968, 7.

120. "Aprestas Para la Olimpiada," *Excelsior,* 20 Oct. 1968, 1; Bernardo Ponce, "Perspectiva: Juegos Olimpicos," *Excelsior,* 21 Oct. 1968, 6.

2—Image Preserved—Early Controversies and the Cultural Olympics

1. Bob Ottum, "Getting High in Mexico City," *Sports Illustrated* (25 Oct. 1965): 30–31.

2. "Jones of U.S. Lowers World Mark," 19; "The Highest Olympics," *Sports Illustrated* (4 Nov. 1963): 7.

3. "Olympics without Oxygen?," *Newsweek* (1 Nov. 1965): 63.

4. "The Dissenters," *Sports Illustrated* (2 May 1966): 12.

5. "Olympics without Oxygen?," 63; "In the High, Thin Air," *Time* (31 Dec. 1965): 70.

6. "Olympics without Oxygen?," 63.

7. Ottum, "Getting High," 31.

8. Ibid., 30.

9. "The Effects of the Altitude in Mexico," *Bulletin du Comité International Olympique* 93 (Feb. 1966): 82.

10. Ibid.

11. "Planning for the 1968 Olympic Games," *Parks and Recreation* 1 (Oct. 1966): 851.

12. "Friends in High Places," *Time* (30 December 1966): 44.

13. "Newsletter," *Comité International Olympique* 1 (Oct. 1967): 22; "In the High, Thin Air," 70.

14. *NARA,* RG 59, Box 325, folder 15-1 CUL MEX 4/1/68, memo 3 July 1968, Department of State to All Diplomatic Posts. David Caute, *The Dancer Defects: The Struggle for Cultural Supremacy during the Cold War* (New York: Oxford University Press, 2003); Penny Von Eschen, *Satchmo Blows Up the World: Jazz Ambassadors Play the Cold War* (Cambridge, MA: Harvard University Press, 2004); Richard T. Arndt, *The First Resort of Kings: American Cultural Diplomacy in the Twentieth Century* (Washington: Potomac Books, Inc., 2005); Frances S. Saunders, *The Cultural Cold War: The CIA and the World of Arts and Letters* (New York: The New Press, 1999); Frank Ninkovich, "The Currents of Cultural Diplomacy: Art and the State Department, 1938–47," *Diplomatic History* (Summer 1977): 215–37.

15. *NARA,* RG 59, Box 325, folder 15-1 CUL MEX 4/1/68, memo 17 July 1968, Amembassy Quito to Department of State.

16. See series of memos from various embassies to the Department of State, ibid.

17. Andrew Strenk, "Amateurism: Myth and Reality," in Jeffrey Segrave and Donald Chu, eds., *Olympism* (Champaign, IL: Human Kinetics, 1981), 59.

18. S.W. Pope, *Patriotic Games: Sporting Traditions in the American Imagination, 1876–1926* (New York: Oxford University Press, 1997).

19. Guttmann, *Games Must Go On,* 116.

20. Strenk, "Amateurism," 61–66.

21. As cited in Strenk, "Amateurism," 64–65.

22. Ibid., 58. For one athlete's perspective on the amateurism debate, see Don Schollander and Duke Savage, *Deep Water* (New York: Crown Publishers, Inc., 1971), 161–73, 218–23, 263–65.

23. Jose Barrenechea, Jr., "Afirma Pavlov: En la 'URSS no hay Profesionalismo,'" *Excelsior,* 11 Oct. 1968, 4; see also R.G. Osterhoudt, "Capitalist and Socialist Interpretations of Modern Amateurism: An Essay on the Fundamental Difference," in Segrave and Chu, eds., *Olympism,* 42–45.

24. Strenk, "Amateurism," 57.

25. S. Ya. Chikin, "Formation of the Physically Improved Man—An Important Problem," *Theory and Practice of Physical Culture* 10 (1963): 13–19, translated in *Yessis Translation Review* 1:4 (March 1966): 6; V. Mikhailov, "The Law of the Dollar," *Physical Culture and Sport* 7 (1966): 13–14, translated in *Yessis Translation Review* 2:2 (June 1967): 52; Avery Brundage, "I Must Admit—Russian Athletes Are Great!" *Saturday Evening Post* (30 April 1955): 29, 111; David Cort, "The Olympics: Myth of the Amateur," *The Nation* 199 (28 Sept. 1964): 157.

26. "The New Battery of Preparedness for Work and Defense of the U.S.S.R.," *Theory and Practice of Physical Culture* 3 (1972): 2–4, translated in *Yessis Translation Review,* 7:3 (Sept. 1972): 80.

27. F.P. Shuvalov, "The Legacies of Lenin Are Being Fulfilled," *Theory and Practice of Physical Culture* 4 (1966): 6–8, translated in *Yessis Translation Review,* 2:1 (March 1967): 3; Riordan, *Sport, Politics, and Communism,* 70–71; Chikin, "Formation of the Physically Improved Man," 5; O'Mahony, *Sport in the U.S.S.R.,* 157–75.

28. Riordan, "Sport Policy of the Soviet Union," in Pierre Arnaud and James Riordan, eds. *Sport and International Politics* (New York: Taylor and Francis, 1998): 73.

29. Victor Peppard and James Riordan, *Playing Politics: Soviet Sport Diplomacy to 1992* (Greenwich, CT: JAI Press, 1993), 62.

30. Caute, *Dancer Defects*; Patrick Major and Rana Mitter, eds., *Across the Blocs: Cold War Cultural and Social History* (London: Frank Cass, 2004).

31. Major and Mitter, *Across the Blocs*; also Riordan, *Sport, Politics, and Communism,* 127–45; O'Mahony, *Sport in the U.S.S.R.,* 151–75.

32. Peppard and Riordan, *Playing Politics,* 67–68; Schollander and Savage, *Deep Water,* 145–73.

33. Peppard and Riordan, *Playing Politics,* 69.

34. Riordan, *Sport, Politics, and Communism,* 83–99; Anatoly Isaenko, interview with the author, Columbus, GA, 18 Oct. 2002.

35. Yuri A. Rastvorov, "Red Amateurs Are Pros," *Life* (6 June 1955): 98.

36. Ibid., 97; Brundage, "I Must Admit," 112.

37. S.W. Pope, *Patriotic Games,* 19.

38. As cited in ibid., 23.

39. Ronald A. Smith, *Sports and Freedom: the Rise of Big-Time College Athletics* (New York: Oxford University Press, 1990), 168.

40. Wes Santee, "Names, Places and Pay-offs—Santee Blows the Whistle," *Life* (19 Nov. 1956): 99.

41. Cort, "The Olympics," 158.

42. As cited in Guttmann, *Games Must Go On,* 130.

43. As cited in Brichford, "Avery Brundage and Racism."

44. *NARA,* RG 59, Box 367, folder EDU 15-1, JAPAN, memo 17 March 1964, Amembassy Cape Town to Secretary of State; Ian Robertson and Phillip Whitten, "The Olympics: Keep South Africa Out," *The New Republic,* 158:15 (13 Apr. 1968): 13; Brichford, "Avery Brundage and Racism," 131. For more on cricket, see C.L.R. James, *Beyond a Boundary* (Durham: Duke University Press, 1993).

45. Espy, *Politics*, 100; Lloyd Garrison, "South Africa Allowed to Compete in Olympic Games at Mexico City," *New York Times*, 16 Feb. 1968, 41; Lee Griggs, "The Last Living Amateur Is still a King among Kings," *Sports Illustrated* (22 May 1967): 73.

46. William Barry Furlong, "A Bad Week for Mr. B," *Sports Illustrated* (11 Mar. 1968): 19; Robertson and Whitten, *The New Republic*, "Keep South Africa Out," 14; Garrison, "South Africa Allowed to Compete."

47. Ibid.

48. "5 More African Nations Join Boycott of Olympics," *New York Times*, 18 Feb. 1968, L++:1, 2.

49. Ibid.

50. Ibid.; "Boycott in Mexico," *Newsweek* (11 Mar. 1968): 84.

51. "Kenya, Sudan, and Iraq Join Boycott of Summer Olympics," *New York Times*, 21 Feb. 1968, 39; "Special Meeting Called Unneeded," *New York Times*, 27 Feb. 1968, 48.

52. "South Africa Blacks Attack Boycott," *New York Times*, 3 Mar. 1968, S:7; also Arthur Daley, "Some Second Thoughts," *New York Times*, 23 Feb. 1968, 23.

53. As quoted in "Brundage Stands Firm on South Africa," *New York Times*, 24 Mar. 1968, V:14.

54. "Nations Divided on Games Boycott," *New York Times*, 10 Mar. 1968, S:7.

55. "Lausanne Is Site of Olympic Talks," *New York Times*, 13 Mar. 1968, 57; Furlong, "Bad Week," 19.

56. "Amateur's Champion," *New York Times*, 27 Feb. 1968, 48.

57. "Brundage States He Opposes Move," *New York Times*, 12 Mar. 1968, 53.

58. Ibid.

59. "Brundage Calls Executive Unit to April Session," *New York Times*, 13 Mar. 1968, 57; "Versión de Brundage al casa de Sudáfrica," *El Nacional*, 16 Sept. 1968, 2:1; Lloyd Garrison, "Olympic Unit, in Reversal, Votes to Bar South Africa," *New York Times*, 22 Apr. 1968, 62.

60. Bass, *Not the Triumph but the Struggle*, 178; "Versión de Brundage al casa de Sudáfrica," 1.

61. Espy, *Politics*, 105; Tex Maule, "Switcheroo from Yes to Nyet," *Sports Illustrated* (29 Apr. 1968): 29.

62. "Airgram Memo," 14 May 1968 from Amembassy Moscow to State Department, *NARA*, RG 59, Box 325, folder 15-1, MEX CUL 4/1/68.

63. Ibid.; "Olympian Retreat," *Newsweek* (6 May 1968): 90–91.

64. "Result Is Decided Early in Polling," *New York Times*, 24 Apr. 1968, 35.

65. "Telegram," 25 Apr. 1968 from Amembassy Cape Town to Secretary of State, *NARA*, RG 59, Box 325, folder 15-1 MEX CUL, 4/1/68.

66. "Reversal in Lausanne," *New York Times*, 22 Apr. 1968, 46; "Invitation Withdrawn," *Time*, 3 May 1968, 66–67; "Telegram," 23 Apr. 1968 from Amembassy Pretoria to State Department, *NARA*, RG 59, Box 323, folder 15-1, MEX CUL, 4/1/68.

67. "Favorable Vote Seen as Certain," *New York Times*, 23 Apr. 1968, 53.

68. "For the Honor of the Games," *National Review* 20:38 (24 Sept. 1968): 949; "Czech TV Resumes," *New York Times*, 25 Aug. 1968, 41; "Ban on Soviet Urged," *New York Times*, 24 Apr. 1968, 35.

69. State Department Telegram, 12 June 1968, from Amconsul Salisbury to State Department, *NARA*, RG 59, Box 325, folder 15-1, MEX CUL 4/1/68; "Rodesia de Sur, Imposibilitada Para Participar en los Juegos Olímpicos," *El Universal*, 7 June 1968, 18; "Opina Brundage que Sigue Vigente la Invitación Olímpica a Rodesia," *El Universal*, 8 June 1968, 1.

70. Richard Joseph, "Travel Notes," *Esquire* 68:5 (Nov. 1967): 66.

71. For an excellent assessment of the role of Pedro Rámirez Vázquez in preparing for the Olympics, see Ariel Rodríguez Kuri, "Hacia México 68: Pedro Ramírez

Vázquez y el proyecto olímpico," *Secuencia* 56 (May–Aug. 2003): 37–73. Also see Zolov, "Showcasing the 'Land of Tomorrow,'" 161–68. For one perspective on the cost efficiency of the Mexico City Olympics, see "En México se ha Hecho la Olimpiada 'más Taquillera,'" *Excelsior,* 9 Nov. 1968, 17. For other information regarding the planning and preparation for the Olympics, see Ariel Rodríguez Kuri, "El otro 68: Política y Estilo en la Organización de los Juegos Olímpicos de la Ciudad de México," *Relaciones* 19 (Fall 1998): 109–29.

72. Zolov, "Showcasing the 'Land of Tomorrow.'"

73. "Television Programs Dedicated to the Events of the Cultural Olympiad," *El Nacional,* 10 Sept. 1968, 8. See, for instance, *Excelsior,* 3 Nov. 1968, A:38; *El Universal,* 5 Nov. 1968, 10; *El Universal,* 5 May 1968, B:32; *El Universal,* 9 June 1968, D:34; *Excelsior,* 12 Oct. 1968, 19; *Excelsior,* 10 Oct. 1968, 5.

74. Sanka Knox, "Olympics Press Culture Activity," *New York Times,* 16 July 1968, 33.

75. Ramon Morones, "Duke Ellington en México," *Excelsior,* 25 Sept. 1968, 18.

76. "Olympic Games Adding Culture," *New York Times,* 11 Feb. 1968, 94.

77. Zolov, "Showcasing the 'Land of Tomorrow,'" 177–79; Ana Mary Ugalde, interview with the author, Mexico City, 10 Nov. 2001.

78. Ibid.

79. Karel Wendl, "Route of Friendship: A Cultural/Artistic Event of the Games of the XIX Olympiad in Mexico City—1968," *Olympika: The International Journal of Olympic Studies* 7 (1998): 113–34; "21 Esculturas Monumentales Dejará Como Testimonio la Olimpíada Cultural," *El Universal,* 5 June 1968, 8; "La Ruta de la Amistad," *Excelsior Magazine Dominical,* 13 Oct. 1968, 5; "New Goal: Mexico's 1968 Olympics" and "Artists on the Mexican Scene," *Harper's Bazaar* 101:1 (July 1968): 74–75; "Olympic Games Adding Culture"; Grace Glueck, "Not All Rowing or Discus Throwing," *New York Times,* 21 June 1968, D:30.

80. Letter from Edmund Willard to Under Secretary of State for Latin American Affairs, 17 Nov. 1967, and reply, 4 Dec. 1967, *NARA,* RG 59, Box 325, folder 15 CUL Mex 1/1/67; Enrique Loubet, "Una Pintura de Gauguin que Vale 5 Millones de Pesos Envía Francia Como Aportación a la Olímpiada Cultura," *Excelsior,* 9 Sept. 1968, A:16; Augustin Salmon, "Se Efectuará en México el Primer Curso de Folklore Internacional, Dentro de la Olimpiada Cultura," *Excelsior,* 13 Sept. 1968, A:17; Fausto Fernandez Ponte, "Paz, Cultura y Deporte, Propósitos Olímpicos de México," *Excelsior,* 13 Sept. 1968, A:5; "Cien Países Participarán en Este Suceso de la Olimpiada Cultural," *Excelsior,* 7 Sept. 1968, 16; "A Well Designed Warm-up for the Olympics," *Life* 64:20 (17 May 1968): 55; "Amity and Art," *Architectural Forum* 129:3 (Oct. 1968): 67–70; Sidney Wise, "Culture to Supplement Olympic Sports," *New York Times,* 14 July 1968, V:10; "Dali Painting for Olympics," *New York Times,* 28 Aug. 1968, 58; "Mexico's Olympic Stamps," *New York Times,* 27 Oct. 1968, 34; Glueck, "Not All Rowing"; Knox, "Olympics Press Culture."

81. Dept. of State Memorandum, "Statement on Mexican Olympic Cultural Program," 22 June 1968, *NARA,* RG 59, Box 325, folder 15-1 Mex CUL 4/1/68.

82. Yale Richmond, *Cultural Exchange and the Cold War: Raising the Iron Curtain* (University Park, PA: Pennsylvania State University Press, 2003); Dept. of State Airgram, from Amembassy Mexico City to Dept. of State, 7 Apr. 1968, *NARA,* RG 59, Box 325, folder 15-1 Mex CUL 4/1/68.

83. Octavio Paz, *The Labyrinth of Solitude* (New York: Grove Press, 1985), 29.

84. Dept. of State Airgram, from Amembassy Mexico to SecState, 7 Apr. 1968, *NARA,* RG 59, Box 325, folder 15-1 Mex CUL 4/1/68.

85. "La Olimpiada Cultural," *El Universal Revista de la Semana,* 3 Nov. 1968, 1–10. Glueck, "Not All Rowing"; "Letter from Mexico City," *Holiday* (Oct. 1967): 16.

86. Pan Dodd Eimon, "The City Tells Its Story," *The American City* 83:8 (Aug.

1968): 133–34; "Abirán el 12 de Este, en Coapa, Tres Villas de Viviendas Olímpicas," *Excelsior,* 1 Sept. 1968, 1. Henry Giniger, "A Sports Capital-to-Be," *New York Times,* 13 Jan. 1968, 28; "Better Act Now if You're Going to [the] Olympics," *U.S. News and World Report,* 24 June 1968, 56.

87. *Boletin Oficial, XIX Olimpiada* 2 (Oct. 1965): 2–3; "40 Millones de Flores Durante la Olimpiada," *Excelsior,* 3 Sept. 1968, 22; "200 Autobuses Para el Transporte de los Atletas," *El Universal,* 20 June 1968, 22; Eimon, "City Tells Its Story"; "If You Plan to See the Olympics," *Sunset* 140:1 (Jan. 1968): 28; "Mexico's Olympics . . . not Yet Sold Out," *Sunset* 140:7 (July 1968): 26; "Letter from Mexico City," *Holiday* (Oct. 1967): 18; "The Scene a la Mexicana," *Time* (18 Oct. 1968): 79; Ugalde interview.

88. Robert S. Strother, "Mexico's Sky-High Olympiad," *Reader's Digest* 93:557 (Sept. 1968): 33; "Mostraron los tableros electrónicos olímpicos," *El Nacional,* 1 Aug. 1968, 2:2. An excellent summary of all the major projects is found in "Obras Olímpicas," *Excelsior Magazine Dominical,* 29 Sept. 1968, 1–15. See also Henry Giniger, "Mexicans Rushing Olympics' Complex," *New York Times,* 21 July 1968, V:5; "Entre los Mejores del Mundo Estará el Tablero del Estadio Olímpico de la C.U.," *El Universal,* 12 June 1968, 18.

89. Edmundo Conteras J., "La Alberca Olímpica Está Considerada Como un Auténtico Alarde de la Técnica Moderna," *El Universal,* 18 June 1968, 19; "Obras Olímpicas," 1–15; "Excelsior Visita las Obras Olímpicas," *Excelsior,* 6 Sept. 1968, 1; Giniger, "Mexicans Rushing Olympics' Complex."

90. Henry Giniger, "Olympic Building Is Behind Schedule," *New York Times,* 8 Sept. 1968, V:10.

91. "Diaz Inaugurates Seven Olympic Sites," *New York Times,* 14 Sept. 1968, 6; "Todo Listo Para los Juegos Olímpicos," *Excelsior,* 5 Oct. 1968, 1; "The Olympics' Extra Heat," *Newsweek* (28 Oct. 1968): 79.

3—Image Tarnished—The Revolt of the Black Athlete

1. Kenny Moore, "A Courageous Stand," *Sports Illustrated* (5 Aug. 1991): 70–71; C.D. Jackson, *Why? The Biography of John Carlos* (Los Angeles: Milligan Books, 2000), 164–68; John Underwood, "The Non-Trial Trials," *Sports Illustrated* (8 July 1968): 11–13.

2. Jackson, *Why?,* 164–68.

3. For an excellent and detailed description of the protest and its symbolic significance, see Amy Bass, *Not the Triumph,* 237–46; also see Douglas Hartmann, *Race, Culture, and the Revolt of the Black Athlete: The 1968 Olympic Protests and Their Aftermath* (Chicago: University of Chicago Press, 2003), 3–26.

4. Mark Ribowsky, *A Complete History of the Negro Leagues* (New York: Carol Publishing Group, 1995), 280.

5. A.S. Young, "The Black Athlete in the Golden Age of Sports, Part II: Jackie Opens the Door—Wide!" *Ebony* 24:2 (Dec. 1968): 130.

6. Arthur Ashe, *A Hard Road to Glory: Baseball* (New York: Amistad Press, 1988), 44–46; Arthur Ashe, *A Hard Road to Glory: Football* (Amistad Press, 1988), 48–53; Arthur Ashe, *A Hard Road to Glory: Basketball* (Amistad Press, 1988), 22–25. It should be noted that segregation remained steadfast in college sports in the South until after the *Brown* decision and in some cases well into the 1960s. The long, slow desegregation of college sports is the story of many "Jackie Robinsons" at many different institutions and a story that lies outside the scope of this work. See Charles Martin, "Jim Crow in the Gymnasium: The Integration of College Basketball in the American South," *The International Journal of the History of Sport* 10:1 (April 1993): 68–86; Nelson George, *Elevating the Game: Black Men and Basketball* (New York: HarperCollins Publishers, 1992), 132–43; Neil D. Isaacs, *All the Moves: A History of College Basketball* (New

York: J.B. Lippincott Co., 1975), 188–211; David K. Wiggins, "'The Future of College Athletics Is at Stake': Black Athletes and Racial Turmoil on Three Predominantly White University Campuses, 1968–1972," *Journal of Sport History* 15:3 (Winter 1988): 304–33; David K. Wiggins, "Prized Performers, but Frequently Overlooked Students: The Involvement of Black Athletes in Intercollegiate Sports on Predominately White University Campuses, 1890–1972," *Research Quarterly for Exercise and Sport* 62 (June 1991): 164–77.

7. John Hoberman, *Darwin's Athletes* (New York: Houghton Mifflin, 1997), 32.

8. Rhoden, *Forty Million Dollar Slaves*; Zirin, *What's My Name.*

9. William Van Deburg, *New Day in Babylon* (Chicago: University of Chicago Press, 1992), 84; see also Jack Olsen, "The Cruel Deception," *Sports Illustrated* (1 July 1968): 15–16; Harry Edwards, *Revolt of the Black Athlete* (New York: Free Press, 1969).

10. "For a Moment, Black Hero before a White Crowd," *Life* 64:11 (15 March 1968): 22.

11. Edwards, *Revolt,* 23.

12. "A Slap in the Face to Black Olympic Heroes," *Ebony* (April 1985): 91–98; Edwards, *Revolt,* 16–17; Arthur Ashe, *A Hard Road to Glory: Basketball,* 38–39; Bill Russell, *Go Up for Glory* (Berkeley: Berkeley Publishing Group, 1980); Phillip Hoose, *Necessities* (New York: Random House, 1989).

13. Mal Whitfield, "Let's Boycott the Olympics," *Ebony* 19:5 (March 1964): 98.

14. Ibid., 100.

15. Charles Kaiser, *1968 in America: Music, Politics, Chaos, Counterculture, and the Shaping of a Generation* (New York: Weidenfeld and Nicolson, 1988), 136.

16. Ibid., 139.

17. Hartmann, *Race, Culture, and the Revolt,* 60–92.

18. Kaiser, *1968 in America,* 141–42.

19. Ibid., 143–44.

20. Ibid., 145.

21. Arthur Ashe, *A Hard Road to Glory: Boxing,* 59.

22. William Strathmore, *Muhammad Ali: The Unseen Archives* (Bath, UK: Parragon Publishing, 2001), 44–110; Zirin, *What's My Name,* 69–72.

23. "Muhammad Ali," *San Francisco Express Times,* 2 May 1968, 7.

24. Ibid.; Michael Oriard, "Muhammad Ali: The Hero in the Age of Mass Media," in *Muhammad Ali: The People's Champ,* ed. Elliott J. Gorn (Urbana: University of Illinois Press, 1995), 5–22; Bass, *Not the Triumph,* 32–33; *Fields of Fire,* HBO Films.

25. Charles V. Hamilton, "An Advocate of Black Power Defines It," *New York Times Magazine* (14 April 1968): 22.

26. Jack Scott, "The White Olympics," *Ramparts* (May 1968): 59.

27. Edwards, *Revolt,* 43. See, for instance, "Black Manifesto—Blueprint for African-Americans," *The Black Liberator* (June 1969): 1; also "Racist Olympics," *San Francisco Express Times* 1:32 (28 Aug. 1968): 7.

28. Van Deburg, *New Day in Babylon,* 97–101.

29. Bob Beamon and Milana Walter Beamon, *The Man Who Could Fly: The Bob Beamon Story* (Columbus, MS: Genesis Press, 1999), 93–94; "The Angry Black Athlete," *Newsweek* (15 July 1968): D:57; Phil Pepe, *Stand Tall: The Lew Alcindor Story* (New York: Grosset & Dunlap, 1970), 38; Moore, "A Courageous Stand," 66; Jackson, *Why,* 140–44.

30. Dick Schaap, "The Revolt of the Black Athletes," *Look* 32 (6 Aug. 1968): 72; Scott, "The White Olympics," 57; Arnold Hano, "The Black Rebel Who 'Whitelists' the Olympics," *New York Times Magazine* 6 (12 May 1968): 42–44. The best in the world in 1968 could throw the discus just over 200 feet. Al Oerter won the gold medal at the Olympics with a throw of 212 feet (improving on his world record by over five feet), while both the silver and bronze medallists threw 206 feet. See Nigel Blundell

and Duncan Mackay, *The History of the Olympics* (London: PRC Publishing, 1999), 211; "Pride and Precocity," *Time* (25 Oct. 1968): 62

31. David K. Wiggins, "'The Year of Awakening': Black Athletes, Racial Unrest and the Civil Rights Movement of 1968," *The International Journal of the History of Sport* 9:2 (Aug. 1992): 188–91.

32. Edwards, *Revolt,* 42; "Cause for Alarm," *Sports Illustrated* (25 Sept. 1967): 11.

33. Scott, "The White Olympics," 59; Frank Murphy, *The Last Protest: Lee Evans in Mexico City* (Kansas City: Windsprint Press, 2006), 217–23.

34. Edwards, *Revolt,* 41–46.

35. Ibid., 50–56; Moore, "A Courageous Stand," 68.

36. Pete Axthelm, "Boycott Now—Boycott Later," *Sports Illustrated* (26 Feb. 1968): 24–26.

37. See Bass, *Not the Triumph*; "Cal Breaks Black Boycott: Nice Guys Finish Last," *San Francisco Express Times,* 29 Feb. 1968, 4.

38. Axthelm, "Boycott Now—Boycott Later," 25.

39. Ibid.

40. Ibid.

41. Dave Anderson, "Negro Athletes Apprehensive, but Compete in Meet Anyway," *New York Times,* 17 Feb. 1968, 19.

42. Edwards, *Revolt,* 80–86.

43. Ibid.; see also Homer Bigart, "Militants Lose 7th Ave. Scuffle," *New York Times,* 17 Feb. 1968, 19; Frank Litsky, "9 Negroes Appear in Garden Action," *New York Times,* 17 Feb. 1968, 19.

44. Edwards, *Revolt,* 80–86.

45. Ibid., 88; Pete Axthelm, "Boos and a Beating for Tommie," *Sports Illustrated* (29 Jan. 1968): 56; Scott, "The White Olympics," 60; Moore, "A Courageous Stand," 68; Lew Alcindor with Jack Olsen, "A Year of Turmoil and Decision," *Sports Illustrated* (10 Nov. 1969): 35.

46. Alcindor with Olsen, "A Year of Turmoil," 35.

47. Robert Lipsyte, "The Spirit of the Olympics," *New York Times,* 1 Aug. 1968, 34.

48. Jonathan Rodgers, "A Step to an Olympic Boycott," *Sports Illustrated* (4 Dec. 1967): 31; "If They Run, They'll Win," *Ebony* 23:12 (Oct. 1968): 188.

49. "Olympic Boycott?" *Newsweek* (4 Dec. 1967): 59; "Should Negroes Boycott the Olympics?" *Ebony* 23: 4 (March 1968): 115.

50. "Negro Olympic Boycott Is Off Target," *Life* 63:23 (8 Dec. 1967): 4; "Louis Frowns on Olympic Boycott," *New York Times,* 3 Apr. 1968, 54; Robert Lipsyte, "Politics and Protest," *New York Times,* 10 Feb. 1968, 41.

51. "Olympic Boycott?" *Newsweek* (4 Dec. 1967): 59.

52. "U.S. Olympic Boycott Leaders Remain Undecided on Course," *New York Times,* 23 June 1968, V:1; "Negro Vote Barring Games Boycott Told," *New York Times,* 1 Aug. 1968, 35; Zirin, *What's My Name,* 73–100.

53. C. Gerald Fraser, "Negroes Call Off Boycott, Reshape Olympic Protest," *New York Times,* 1 Sept. 1968, 5, 1; "Notas Olimpicas," *Excelsior,* 2 Sept. 1968, 3; "No Habrá Boicot Negro a los Juegos," *Excelsior,* 12 Sept. 1968, 1, 9.

54. "A Negro Boycott: Fair Play or Fumble?" *Senior Scholastic* (15 Feb. 1968): 10.

55. Fraser, "Negroes Call Off Boycott," 4; Elaine Brown, *A Taste of Power: A Black Woman's Story* (New York: Pantheon Books, 1992); Sara Evans, *Personal Politics: The Roots of Women's Liberation in the Civil Rights Movement and the New Left* (New York: Vintage, 1979), 83–101. The precise connection between female athletes and the Olympic Project for Human Rights remains a subject for further study. The best discussion of this topic is in Bass, *Not the Triumph,* 189–91, 214–26.

56. Pepe, *Stand Tall,* 114.

57. Alcindor, "A Year of Turmoil and Decision"; Sam Goldaper, "Alcindor Clarifies TV Remark, Criticizes Racial Bias in U.S.," *New York Times,* 23 July 1968, 31.

58. Pepe, *Stand Tall,* 114; "If They Run, They'll Win," 188; Fausto Fernandez Ponte, "Negros, Sólo Para la Guerra," *Excelsior,* 14 Sept. 1968, 1; Zirin, *What's My Name,* 80.

59. Fraser, "Negroes Call Off Boycott," 4; "Los Atletas Negros no piden la Renuncia de A. Brundage," *El Nacional,* 26 Sept. 1968, 3:2.

4—Image Shattered—Tlatelolco

1. "Recio Combate al Despersar el Ejército un Mitin de Huelguistas," *Excelsior,* 3 Oct. 1968, 1, 13+.

2. Krauze, *Biography of Power,* 715–22; "Mexico Washes away the Bloodstains," *San Francisco Express Times* 1:42 (6 Nov. 1968): 3, 5. Accounts of the student movement and this massacre have long been based on personal interviews, newspaper articles, and speculation (often well-reasoned and justified but unsubstantiated). The Mexican government was understandably reluctant to release any information regarding the massacre, and the U.S. government generally does not release files for 30 years, so many important sources went untapped. Beginning in 1998, the U.S. government began to declassify some of the documents relevant to the massacre, a process that continues today. In Mexico the election of Vicente Fox in 2000 sparked calls for the Mexican government to investigate the incident and release its own documents. Fox acceded to these requests in November 2001, announcing the release of thousands of documents and calling for a full investigation, which is ongoing. The newly released documents from both governments have answered many of the questions stemming from the massacre, leaving only a handful of significant questions unanswered, and making possible a much fuller description of the student movement and the massacre. Many of these documents are cited individually below. Many are also available online at <http://www.gwu.edu/~nsarchiv/NSAEBB/NSAEBB99/>, where they have been capably organized and abstracted by Kate Doyle. This website will hereafter be cited as "Doyle."

3. Juan Martinez, interview. See also Mexico City Sitrep, CIA Station in Mexico, confidential intelligence information cable, 2 Aug. 1968, National Security Archive, Doyle document 52; also Mexico City Sitrep, CIA Station in Mexico, confidential intelligence information cable, 10 Aug. 1968, Doyle document 58, which explains that such rumors of cremation of bodies can not be true, as "there is no crematorium at the military hospital." Dept. of State Airgram, 20 Oct. 1968, "Review of Mexico City Student Disturbances," *NARA,* RG 59, Box 2340, folder POL 13.2 Mex, 9/1/68, page 8; Pedro Aguilar Cabrera, interview; Krauze, *Biography of Power,* 715–22; Lynn V. Foster, *A Brief History of Mexico* (New York: Facts on File, Inc., 1997), 199–201; Elaine Carey, *Plaza of Sacrifices: Gender, Power, and Terror in 1968 Mexico* (Albuquerque: University of New Mexico, 2005), 134–39; Paco Ignacio Taibo II, *'68* (New York: Seven Stories Press, 2004), 105; Elena Poniatowska, *La Noche de Tlatelolco* (Mexico: Biblioteca ERA, 1993). This book is translated into English as *Massacre in Mexico.* The U.S. State Department listed the following figures: "At least forty, and [perhaps] five times that many were killed, 400 to 500 were wounded and over one thousand five hundred were arrested." See Dept. of State Airgram, 20 Oct. 1968, "Review of Mexico City Disturbances," *NARA,* RG 59, Box 2340, folder POL 13.2 Mex 9/1/68, page 15. Sources reporting to the FBI estimated as many as 200 dead. See White House, secret memorandum, "Mexican Riots—Extent of Communist Involvement," 5 Oct. 1968, Lyndon B. Johnson Library, National Security Files, CO-Mexico, Vol IV, Box 60, "Mexico, memos & misc., 1/68–10/68," Doyle document 102.

4. Octavio Paz, *The Other Mexico: Critique of the Pyramid* (New York: Grove Press, 1985), 220–37. For a thorough examination of this process, see Julia Preston and Samuel Dillon, *Opening Mexico: The Making of a Democracy* (New York: Farrar, Straus and Giroux, 2004); also see Evelyn P. Stevens, *Protest and Response in Mexico* (Cambridge, MA: The MIT Press, 1974), 99–184; Diane Davis, "Social Movements in Mexico's Crisis," *Journal of International Affairs* 43:2 (Winter 1990): 343–67; Carlos Monsiváis, "From '68 to Cardenismo: Toward a Chronicle of Social Movements," *Journal of International Affairs* 43:2 (Winter 1990): 386–87.

5. Brooks, "Mexico," 19–20; Stevens, *Protest and Response*, 99–184; Carey, *Plaza of Sacrifices*, 22–32.

6. Ibid.

7. Ibid.

8. Kaiser, *1968 in America*, 150–65; Ronald Fraser, *1968: A Student Generation in Revolt* (New York: Pantheon Books, 1988), 1–14; Airgram 3 Nov. 1968, "Generalizations on Student Unrest," *NARA*, RG 59, Box 2340, folder POL 13.2 MEX, 9/1/68; Gerard De Groot, ed., *Student Protest: The Sixties and After* (New York: Addison Wesley Publishing Co., 1998), 5.

9. Jeremi Suri, *Power and Protest: Global Revolution and the Rise of Détente* (Cambridge, MA: Harvard University Press, 2003), 88–128; Herbert Braun, "Protests of Engagement: Dignity, False Love, and Self-Love in Mexico during 1968," *Comparative Studies in Society and History* 39:3 (July 1997): 511–49.

10. Dept. of State Airgram, 3 Nov. 1968, "Student Unrest: Comments on Enclosure CA-10592," *NARA*, RG 59, Box 2350, Pol 13-2, Doyle document 24; Dept. of State Telegram, from Amembassy Mexico to SecState, 14 June 1968, *NARA*, RG 59, Box 2341, folder POL 14 Mex 1/1/67.

11. John Spitzer and Harvey Cohen, "In Mexico, '68," *Ramparts Magazine* 7:6 (26 Oct. 1968): 39; Stevens, *Protest and Response*, 185–240; Carey, *Plaza of Sacrifices*, 39; Henry Giniger, "Students' Strike Embarrasses Mexico," *New York Times*, 9 Sept. 1968, 1; Ernesto Viva, "Exclusive: Day-by-day Story of Mexican Student Revolt," *San Francisco Express Times* 1:29 (7 Aug. 1968): 5; "Mexican Students Fight Riot Police," *New York Times*, 31 July 1968, 1; Dept. of State Airgram, 7 Aug. 1968, "Roundup of Recent Political Developments," *NARA*, RG 59, Box 2337, folder POL 2 Mex 7/1/68.

12. Spitzer and Cohen, "In Mexico," 40; Henry Giniger, "Reds Deny Role in Mexico Riots," *New York Times*, 5 Aug. 1968, 3; Bureau of Intelligence and Research, confidential intelligence note, "Mexican President's Decision to Use Force against Students May Exacerbate Differences," 29 Aug. 1968, *NARA*, RG 59, Box 2343, Pol 23-8 Mex, Doyle document 32.

13. Editorials regarding the student movement appeared in the Mexican papers almost daily throughout the summer of 1968, sometimes three or four a day. There are far too many examples to cite them all here, but a few of the most salient include: Jose Alvarado, "La Generación de 1968," *Excelsior*, 2 Oct. 1968, 7, which summarizes the variety of opinions in Mexico about the students; "Las Olimpiadas Como Compromiso," *Excelsior*, 1 Sept. 1968, 7, arguing that the Mexican government must be especially careful in dealing with the students due to the increased visibility of the Olympics; Alfonso Trueba, "A los Estudiantes," *Excelsior*, 3 Sept. 1968, 7, in which an "older man" argues that the students need to temper their views; Sergio Villegas, "Movimiento Estudiantil," *Excelsior*, 8 Sept. 1968, 7; "Exhorto al Estudio," *Excelsior*, 13 Sept. 1968, A:6; an untitled editorial in *El Nacional*, 26 Sept. 1968, 6, calling for a truce between the students and the government during the Olympics; a full page of three editorials in *Excelsior*, 30 Sept. 1968, 7.

14. The full extent of communist involvement in the student movement is one question still largely unanswered by recently declassified government documents. For the most part, U.S. government sources echo the claim of the Mexican government

that the movement was orchestrated by a core of extremists, while at the same time doubting whether a small group of such extremists could maintain such a large movement over an extended period of time. See Intelligence note, "Mexico, Current Unrest Springs from Widespread Student Disaffection and Alienation," 10 Oct. 1968, *NARA*, RG 59, Box 2343, Pol 23-8, Doyle document 39; James N. Goodsell, "Mexico: Why the Students Rioted," *Current History* 58:329 (Jan. 1969): 32; CIA secret intelligence summary, "Students Stage Major Disorders in Mexico," 2 Aug. 1968, Doyle document 53; also Spitzer and Cohen, "In Mexico", 40; Giniger, "Students' Strike"; Sheldon G. Weeks, "Mexican Students' Demands," *New York Times*, 11 Aug. 1968, IV:11; Ignacio Taibo, '*68*.

15. For a more detailed description of the political makeup of the student movement, see Carey, *Plaza of Sacrifices*, 47–64; Ignacio Taibo, '*68*, 16–23, 56–59; Martinez, interview; Stevens, *Protest and Response*, 185–240; "Mexican Student Protests Spread to 2 Other Cities," *New York Times*, 1 Aug. 1968, 4; Dept. of State Telegram, from Amembassy Mexico to SecState, 29 July 1968, *NARA*, RG 59, Box 2343, folder 23-8 Mex 1/1/68, POL 23 Mex to POL-MEX-US.

16. Henry Giniger, "Mexico Classes on Tomorrow: Riots Leave Nation Disturbed," *New York Times*, 4 Aug. 1968, 20; see Intelligence note, "Mexican Student Riots Highly Embarrassing but Not a Threat to Stability," 6 Aug. 1968, *NARA* RG 59, Box 2343, Pol 23-8, Doyle document 29; CIA Station in Mexico, confidential intelligence information cable, "Mexico City Sitrep," 31 July 1968, National Security Archive, Doyle document 48; CIA, secret intelligence summary, "Mexican Students Still Spar with Government," 13 Sept. 1968, National Security Archive, Doyle document 69; U.S. Embassy in Mexico, confidential telegram, "Student Disorders," 27 Aug. 1968, *NARA*, RG 59, Box 2340, Pol 13-2, Doyle document 10; Jonathan Heath, *Mexico and the Sexenio Curse: Presidential Successions and Economic Crises in Modern Mexico* (Washington: Center for Strategic and International Studies, 1999), 18; Viva, "Exclusive: Day-by-day Story," 5; Defense Intelligence Agency, confidential intelligence information report, "Status of Brig Gen José Hernández Toledo," 23 Oct. 1968, National Security Archive, Doyle document 90.

17. Dept. of State Intelligence Note, from Thomas L. Hughes to The Secretary, 29 Aug. 1968, *NARA*, RG59, Box 2343, folder 23-8 Mex 1/1/68, POL 23 Mex to POL-MEX-US.

18. Henry Giniger, "50,000 Mexico City Students March in New Protest against Police and Army," *New York Times*, 2 Aug. 1968, 11; Krauze, *Biography of Power*, 702.

19. Dept. of State Airgram, 20 Oct. 1968, "Review of Mexico City Student Disturbances," *NARA*, RG 59, Box 2340, folder POL 13.2 Mex 9/1/68, page 11; Bureau of Intelligence and Research, confidential working draft, "Student Violence and Attitudes in Latin America," ca. 15 Nov. 1968, Lyndon B. Johnson Library, National Security Files Intelligence File, Box 3, "Student Unrest," Doyle document 43; CIA secret intelligence summary, "Students Stage Major Disorders in Mexico," 2 Aug. 1968, Doyle document 53. Also Ignacio Taibo, '*68*, 50, 73–76.

20. Paz, *Other Mexico*, 232; Krauze, *Biography of Power*, 694–702; Davis, "Social Movements," 343–67; Monsiváis, "From '68 to Cardenismo," 386–87; Henry Giniger, "Mexican Students Stage Unusual Protest against President," *New York Times*, 14 Aug. 1968, 14; Giniger, "The Calm Exterior Is Deceiving," *New York Times*, 18 Aug. 1968, IV:5; Giniger, "Mexico Students Urge a New Party," *New York Times*, 22 Aug. 1968, 7; Dept. of State Airgram, 4 Sept. 1968, "Roundup of Recent Political Developments," *NARA*, RG 59, Box 2337A, folder POL 2 Mex 9/1/68.

21. Henry Giniger, "Gunfire and Fighting Break Out in Students' Protest in Mexico," *New York Times*, 29 Aug. 1968, 5.

22. U.S. intelligence documents support the assertion that this was a turning point, as they uniformly argue that Díaz Ordaz and the Mexican government took a

much more aggressive posture after the protests of the 27th. Several documents mention Díaz Ordaz specifically and his personal motivations for silencing the insults against him, while others point to a failure of the early conciliatory strategy of the government in general and a need to crush the movement before it grew even larger. Still others mention the Olympics as an impending "deadline" forcing the government to become more assertive. See Dept. of State Telegram, from Amembassy Mexico to SecState, 19 Sept. 1968, *NARA*, RG 59, Box 2340, folder POL 13.2 Mex 9/1/68; U.S. Embassy in Mexico, confidential telegram, "August 27 Student Demonstration," 29 Aug. 1968, *NARA*, RG 59, Box 2340, folder Pol 13.2 Mex, Doyle document 11; U.S. Embassy in Mexico, confidential telegram, "Civil Disorder—Student Activities," 30 Aug. 1968, *NARA*, RG 59, Box 2340, Pol 13-2 Mex, Doyle document 12; White House, confidential cable, "Student Situation in Mexico," 29 Aug. 1968, Lyndon B. Johnson Library, National Security Files, CO-Mexico, Vol. IV, Box 60, "Mexico, memos & misc., 1/68–10/68," Doyle document 99. Henry Giniger, "Diaz Warns Dissident Mexican Students against Provocation," *New York Times*, 2 Sept. 1968, 11; "Student Defiance Persists in Mexico," *New York Times*, 4 Sept. 1968, 95; Dept. of State Telegrams, from Amembassy Mexico to SecState, 1 Sept. 1968 and 6 Sept. 1968, *NARA*, RG 59, Box 2341, POL 15-1 Mex 1/1/68. Also Ignacio Taibo, *'68*, 70–73; Carey, *Plaza of Sacrifices*, 99–105.

23. Dept. of State Airgram, 20 Oct. 1968, "Review of Mexico City Student Disturbances," *NARA*, RG 59, Box 2340, folder POL 13.2 Mex 9/1/68, page 13.

24. Angel T. Ferreira, "Clara Respuesta de Díaz Ordaz a las Demandas Estudiantiles," *Excelsior*, 2 Sept. 1968, 1, 11; State Department letter, "[Mexican Request for Military Radios]," 24 May 1968, *NARA*, RG 59, Box 1699, Def 19-8 Mex, Doyle document 84; State Department memorandum, "Out-of-Channels Request from Mexico," 18 July 1968, *NARA*, RG 59, Box 1578, Def 12-5 Mex, Doyle document 85; ibid.; Henry Giniger, "Mexican Army Seizes National University to End Agitation by Students," *New York Times*, 20 Sept. 1968, 1; "Students Battle Mexican Police," *New York Times*, 21 Sept. 1968, 9; Giniger, "Tension in Mexico Produces a 'Dialogue of the Deaf,'" *New York Times*, 21 Sept. 1968, 8; "Mexico Frees 250; Others Are Seized," *New York Times*, 22 Sept. 1968, 20.

25. Henry Giniger, "3 Dead, Many Hurt in Mexico City Battle," *New York Times*, 25 Sept. 1968, 1; Henry Giniger, "On an Embattled Campus, 8 Mexican Student Leaders Stress Moderate Aims," *New York Times*, 27 Sept. 1968, 16; ibid.; Henry Giniger, "40 Are Wounded in Mexico City as Police Clash with Students," *New York Times*, 24 Sept. 1968, 1; Giniger, "Hundreds Seized in Mexico Clashes," *New York Times*, 23 Sept. 1968, 1; Giniger, "Mexico City Death Toll Increases in Continuing Student Clashes," *New York Times*, 26 Sept. 1968, 21; Carey, *Plaza of Sacrifices*, 122–25.

26. *Plaza of Sacrifices*, 122–25.

27. Dept. of State Telegram, from Amembassy Mexico to SecState, 2 Aug. 1968, *NARA*, RG 59, Box 2343, folder 23-8 Mex 1/1/68, POL 23 Mex to POL-MEX-US.

28. Dept. of State Memorandum, from Covey T. Oliver to the Secretary, 28 Aug. 1968, *NARA*, RG 59, Box 2343, folder 23-8 Mex 1/1/68, POL 23 Mex to POL-MEX-US.

29. See *El Nacional*, 26 Sept. 1968, 6; "Las Olimpiadas Como Compromiso," *Excelsior*, 1 Sept. 1968, 7; Dept. of State Memorandum, from Covey T. Oliver to Acting Secretary, 1 Oct. 1968, *NARA*, RG 59, Box 2343, folder 23-8, Mex 1/1/68, POL 23 Mex to POL-MEX-US; Assistant Secretary of State for Latin America, confidential information memorandum, "Mexico—Prospects Following Occupation of the National University," 20 Sept. 1968, *NARA*, RG 59, Box 2340, Pol 23-8, Doyle document 33; Bureau of Intelligence and Research, confidential intelligence note, "Mexican Government's Use of Force Probably Forecloses the Possibility of a Compromise Solution to the Student Conflict," 26 Sept. 1968, *NARA*, RG 59, Box 2340, Pol 13-2 Mex, Doyle document 35.

30. Dept. of State Memorandum, from Covey T. Oliver to Acting Secretary, 1 Oct. 1968, *NARA*, RG 59, Box 2343, folder 23-8, Mex 1/1/68, POL 23 Mex to POL-MEX-US; Assistant Secretary of State for Latin America, confidential information memorandum, "Mexico—Prospects Following Occupation of the National University," 20 Sept. 1968, *NARA*, RG 59, Box 2340, Pol 23-8, Doyle document 33; Bureau of Intelligence and Research, confidential intelligence note, "Mexican Government's Use of Force Probably Forecloses the Possibility of a Compromise Solution to the Student Conflict," 26 Sept. 1968, *NARA*, RG 59, Box 2340, Pol 13-2 Mex, Doyle document 35.

31. Poniatowska, *Massacre in Mexico*, 210; Preston and Dillon, *Opening Mexico*.

32. Pedro Ocampo Ramirez, "La Universidad con Estudiantes," *Excelsior*, 2 Oct. 1968, 6; Dept. of State Memorandum, from Covey T. Oliver to Acting Secretary, 1 Oct. 1968, *NARA*, RG 59, Box 2343, folder 23-8, Mex 1/1/68, POL 23 Mex to POL-MEX-US; Assistant Secretary of State for Latin America, confidential information memorandum, "Mexico—Prospects Following Occupation of the National University," 20 Sept. 1968, *NARA*, RG 59, Box 2340, Pol 23-8, Doyle document 33; Bureau of Intelligence and Research, confidential intelligence note, "Mexican Government's Use of Force Probably Forecloses the Possibility of a Compromise Solution to the Student Conflict," 26 Sept. 1968, *NARA*, RG 59, Box 2340, Pol 13-2 Mex, Doyle document 35.

33. "Viente Muertos, 75 Heridos y 400 Presos," *Excelsior*, 3 Oct. 1968, 1,9; also *Excelsior*, 4 Oct. 1968, A:27; "Recio Combate," 1, 13+; Miguel Billa Larenza, interview with the author, Mexico City, 12 Nov. 2001; "A La Opinion Publica," *Excelsior*, 4 Oct. 1968, 10.

34. Krauze, *Biography of Power*, 719–20; Poniatowska, *Massacre in Mexico*, 202–8; Mark Kurlansky, *1968: The Year that Rocked the World* (New York: Ballantine Books, 2004). Krauze's theory was based on the accounts of members of student leadership who insisted that the first shots fired from the apartment building were not fired by students but by members of the secret police or Olympia Battalion. Intelligence reports in recently declassified documents corroborate that the first shots seem to have come from the balcony, but none as yet have confirmed the conspiracy suggested by Krauze. See Dept. of State Telegram, 10 Oct. 1968, *NARA*, RG 59, Box 2340, folder POL 13.2 Mex 9/1/68; CIA Station in Mexico, confidential cable, "Mexico City," 3 Oct. 1968, Lyndon B. Johnson Library, National Security Files CO-Mexico, Vol. IV, Box 60, "Mexico, memos & misc., 1/68–10/68 (cont.)," Doyle document 74.

35. Student testimonials and witnesses agree that the students rarely employed firearms. In some of the clashes, students did use guns, although students so armed were a distinct minority. In one press release, which could very well have been created, or at least influenced, by government officials, the Mexican police displayed a huge collection of weapons confiscated after over 50 clashes with the students. Even in this display, there are only a few handguns and rifles, with the bulk of the weapons being bottles and Molotov cocktails. See "299 Detenidos en los Disturbios Ocurridos en el Politecnico," *El Nacional*, 25 Sept. 1968, 6; Manuel Campos Diaz y Sanchez, "Gritos y Escándalo al Rendir Declaraciones los 54 Consignados por los Disturbios Estudiantiles," *Excelsior*, 25 Sept. 1968, 1.

36. "Recio Combate."

37. Billa Larenza, interview; Juan Aguilera, "Darkness in Tlatelolco," *Excelsior*, 4 Oct. 1968, 1. Official Mexican government statistics listed 37 killed. Other estimates have ranged much higher, even into the thousands. Most contemporary sources estimate the true figure at around 300. See, among others, "Mexico: Massacre in Tlatelolco Square," <http://english/pravda/ru/diplomatic/2002/10/04/37695.html>.

38. Poniatowska, *Massacre in Mexico*. Poniatowska's classic collection has been joined by several other collections of interviews and testimonials about the student movement and the massacre, including Luis Franco Ramos, ed., *Pensar el 68* (Mexico: Cal 7 Arena, 1988); Renata Sevilla, *Tlatelolco: Ocho Años Despues* (University of Florida,

Latin America Collection, LA 428.7 .S4x); Juan Miguel de Mora, *Tlatelolco 1968: Por Fin Toda la Verdad* (Mexico D.F.: Edamex, 1979); Ignacio Taibo, *'68,* and Jose Revueltas, *México 68: Juventud y Revolucion* (Mexico: Ediciones Era, 1978). For another study, see Medina Valdés Gerardo, *El 68, Tlatelolco y el Pan* (Mexico D.F.: Epessa, 1990).

39. Dept. of State Airgram, from Amembassy Mexico to SecState, 25 Dec. 1968, "Communists Reveal Demoralizing Effect of October 2 Incident," *NARA,* RG 59, Box 2339, folder POL 12 Mex 1/1/68; Dept. of State Airgram, 20 Oct. 1968, "Review of Mexico City Student Disturbances," *NARA,* RG 59, Box 2340, folder POL 13.2 Mex 9/1/68, page 16; Hay interview; Enrique Loubet, Jr., "Reitera Brundage su Confianza en México," *Excelsior,* 4 Oct. 1968, 1; Ignacio Tabio, *'68,* 110–12; Carey, *Plaza of Sacrifices,* 145–47.

40. Dept. of State Telegram, from Amembassy Mexico to SecState, 3 Oct. 1968, *NARA,* RG 59, Box 2340, folder POL 13.2 Mex 9/1/68.

41. U.S. intelligence officers speculated as early as 19 July that the student protests might interfere with the Olympics and that the Mexican government would go to great lengths to ensure the security of the Games. As the summer wore on, mention of the "Olympic deadline" to end the movement grew more frequent. See CIA, secret intelligence summary, "Student Unrest Troubles Mexico," 19 July 1968, National Security Archive, Doyle document 45; CIA, secret intelligence summary, "Mexican Government Stalls Student Movement," 6 Sept. 1968, National Security Archive, Doyle document 66; Poniatowska, *Massacre in Mexico,* 310; Jose Alvarado, "La Juventud Merece Respeto," *Excelsior,* 11 Sept. 1968, 7.

42. Dept. of State Memorandum, from Covey T. Oliver to the Secretary, 26 Sept. 1968, *NARA,* RG 59, Box 2343, folder 23-8 Mex 1/1/68, POL 23 Mex to POL-MEX-US; Goodsell, "Why Students Rioted," 33; U.S. Dept. of State Telegram, 5 Oct. 1968, *NARA,* RG 59, Box 2340, folder POL 13.2 Mex 9/1/68. One recent study that does emphasize the "Olympic deadline" is Elaine Carey, *Plaza of Sacrifices,* 107–10, 140–57. U.S. Dept of State Intelligence Notes, from Thomas L. Hughes to the Secretary, 6 and 16 Aug. 1968, *NARA,* RG 59, Box 2343, folder 23-8 Mex 1/1/68, POL 23 Mex to POL-MEX-US; Bureau of Intelligence and Research, secret intelligence note, "Mexican Student Demonstrations Continue Despite Government Efforts," 16 Aug. 1968, *NARA,* RG 59, Box 2343, Pol 23-8, Doyle document 30; U.S. Embassy in Mexico, secret telegram, "[Mexican Government Continues Crack Down]," 27 Sept. 1968, *NARA,* RG 59, Box 2340, Pol 13-2, Doyle document 16; U.S. Embassy in Mexico, confidential telegram, "Sitrep September 27, 1968," 27 Sept. 1968, *NARA,* RG 59, Box 2340, Pol 13-2, Doyle document 17.

43. Poniatowska, *Massacre in Mexico,* 310; Tariq Ali and Susan Watkins, *1968: Marching in the Streets* (New York: The Free Press, 1998), 166; Henry Giniger, "Mexico Keeps Up Calm Exterior," *New York Times,* 15 Aug. 1968, 11.

44. Dept. of State Telegram, from Amembassy Mexico to SecState, 6 Oct. 1968, *NARA,* RG 59, Box 2343, folder 23-8 Mex 1/1/68, POL 23 Mex to POL-MEX-US.

45. Poniatowska, *Massacre in Mexico,* 218, 221.

46. The ad appeared in the Oct. 17 *El Dia,* cited in Dept. of State Telegram, 17 Oct. 1968, *NARA,* RG 59, Box 2340, folder POL 13.2 Mex 9/1/68.

47. "Spell of the Olympics," *Newsweek* (21 Oct. 1968): 65.

48. Dept. of State Telegram, from Amembassy Mexico to SecState, 9 Oct. 1968, *NARA,* RG 59, Box 2343, folder 23-8 Mex 1/1/68, POL 23 Mex to POL-MEX-US.

49. "Plena Protección a Visitantes y Competidores," *Excelsior,* 4 Oct. 1968, 1+; Dept. of State Telegram, from Amembassy Rome to SecState, 9 Oct. 1968, *NARA,* RG 59, Box 2340, folder POL 13.2 Mex 9/1/68; Carey, *Plaza of Sacrifices,* 140.

50. "Plot to Kill the Olympics," *Newsweek* (2 Sept. 1968): 59.

51. Poniatowska, *Massacre in Mexico,* 201.

52. Ibid., 307.

53. Ibid.; U.S. intelligence sources support the assertion that concern for the safety of the Olympics was a major impetus for the crackdown. One study, issued two weeks after the massacre, noted that there had been "an intense concern among almost all Mexicans that the student situation would either prevent or hamper the Olympics." See Defense Intelligence Agency, confidential intelligence information report, "Army Participation in Student Situation, Mexico City," 18 Oct. 1968, Doyle document 88.

54. "Alarmista versión de que el COI aplazará la Olimpiada," *El Nacional,* 26 Sept. 1968, 3:2a; "Desmiente el COI el possible aplazamiento de la XIX Olimpiada," *El Nacional,* 27 Sept. 1968, 3:3a; "Los Juegos no se suspenderán, afirma Brundage," *El Nacional,* 28 Sept. 1968, 1.

55. Daley and Kiernan, *Story of the Olympic Games,* 420–21.

56. See, for example, Dept. of State Telegrams, from Amembassy Mexico to SecState, 6 Sept., 2 Oct., and 14 Oct. 1968, *NARA,* RG 59, Box 2340, folder 13.2 Mex 9/1/68; *New York Times,* 13 Oct. 1968.

5—The World Watches—October '68

1. "Llega la Antorcha a Barcelona," *Excelsior,* 1 Sept. 1968, 8; "La Antorcha Olimpica," *Excelsior Magazine Dominical,* 13 Oct. 1968, 2; Manuel Arvizu, "España Sigue de Fiesta por la Antorcha," *Excelsior,* 8 Sept. 1968, 1, 10; "Hoy Llegará el Fuego Olímpico a Sevilla," *Excelsior,* 9 Sept. 1968, 1;11-A; "La Antorcha Olímpica Navega Hacia América," *El Nacional,* 12 Sept. 1968, 2; "Surca el Atlántico el Fuego Olímpico," *Excelsior,* 16 Sept. 1968, 8, 11; Jose Luis Hernandez Sosa, "Apoteótico Recibimiento Espera en Veracruz a la Flama Olímpica," *El Nacional,* 29 Sept. 1968, 9; "Olympic Torch Is Hailed on Reaching Columbus' Home Port of Genoa," *New York Times,* 28 Aug. 1968, 56. For a detailed itinerary of the journey of the torch, see "La Antorcha Olimpica en Ruta Hacia Mexico," *Excelsior,* 1 Sept. 1968, 10. See also Manuel Arvizu, "Está en Madrid la Antorcha Olímpica," *Excelsior,* 6 Sept. 1968, 1; Miguel Angel Martinez Agis, "Multitudes a Todo lo Largo de la Ruta, de Teotihuacán Hasta el Estadio Olímpico," *Excelsior,* 13 Oct. 1968, 1; Steve Cady, "Parade of 7,226 Athletes to Open Olympic Ceremonies Today," *New York Times,* 12 Oct. 1968, 45; <http://olympic-museum.de/torches/torch1968.htm>. For a description of the final ceremony at the pyramids, see Carlos Denegri, "Mariachis, Globos, Palomas, Gran Fiesta," *Excelsior,* 12 Oct. 1968, 1.

2. Film: *Olimpiada en Mexico,* Mexican Olympic Committee, Mexico City. For further description of the Opening Ceremonies, see Carlos Dunegri, "Esplendorosa Apertura de los Juegos, Bajo el Signo de la Paz," *Excelsior,* 13 Oct. 1968, 1; Jaime Reyes Estrada, "'Maravilloso, Extraordinario . . . ,'" *Excelsior,* 13 Oct. 1968, 5; Manuel Seyde, "El Más Impresionante Desfile de la Historia Olímpica," *Excelsior,* 13 Oct. 1968, 1; "The Olympics," *Time* (18 Oct. 1968): 78.

3. "Girl Who Carries Torch for Mexico also Loves Sports," *New York Times,* 13 Oct. 1968, S:3.

4. Zolov, "Showcasing the 'Land of Tomorrow,'" 179; Bass, *Not the Triumph,* 106–7; "Figuras Olimpicas: Enriqueta Basilio," *El Nacional,* 20 Sept. 1968, 2A:2; Eduardo Ramirez, "Precisión y Brillo en el ensayo de la inauguración," *El Nacional,* 23 Sept. 1968, 1; Arthur Daley, "Amid Matchless Pageantry," *New York Times,* 13 Oct. 1968, V:2.

5. Neil Amdur, "Temu of Kenya Wins 10,000-Meter Run to Gain First Gold Medal of Olympics," *New York Times,* 14 Oct. 1968, 60; Collins, *Olympic Dreams,* 199; "In Mexico, Burst of African Energy," *Life* 65:17 (25 Oct. 1968): 40–41.

6. Manuel Barragan, "Más de 250 Records Nacionales se Lograron en el Atletismo Olímpico," *El Universal,* 6 Nov. 1968, 4; Neil Amdur, "Matson and Hines

Win Shot-Put and 100 Dash for First U.S. Gold Medals," *New York Times*, 15 Oct. 1968, 54; Arthur Daley, "Man with Frustrations," *New York Times*, 15 Oct. 1968, 54; Amdur, "Oerter Takes Record 4th Straight Olympic Gold Medal by Winning Discus," *New York Times*, 15 Oct. 1968, 50; "Oerter Planned His Campaign to Reach Peak in Rarefied Air," *New York Times*, 15 Oct. 1968, 51; Arthur Daley, "The Record Smashers," *New York Times*, 22 Oct. 1968, 51.

7. Fauso Ponce, "Monstruos del Atletismo," *Excelsior Magazine Dominical*, 27 Oct. 1968, 1–2; Joseph M. Sheehan, "Smith Takes Olympic 200 Meters and Seagren Captures Pole Vault for U.S.," *New York Times*, 17 Oct. 1968, 58.

8. Bob Ottum, "Bully Buildup in Old Mexico," *Sports Illustrated* (30 Oct. 1967): 20.

9. Powell's record still stands, making him and Beamon the only men ever to jump over 29 feet. Beamon and Beamon, *Man Who Could Fly*, 95–114; Fausto Ponce, "Beamon: Besó la Pista en que Consumó su Proeza," *Excelsior*, 19 Oct. 1968, 1; Manuel Seyde, "Temas del dia," *Excelsior*, 19 Oct. 1968, 2; Fausto Ponce, "Gloriosa Página Atlética de Beamon; Saltó 8.90 Mts.," *Excelsior*, 19 Oct. 1968, 7; Neil Amdur, "Beamon's 29-2 1/2 Long Jump and Evans's 43.8-Second 400 Set World Marks," *New York Times*, 19 Oct. 1968, 44.

10. Kenny Moore, "The Eye of the Storm," *Sports Illustrated* (12 Aug. 1991): 64.

11. "Evans Puts Aside Racial Problems," *New York Times*, 19 Oct. 1968, 44.

12. The so-called "metric mile."

13. Jon Entine, *Taboo* (New York: Public Affairs, 2000), 54.

14. Neil Amdur, "Keino Breaks Olympic Record in 1,500-Meter Run, with Ryun of U.S. Second," *New York Times*, 21 Oct. 1968, 60; Joseph Durso, "Americans Gain Four Gold Medals," *New York Times*, 20 Oct. 1968, V:3; Marc Bloom, "African King," *Runner's World* 26:9 (1991): 20–21.

15. Joseph L. Arbena, "Mexico City 1968," in Findling and Pelle, eds., *Encyclopedia of the Modern Olympic Movement*, 179; Joseph M. Sheehan, "Altitude Barrier Cracked at Olympics," *New York Times*, 27 Oct. 1968, V:3.

16. Joseph Durso, "Fosbury Flop Is a Gold Medal Smash," *New York Times*, 22 Oct. 1968, 51.

17. Arthur Daley, "The Fosbury Flop," *New York Times*, 23 Oct. 1968, 50.

18. Robert Lipsyte, "A Hero of Our Times," *New York Times*, 21 Oct. 1968, 60; "La Caslavska, Aclamada al Llegar a Praga," *Excelsior*, 29 Oct. 1968; "Czech Olympic Gymnast Bride of Teammate in Mexico," *New York Times*, 27 Oct. 1968, V:3; Oñate Moreno, "Natasha dará pelea a la gran Vera Caslavska," *El Nacional*, 26 Sept. 1968, 1; Guttmann, *The Olympics*, 132.

19. "Americans Sweep Swimming Event," *New York Times*, 23 Oct. 1968, 50; Collins, *Olympic Dreams*, 201; Neil Amdur, "Debbie Meyer Takes 800 Free-Style Swim; Robie Scores Upset in Butterfly," *New York Times*, 25 Oct. 1968, 54; John R. McDermott, "Three Who Reached for Olympic Gold," *Life* 65:18 (1 Nov. 1968): 52–63; Steve Cady, "Gold Rush Really Starts for Foreman Tonight," *New York Times*, 26 Oct. 1968, 45; "Foreman and Harris Gain Triumphs in Olympic Ring," *New York Times*, 27 Oct. 1968, V:1; "U.S. Basketball Team Another Iba Masterpiece," *New York Times*, 24 Oct. 1968, 60.

20. "The Olympics' Extra Heat," *Newsweek* (28 Oct. 1968): 74.

21. Jackson, *Why?*, 194–95.

22. Ibid., 197.

23. "John Carlos Hizo Ayer un Tiempo de 19'7/10," *Excelsior*, 13 Sept. 1968, 1; "2 Accept Medals Wearing Black Gloves," *New York Times*, 17 Oct. 1968, 59.

24. Jackson, *Why?*, 201.

25. For a description of the race itself, see "Tommie Smith Hizo Notable Cierre en los 200," *Excelsior*, 17 Oct. 1968, 5. While this article does note that Carlos slowed

significantly in the final 50 meters, it does not speculate as to his intentions. See also Bass, *Not the Triumph,* 238–39; *Fields of Fire,* HBO Films; Murphy, *Last Protest,* 261–62; Tommie Smith with David Steele, *Silent Gesture* (Philadelphia: Temple University, 2007).

26. Jackson, *Why?,* 205.

27. Ibid.; Moore, "A Courageous Stand," 62; <http://tommiesmith.com/about-main.html>.

28. Jackson, *Why?,* 203.

29. C. Robert Paul, Jr. "Setting the 1968 Record Straight," *International Journal of Olympic History* 5:1 (Spring 1997): 15; Edwards, *Revolt,* 104.

30. Enrique Loubet, Jr., "Acción Antirracista de 2 Campeones de EU," *Excelsior,* 17 Oct. 1968, 1+; Jackson, *Why?,* 207.

31. Jackson, *Why?,* 206; John R. McDermott, "Amid Gold Medals, Raised Black Fists," *Life* 65:18 (1 Nov. 1968): 64C.

32. McDermott, "Amid Gold Medals"; Bass, *Not the Triumph,* 238–39; *Fields of Fire,* HBO Films.

33. "The Olympics' Extra Heat," *Newsweek* (28 Oct. 1968): 79.

34. "Carlos Planning to Sue U.S. Group," *New York Times,* 20 Oct. 1968, V:2.

35. Jackson, *Why?,* 208–9; Bass, *Not the Triumph,* 239–70; Jacques Amalric, "Smith y Carlos: Dos Negros en la Olimpiada," *Excelsior,* 27 Oct. 1968, 6; "Velada Acusación a Dirigentes del Comité Olímpico," *Excelsior,* 25 Oct. 1968, 1, 9+; "Sospechas de que 6 Atletas se Dejaron Sobornar," *Excelsior,* 25 Oct. 1968, 1, 12; Roberto Martinez M., "Decepcionados, mas no Arrepentidos, se Fueron Carlos y Smith; Elogian a Mexico," *Excelsior,* 22 Oct. 1968, 29.

36. "U.S. Leaders Warn of Penalties for Further Black Power Acts," *New York Times,* 18 Oct. 1968, 55.

37. "U.S. Women Dedicate Victory to Smith, Carlos," *New York Times,* 21 Oct. 1968; Enrique Loubet, Jr., "Cubanos y Boinas Negras," *Excelsior,* 21 Oct. 1968, 7; Joseph M. Sheehan, "2 Black Power Advocates Ousted from Olympics," *New York Times,* 19 Oct. 1968, 1.

38. Zirin, *What's My Name,* 83; "Otros 5 Atletas Negros se Unen a la Rebelión," *Excelsior,* 19 Oct. 1968, 1.

39. Steve Cady, "Owens Recalls 1936 Sprinter's Ordeal," *New York Times,* 17 Oct. 1968, 59; Fausto Fernandez Ponte, "Jesse Owens y el Problema Negro," *Excelsior,* 19 Sept. 1968, 1.

40. Lapchick, *Politics of Race and International Sport,* 132.

41. Smith, *Silent Gesture,* 180–83; Zirin, *What's My Name,* 90–100; Steve Cady, "U.S. Boxers Spurn Racial Fights," *New York Times,* 23 Oct. 1968, 51. For more on the varied responses to the protest, see "En Europa, las Opiniones Sobre los Negros se Dividen," *Excelsior,* 22 Oct. 1968, 29; Magdalena Saldara, "Opinan Varios Atletas de Color Sobre la Actitud de Carlos y Smith," *Excelsior,* 22 Oct. 1968, 29; "Los Negros Ante el Mundo," *Excelsior,* 21 Oct. 1968, 6.

42. Arthur Daley, "The Incident," *New York Times,* 20 Oct. 1968, V:2.

43. Thomas J. Hamilton, "14 Athletes Set to Leave Today," *New York Times,* 15 Sept. 1968, V:9.

44. Robert Lipsyte, "Return from Olympus," *New York Times,* 26 Oct. 1968, 45.

45. Ibid.

46. Robert E. Rinehart, "'Fists Flew and Blood Flowed': Symbolic Resistance and International Response in Hungarian Water Polo at the Melbourne Olympics, 1956," *Journal of Sport History* 23:2 (Summer 1996): 120–39.

47. "3 U.S. Stars Accused of Using Equipment at Olympics for Pay," *New York Times,* 23 Oct. 1968, 50; Joseph M. Sheehan, "U.S. First Nation to Check Reports," *New York Times,* 24 Oct. 1968, 60; "Final Olympic Heat," *Newsweek* (4 Nov. 1968): 66.

48. Ibid.; Arthur Daley, "What Price Amateurism?" *New York Times,* 25 Oct. 1968, 54; Robert Lipsyte, "Shoes in the Machinery," *New York Times,* 24 Oct. 1968, 60.

49. "Shake Up of IOC Urged by Sayre," *New York Times,* 26 Oct. 1968, 45; "The Olympics," *Time* (1 Nov. 1968): 55.

50. Dept. of State Telegram, from Amembassy Mexico to SecState, 2 Oct. 1968, *NARA,* RG 59, Box 2340, folder POL 13.2 Mex 9/1/68; Dept. of State Airgram, from Amconsul Tijuana to Dept. of State, 23 Oct. 1968, *NARA,* RG 59, Box 2340, folder POL 13.2 Mex 9/1/68; Dept. of State Airgram, from Amconsul Chihuahua to Amembassy Mexico City, 18 Oct. 1968, *NARA,* RG 59, Box 2340, folder POL 13.2 Mex 9/1/68. Editorials calling for the students to remain peaceful were common between the Tlatelolco massacre and the Opening Ceremonies. See, for example, "Yánez Demanda Calmar la Tensión Estudiantil," *Excelsior,* 10 Oct. 1968, 1; Gilberto Keith, "México Olímpico," *Excelsior,* 10 Oct. 1968, 7.

51. Dept. of State Memorandum, 3 Oct. 1968, *NARA,* RG 59, Box 2340, folder POL 13.2 Mex 9/1/68.

52. Dept. of State Telegram, from Amembassy Mexico to SecState, 6 Oct. 1968, *NARA,* RG 59, Box 2343, folder 23-8 Mex 1/1/68, POL 23 Mex to POL-MEX-US.

53. Dept. of State Memorandum, from Covey T. Oliver to the Secretary, 20 Sept. 1968, *NARA,* RG 59, Box 2343, folder 23-8 Mex 1/1/68, POL 23 Mex to POL-MEX-US.

54. David Chester, *The Olympic Games Handbook* (New York: Charles Scribner's Sons, 1971), 164.

55. Acosta interview; Dept. of State Telegram, from Amembassy Mexico to SecState, 10 Oct. 1968, *NARA,* RG 59, Box 2343, folder 23-8 Mex 1/1/68 POL 23 Mex to POL-MEX-US Intelligence Note, Dept. of State, 10 Oct. 1968, *NARA,* RG 59, Box 2343, folder 23-8 Mex 1/1/68 POL 23 Mex to POL-MEX-US; Dept. of State Telegram, from Amembassy Mexico to SecState, 16 Oct. 1968, *NARA,* RG 59, Box 2343, folder 23-8 Mex 1/1/68, POL 23 Mex to POL-MEX-US; Dept. of State Telegram, from Amembassy Mexico to SecState, 11 Oct. 1968, *NARA,* RG 59, Box 2340, folder POL 13.2 Mex 9/1/68; Dept. of State Telegram, from Amembassy Mexico to SecState, 10 Oct. 1968, *NARA,* RG 59, Box 2343, folder 23-8 Mex 1/1/68 POL 23 Mex to POL-MEX-US.

56. Guttmann, *Games Must Go On,* 123; "Los deportistas no usarán estimulantes," *El Nacional,* 26 Sept. 1968, 3:2; "Notas Olimpicas," *Excelsior,* 27 Sept. 1968, 7; Howard A. Rusk, "Olympic Game Health," *New York Times,* 13 Oct. 1968, 88.

57. Collins, *Olympic Dreams,* 201; "Sweden Ordered to Return Medals," *New York Times,* 25 Oct. 1968, 54; "U.S. Wrestler Gets Reprieve after Foe Fails Drug Test," *New York Times,* 26 Oct. 1968, 44.

58. Entine, *Taboo,* 304–16; Hay interview.

59. Hay interview.

60. Ibid.

61. Ibid.

62. Ibid. Arbena, "Mexico City 1968," in *Encyclopedia of the Modern Olympic Movement.*

63. "Apertura y Cierre de una Olimpiada," *Excelsior Magazine Dominical,* 27 Oct. 1968, 8–9; Carlos Denegri, "Con Una Grandiosa Fiesta Terminaron los Juegos Olímpicos," *Excelsior,* 28 Oct. 1968, 1, 11; Steve Cady, "Amid Gun Salutes and Music, Mexico Bids a Colorful 'Adios' to Olympics," *New York Times,* 28 Oct. 1968, 59. For one athlete's interpretation of the 1968 Olympics and its controversies, see Schollander and Savage, *Deep Water,* 255–74.

64. Manuel Seyde, "Temas del dia," *Excelsior,* 28 Oct. 1968, 2; Fausto Fernandez Ponte, "'Gracias a México, el Espíritu Olímpico se Vigorizó': Brundage," *Excelsior,* 29 Oct. 1968, 1; Arthur Daley, "The True Olympic Spirit," *New York Times,* 29 Oct. 1968, 57; Hay interview.

65. Hay interview; "Parade at Olympic Closing Curtailed to Avoid Disorder," *New York Times,* 23 Oct. 1968, 50.

66. Cady, "Amid Gun Salutes."

6—Settling the Score

1. Hay interview; Manuel Barragan, "La Nueva Cita Olímpica es Para 1972 en Munich," *El Universal*, 7 Nov. 1968, 4.

2. "Pope Praises Olympic Games," *New York Times*, 24 Oct. 1968, 60.

3. "Gran Elogio a los Juegos Olimpicos de Mexico en 'El Comercio,' de Lima," *Excelsior*, 3 Nov. 1968, 3; for more on the financing of the Games, see Rodríguez Kuri, "Hacia México 68"; also Rodríguez Kuri, "El otro 68."

4. "Se Cumplió el Ideal Olímpico, Dice Ramírez Vázquez," *Excelsior*, 26 Oct. 1968, 7; Enrique Maza, "Conflicto y Olimpiada: Lo Posible en México," *Excelsior*, 29 Oct. 1968, 6; Ramon de Ertze Garamendi, "Suma y Resta: Clausura Olímpica," *Excelsior*, 28 Oct. 1968, 6; "Agradecimiento del COM Para el Presidente D.O.," *Excelsior*, 1 Nov. 1968, 3; "DeGaulle Elogia la Olimpiada," *Excelsior*, 1 Nov. 1968, 1; "Johnson Felicita a los Atletas Olímpicos," *El Universal*, 1 Nov. 1968, 2; "Mensaje de RMN por los Juegos," *Excelsior*, 7 Nov. 1968, 1. For similar praise, see Memorandum for the President, from Dean Rusk, 11 Dec. 1968, *NARA*, RG 59, Box 2339, folder POL 7 Mex 1/1/68; "Aportaciones Relevantes de la Olimpiada en Mexico," memo from private collection of Pedro Ramirez Vasquez, Mexico City, Mexico.

5. Arbena, *Sport in Latin America*, 359; Jose Barrenechea, Jr., "México Pasará a la Historia de los Juegos Olímpicos," *Excelsior*, 8 Oct. 1968, 4; "En la Olimpiada, Mexico Demonstro lo que es Capaz de Hacer, ce la CANACO," *Excelsior*, 1 Nov. 1968, 25.

6. Ibid.; "XIX Olympiad: Spirited Success," *America* 119:15 (9 Nov. 1968): 423; similar thinking is expressed in Carlos Ravelo, "Se Aprovechará la Publicidad que Dejó la Olimpiada," *Excelsior*, 7 Nov. 1968, 1.

7. Ibid.; also "Afluye Dinero a Mexico, Dice Ortiz Mena," *Excelsior*, 8 Nov. 1968, 14; "Incremento Turístico Hacia Nuestro País, Resultado de la Olimpiada '68," *Excelsior*, 8 Nov. 1968, 13.

8. Expenditures listed here are in U.S. dollars. "XIX Olympiad: Spirited Success," *America* 119:15 (9 Nov. 1968): 423; Dept. of State Airgram, from Amembassy Mexico to Dept. of State, "Projected Mexican Economic Growth in 1968—Revised Appraisal," 2 Dec. 1968, *NARA*, RG 59, Box 642, folder E 5 Mex 1/1/67; "Gasto de los Turistas Olímpicos," *Excelsior*, 24 Oct. 1968, 1, 13. Interpretation of these figures differs depending on the source, as some sources include certain types of civic improvements and other outlays under Olympic expenses, while others do not. For a slightly different financial breakdown, see Arbena, "Mexico City 1968," in *Encyclopedia of the Modern Olympic Movement*, 181.

9. Retailers ran advertising campaigns encouraging Mexicans to buy a television, or a new color television, in time for the Olympics. See, for example, *Excelsior*, 18 Sept. 1968, 9; Dept. of State Telegram, from Amembassy Mexico to SecState, "Mexican Economy in 1968," 2 Feb. 1969, *NARA*, RG 59, Box 642, folder E 2 Mex 1/1/69.

10. A sampling of projects undertaken in 1969 included a plant for making an alcoholic beverage from henequen, a cement factory, several shoe factories, two ice-making plants, a fruit-processing plant, and many others. Initial State Department assessment of these projects was "Welcome as these projects are, none of the projects will employ any significant number of the greatly under-employed . . . peasants." Dept. of State Airgram, from American Consulate Merida to Dept. of State, 23 Jan. 1969, *NARA*, RG 59, Box 642, folder E 5 Mex 1/1/67; Dept. of State Airgram, from Amembassy Mexico to Dept. of State, 29 Aug. 1968, "*The Economist* publishes critical article on Mexican economy," *NARA*, RG 59, Box 642, folder E 2 Mex 6/1/68; Judith Adler Hellman, *Mexico in Crisis* (New York: Holmes and Meier, 1978).

11. Samuel Schmidt offers a sound analysis of the economic decline of the 1970s. He points to significant problems afflicting the Mexican economy, such as maldistribution of income, state protection of industry and the business class, tax eva-

sion and generally low income from taxes, increasing debt, and overproduction, none of which would have been eased by Olympic spending. See Schmidt, *Deterioration,* 18–30; Douglas W. Richmond, *The Mexican Nation: Historical Continuity and Modern Change* (Upper Saddle River, NJ: Prentice Hall, 2002), 346–53.

12. Blundell and Mackay, *History of the Olympics,* 198.

13. Dept. of State Airgram, from Amembassy MOSCOW to Dept. of State, "Soviet Press on the Mexico Olympics," 1 Nov. 1968, *NARA,* RG 59, Box 325, folder 15 CUL Mex 1/1/67; Dr. Eduardo Borrell Navarro, "Moscú Frente a Washington," *Excelsior,* 28 Oct. 1968, 7.

14. Navarro, "Moscú Frente a Washington."

15. "Soviet Council Names a Minister of Sports," *New York Times,* 19 Nov. 1968, V:15; Dept. of State Telegram, from Amembassy Moscow to SecState, "Soviet Olympic Coverage," 22 Oct. 1968, *NARA,* RG 59, Box 325, folder 15 CUL Mex 1/1/67.

16. Peppard and Riordan, *Playing Politics,* 85. The 1984 boycott year excepted.

17. Arthur Daley, "The Record Smashers," *New York Times,* 22 Oct. 1968, 51.

18. "USOC to Send Boxers on Tours," *New York Times,* 23 Oct. 1968, 50; "Soviet to Resume US Meets," *New York Times,* 22 Oct. 1968, 50; Peppard and Riordan, *Playing Politics,* 84–90; Marilyn Marshall, "Good as Gold," *Ebony* 43:11 (Sept. 1988): 142.

19. M.A. Martinez Agis, "Sin los Negros, 20 Medallas Menos se Hubiera Llevado EE.UU., Opinan," *Excelsior,* 22 Oct. 1968, 29; Fausto Ponce, "En Atletismo se Consumaron las más Grandes Hazañas," *Excelsior,* 28 Oct. 1968, 7; Moore, "The Eye of the Storm," 64.

20. Moore, "The Eye of the Storm," 64.

21. Ibid.

22. Edmundo Garcia Jaen, "Expresan John Carlos y Tommie Smith su Simpatía por México," *Excelsior,* 14 Sept. 1968, 6. Thoughts of the Mexican organizing committee are gleaned largely from the Hay interview. For editorials considering the views of the masses and others, see Genaro Maria Gonzalez, "Olimpiada y Racismo," *Excelsior,* 21 Oct. 1968, 7; Froylan M. Lopez Narvaez, "Poder Negro Protesta Olímpica," *Excelsior,* 18 Oct. 1968, 7. Consideration of the malleable nature of Mexican-U.S. relations is discussed in Stephen D. Morris, *Gringolandia: Mexican Identity and Perceptions of the United States* (New York: Rowman and Littlefield, 2005), 24–40.

23. Ibid.; Jackson, *Why?,* 214–58; Smith, *Silent Gesture,* 186–210.

24. Moore, "Eye of the Storm," 64–72; Zirin, *What's My Name,* 88.

25. Ivan Delventhal, "For Sale, a Gold Medal with a History," *New York Times,* 11 April 2001, C17. See also <http://www.TommieSmith.com>; Moore, "Eye of the Storm," 66; Smith, *Silent Gesture;* Jackson, *Why?*

26. Moore, "Eye of the Storm," 66.

27. Ibid.,

28. Steve Holman, "Significance of '68 Salute Is Still Right on Time," *USA Today,* Oct. 1998, as cited at <http://www.johncarlos.com/1998_article_Holman.htm>; "Radical Sprinters Back on the Track," *Newsweek* (8 March 1982): 12.

29. Peter King, "Why Is This Man Smiling?" *Sports Illustrated* (12 Aug. 1991): 13–14. See, for instance, Hoberman, *Darwin's Athletes,* and Entine, *Taboo.* For a more detailed analysis of black athletes since the 1968 protest, see Bass, *Not the Triumph,* 291–348; Hoose, *Necessities.*

30. Dept. of State Airgram, from Amembassy Mexico to Dept. of State, 3 Nov. 1968, *NARA,* RG 59, Box 2337A, folder POL 2 Mex 11/1/68; Rhoden, *Forty Million Dollar Slaves,* 8.

31. Dept. of State Telegram, from Amembassy Mexico to SecState, 28 Nov. 1968, *NARA,* RG 59, Box 2341, folder 15-1 Mex 1/1/67.

32. Gilberto Keith, "Futuro del Movimiento," *Excelsior,* 3 Oct. 1968, 7; Dept. of State Airgram, from Amembassy Mexico to Dept. of State, 2 Dec. 1968, *NARA,* RG 59, Box 2337A, folder POL 2 Mex 11/1/68; Dept. of State Airgram, from Amembassy

Mexico to Dept. of State, 20 Jan. 1969, *NARA*, RG 59, Box 2337A, folder POL 2 Mex 11/1/68; Dept. of State Airgram, from Amembassy Mexico to Dept. of State, 11 Feb. 1969, *NARA*, RG 59, Box 2337A, folder POL 2 Mex 11/1/68.

33. Donald Hodges and Ross Gandy, *Mexico under Siege: Popular Resistance to Presidential Despotism* (New York: Zed Books, 2002), 100-105; Maclachlan and Beezley, *El Gran Pueblo,* 414–24; Ignacio Taibo, *'68,* 117.

34. Dept. of State Airgram, from American Consulate, Veracruz to Dept. of State, "New Cine Club at Veracruz Possible Vehicle for Communist Propaganda," 20 Oct. 1962, *NARA*, RG 59, Box 2338, folder 812.46/4-1361; Carey, *Plaza of Sacrifices,* 158–73.

35. Hodges and Gandy, *Mexico under Siege,* 99.

36. Dept. of State Airgram, from Amembassy San Jose to Dept. of State, "Seminar for Central American University Student Leaders," 21 Aug. 1964, *NARA*, RG 59, Box 367, folder EDU 9-4 LA 1/1/64; also Dept. of State Airgram, from Amembassy San Jose to Dept. of State, "Seminar for Central American University Leaders," 12 Aug. 1964, ibid. See, for instance, Dept. of State Airgram, from AmEmbassy Mexico City to Dept. of State, "Preparation of 20th World Strength Report of Communist Party Organizations," 29 Nov. 1967, *NARA*, RG 59, Box 2339, folder POL 12 Mex 1/1/67; also Dept. of State Airgram, from Amconsul Mexicali to Dept. of State, "Communist Meeting in Mexicali," 1 Sept. 1967, ibid.; Dept. of State Airgram, from Amconsul Mexicali to Dept. of State, "Increased Communist Activity in Mexicali Consular District," 14 Mar. 1968, *NARA*, RG 59, Box 2339, folder POL 12 Mex 1/1/68; Dept. of State Telegram, from Amembassy Mexico to SecState, 6 Sept. 1968, *NARA*, RG 59, Box 2340, folder POL 23.2 Mex 9/1/68; Dept. of State Airgram, from Amembassy Mexico to Dept. of State, "Labor and the Students—Mexico 1968," 1 Dec. 1968, *NARA*, RG 59, Box 2343, folder 23-8 Mex 1/1/68 POL 23 Mex to POL-MEX-US; Ignacio Taibo, *'68.*

37. *NARA*, RG 59, Box 643, folder E 1 Mex-US 1/1/68.

38. Letter from Paul Pate to Thomas C. Mann, 7 Apr. 1965, *NARA*, RG 59, Box 368, folder EDU 15 Mex 1/1/64; Dept. of State Airgram, from Amembassy Mexico City to Dept. of State, "Mid-Point in the Diaz Ordaz Administration: A Political Assessment," 9 Jan. 1968, *NARA*, RG 59, Box 2341, folder POL 15-1 Mex 1/1/68; Dept. of State Airgram, from Amembassy Mexico to Dept. of State, 3 July 1968, *NARA*, RG 59, Box 2337, folder POL 2 Mex 7/1/68.

39. Dept. of State Airgram, from Amembassy Mexico to Dept. of State, "Mexican-Soviet Cultural and Scientific Convention," 14 July 1968, *NARA*, RG 59, Box 325, CUL 1/1/67 Mex-A; Dept. of State Intelligence Note, 3 June 1968, *NARA*, RG 59, Box 2339, folder POL 7 Mex 1/1/68; Dept. of State Airgram, from Amembassy Mexico to Dept. of State, "Czech Invasion: Consternation on the Left," 24 Nov. 1968, *NARA*, RG 59, Box 2339, folder POL 12 Mex 1/1/68. As explained by W. Dirk Raat, the U.S. had long been suspicious of Mexico's "independent" policies, in particular its refusal to break relations with the Soviet Union and Cuba, indicating at least some level of openness to communism. Raat, *Mexico and the United States,* 158–59.

40. Dept. of State Telegram, from Amembassy Mexico to SecState, 2 Sept. 1968, *NARA*, RG 59, Box 2341, folder POL 15-1 Mex 1/1/68; Dept. of State Airgram, from Amembassy Mexico to Dept. of State, "Communists Reveal Demoralizing Effect of October 2 Incident," 25 Dec. 1968, *NARA*, RG 59, Box 2339, folder POL 12 Mex 1/1/68.

41. Dept. of State Airgram, from Amembassy Mexico City to Dept. of State, "Mid-Point in the Diaz Ordaz Administration: A Political Assessment," 9 Jan. 1968, *NARA*, RG 59, Box 2341, POL 15-1 Mex 1/1/68; Dept. of State Airgram, from AmEmbassy Mexico to Dept. of State, "Developments in the Mexican Left: Struggle with Cuba, PPS Split," 27 Feb. 1968, *NARA*, RG 59, Box 2339, folder POL 12 Mex 1/1/68; Dept. of State Telegram, from Amembassy Mexico to SecState, 9 May 1968, *NARA*, RG 59, Box 2341, POL 15-1 Mex 1/1/68.

42. Assistant Secretary of State for Latin America, confidential information memorandum, "Mexican Situation," 3 Oct. 1968, *NARA*, RG 59, Box 2343, Pol 23-8, Doyle document 37; U.S. Embassy in Mexico, confidential telegram, "Contingency—Scenarios," 5 Nov. 1968, *NARA*, RG 59, Box 2340, Pol 13-2, Doyle document 25; State Dept. letter, "[Mexican Request for Military Radios]," 24 May 1968, *NARA*, RG 59, Box 1699, Def 19-8; State Dept. memorandum, "Out-of-Channels Request from Mexico," 18 July 1968, *NARA*, RG 59, Box 1578, Def 12-5.

43. "Czech and Soviet Athletes Separated at Olympic Meals," *New York Times,* 15 Sept. 1968, V:11.

44. Zolov, "Showcasing the 'Land of Tomorrow.'"

45. Guttmann, *Olympics,* 143; S.L. Price, "The Race Just Started," *Sports Illustrated* (6 Sept. 2004): 52–53.

46. Guttmann, *Olympics,* 163; Robert K. Barney, Stephen R. Wenn, and Scott G. Martyn, *Selling the Five Rings: The International Olympic Committee and the Rise of Olympic Commercialism* (Salt Lake City: University of Utah Press, 2002), 193–98; Roche, *Mega-events and Modernity,* 138; "Balance Positivo," *El Universal,* 1 Nov. 1968, 3; "Es Enormemente Benéfico el Balance que Deja la Olimpíada," *El Universal,* 1 Nov. 1968, 1, 9; "Díaz Ordaz Ante el C.O.I.," *Excelsior,* 8 Oct. 1968, 6; "En los Olímpicos Todos Visten Diferente," *Excelsior Magazine Dominical,* 27 Oct. 1968, 3–5.

47. For an excellent overview of the evolution of the bidding process, see Barney et al., *Selling the Five Rings.* For a more specific examination of the bidding scandals, see the works of Andrew Jennings, including Andrew Jennings and Vyv Simson, *The Lords of the Rings, Dishonored Games: Corruption, Money and Greed at the Olympics* (New York: Spi Books Trade, 1992); Andrew Jennings, *The New Lords of the Rings: Olympic Corruption and How to Buy Gold Medals* (London: Simon & Schuster, 1996); and Andrew Jennings and Clare Sambrook, *The Great Olympic Swindle: When the World Wanted Its Games Back* (London: Simon & Schuster, 2000); also Helen Jefferson Lenskyj, *Inside the Olympic Industry* (Albany: State University of New York Press, 2000).

48. *Los Angeles Times,* 5 March 1963, III:7; 6 March 1963, III:1; 12 March 1963, III:3.

49. Florenzio Acosta, interview; Schaefler, interview. The television rights for the 1968 Olympics generated a total of $4.5 million U.S. for the IOC. That figure had increased to over $1.3 billion for the 2000 Sydney Olympics, and nearly $1.5 billion for 2004 Athens. International Olympic Committee website, <http://www.olympic.org>; also the Museum of Broadcast Communications website, <http://www.museum.tv>; Lenskyj, *Inside the Olympic Industry,* 32; Jennings, *New Lords of the Rings*; Jennings and Sambrook, *Great Olympic Swindle.* For French objections, see "Qué Alegra," *Excelsior,* 19 Oct. 1963, 27; and "El Alcalde de Lyon," *Excelsior,* 20 Oct. 1968, 38.

50. Poniatowska, *Massacre in Mexico,* 218, 221; "Total Cuidado a la Salud de los Atletas Olimpicos," *Excelsior,* 8 Sept. 1968, 2; Simon Reeve, *One Day in September: The Full Story of the 1972 Munich Olympics Massacre and the Israeli Revenge "Operation Wrath of God"* (New York: Arcade Publishing, 2000); Jack Corcoran, "Athletes Leave Fear Behind," *Tallahassee Democrat,* 2 Aug. 2004, 1A; Miron Varouhakis, "Athens Boosts Troop Numbers, Denies Security Glitches," *AOL News,* 4 Aug. 2004. <http://aolsvc.news.aol.com/sports/article.adp?id=20040804111609990001>.

51. Barrie Houlihan, *Sport, Policy, and Politics: A Comparative Analysis* (London: Routledge, 1997), 179–219.

52. S.L. Price, "American Graffiti," *Sports Illustrated* (23 Aug. 2004): 64–66. "Czech and Soviet Athletes Separated," *New York Times* 15 Sept. 1968, V:11.

53. "Distribución de Comedores en la Villa Olímpica," *El Nacional,* 14 Sept. 1968, 2:1; Reeve, *One Day in September,* 24–32.

54. "Terror at the Olympics," *Newsweek* (18 Sept. 1972): 24; Reeve, *One Day in September*; Guttmann, *The Games Must Go On.*

55. Espy, *Politics,* 98.

56. Robert K. Barney, "Avery Brundage," in Findling and Pelle, eds., *Encyclopedia of the Modern Olympic Movement,* 481. For one athlete's commentary on the decline of the Olympic movement, see Schollander and Savage, *Deep Water,* 271–74.

57. Bob Ottum, "Grim Countdown to the Games," *Sports Illustrated* (14 Oct. 1968): 43; *New York Times,* 13 Oct. 1968, IV:4.

58. Editorial, "Tlatelolco Sangriento," *Excelsior,* 3 Oct. 1968, 6; Victor Payan, "Recuento de la Trágica Jornada," *Excelsior,* 4 Oct. 1968, 1, 11+. Dept. of State Telegram, 14 Oct. 1968, *NARA,* RG 59, Box 2340, folder POL 13.2 Mex 9/1/68; Assistant Secretary of State for Latin America, confidential information memorandum, "Mexican Situation," 3 Oct. 1968, *NARA,* RG 59, Box 2343, Pol 23-8, Doyle document 37; CIA, secret intelligence summary, "Challenges to Mexico's Single Party Rule," 17 Jan. 1969, National Security Archive, Doyle document 83; Preston and Dillon, *Opening Mexico,* 80–84; Manuel Moreno Sanchez, "Octavio Paz: El Derecho a Renunciar," *Excelsior,* 28 Oct. 1968, 6; Roderic Ai Camp, "Political Modernization in Mexico," in Jaime E. Rodriguez O., ed. *The Evolution of the Mexican Political System* (Wilmington, DE: Scholarly Resources, Inc., 1993), 248.

59. Dolly J. Young, "Mexican Literary Reactions to Tlatelolco 1968," *Latin American Research Review* 20:2 (1985): 71–85; Ivonne Gutiérrez, ed. *Entre el Silencio y la Estridencia: La Protesta Literaria del 68* (Aldus, 1998); Allen Wells, "Oaxtepec Revisited: The Politics of Mexican Historiography, 1968–1988," *Mexican Studies* 7:2 (Summer 1991): 331–45; Mary Kay Vaughn, "Cultural Approaches to Peasant Politics in the Mexican Revolution," *Hispanic American Historical Review* 79:2 (1999): 269–305; Jaime E. Rodriguez, "Introduction," in Jaime E. Rodriguez O., *Revolutionary Process in Mexico* (Los Angeles: UCLA Latin American Center Publications, 1990), 1–11; Thomas Benjamin, "The Leviathan on the Zocalo: Recent Historiography of the Postrevolutionary Mexican State," *Latin American Research Review* 20:3 (1985): 195–217.

60. Poniatowska, *Massacre in Mexico,* 6.

61. Monsiváis, "From '68 to Cardenismo," 385–87; Barry Carr, *Mexican Communism 1968–1983: Eurocommunism in the Americas?* (San Diego: Center for U.S.-Mexican Studies, 1985), 4; Manuel Moreno Sanchez, "Una Tragedia Mexicana," *Excelsior,* 7 Oct. 1968, 6; Ignacio Taibo, *'68,* 125–41.

62. Dept. of State Airgram, 9 Jan. 1968, "Mid-Point in the Diaz Ordaz Administration: A Political Assessment," *NARA,* RG59, Box 2341, POL 15-1 Mex 1/1/68.

63. Camp, "Political Modernization," 249.

64. Jeremi Suri, *The Global Revolutions of 1968* (New York: W.W. Norton & Co., 2007), xviii; Arthur Marwick, *The Sixties: Cultural Revolution in Britain, France, Italy, and the United States, c. 1958–1974* (New York: Oxford University Press, 1998), 667; Todd Gitlin, *The Sixties: Years of Hope, Days of Rage* (New York: Bantam, 1987), 319–35; Fraser, *Student Generation,* 203–29; John Morton Blum, *Years of Discord: American Politics and Society, 1961–1974* (New York: W.W. Norton, 1992), 287–300; Terry G. Anderson, *The Sixties* (New York: Pearson-Longman, 2004), 103–9, 584–678; Tariq Ali, *Street Fighting Years: An Autobiography of the Sixties* (London: Collins, 1987).

65. Fraser, *Student Generation,* 203–29; Marwick, *The Sixties,* 585–87; Gitlin, *The Sixties,* 319–35.

66. Carlos B. Gil, ed., *Hope and Frustration: Interviews with Leaders of Mexico's Political Opposition* (Wilmington: Scholarly Resources, Inc., 1992), 35–39; Carr, *Mexican Communism,* 4–5; Roderic Ai Camp, "Potential Strengths of the Political Opposition and What It Means to the PRI," in Camp, ed., *Mexico's Political Stability: The Next Five Years* (Boulder: Westview Press, 1986), 185–88; John Bailey and Leopoldo Gomez, "The PRI and Political Liberalization," *Journal of International Affairs* 43:2 (Winter 1990) 303; Preston and Dillon, *Opening Mexico.*

67. Roderic Ai Camp, *Generals in the Palacio: The Military in Modern Mexico* (New York: Oxford University Press, 1992); Julio Scherer García and Carlos Monsiváis, *Parte de Guerra, Tlatelolco 1968: Documentos de General Marcelino García Barragán, los hechos y la historia* (Nuevo Siglo Aguilar, 1999); Defense Intelligence Agency, confidential intelligence information report, "General Officers in Disfavor with Secretary of Defense," 14 Mar. 1969, National Security Archive, Doyle document 91; David Rondfeldt, *The Modern Mexican Military: Implications for Mexico's Stability and Security,* excerpted in Judith Gentleman, "Prospects for Stability and Change in Mexico," *Latin American Research Review* 23:3 (1988): 194–95; Camp, "Political Modernization," 251.

68. See, among others, "Mexico Moves to Open Massacre Files," <http://www.rose-hulman.edu/~delacova/tlatelolco/files.htm>; Salvador Zarco, "A Reflection on the Tlatelolco Massacre of October 2, 1968," <http://flag.blackened/net/revolt/mexico/history/tlatelolco_1968.html>; Jana Schroeder, "The Truth about Tlatelolco, 1968," <http://www.worldpress.org/Americas/375.cfm>. To view examples of these pictures, follow links at <http://www.gwu.edu/~nsarchiv/NSAEBB/NSAEBB99>; Davis, "Social Movements," 361–62; Dept. of State Telegram, from Amembassy to SecState, 20 Aug. 1968, *NARA,* RG 59, Box 2341, folder POL 14 Mex 1/1/67. A poignant recollection of the event and its impact on Mexican history is Oscar Menéndez, *Códica Tlatelolco 1968–1988* (Plaza and Valdes Publishers, 1988).

Bibliography

Primary Sources

Archives and Institutes (Public)

Academia Olympica Mexicana, Avda. del Conscripto y Anillo Periferico, Mexico City, Mexico.

Amateur Athletic Foundation of Los Angeles (Archives online at <http://www.aafla.org>).

Avery Brundage Collection (University of Illinois, Champaign-Urbana, IL).

Comite Olimpico Mexicano (Mexican Olympic Committee), Avda. del Conscripto y Anillo Periferico Lomas de Sotelo, Mexico City, Mexico.

International Centre for Olympic Studies (University of Western Ontario, London, Ontario, Canada).

National Archives and Records Administration (Washington, D.C.).

National Security Archive, Tlatelolco Massacre (Archives online at <http://www.gwu.edu/~nsarchiv/NSAEBB/NSAEBB99/>, catalogued by Kate Doyle).

United States Olympic Committee (Colorado Springs, CO).

Private Collections

Acosta, Florenzio and Magda. (Member, MOC, and translator with MOC, 1968) Mexico City, Mexico.

Ramirez Vazquez, (architect) Pedro. (President, Mexican Olympic Committee, 1965–1968) Mexico City, Mexico.

Ugalde, Ana Mary. (Translator with Mexican Olympic Committee, 1968) Mexico City, Mexico.

Personal Interviews

Acosta, Florenzio. Member of Mexican Olympic Committee, 1968. Mexico City. 16 November 2001.

Acosta, Magda. Translator for MOC, 1968. Mexico City. 16 November 2001.

Aguilar Cabrera, Pedro. Student in Mexico City, 1968. Mexico City. 14 November 2001.

Billa Larenza, Miguel. Student in Mexico City, 1968. Mexico City. 12 November 2001.

Daniell, Lorna. Resident of Mexico City, 1968. Mexico City. 16 November 2001.

Hay, Dr. Eduardo. Mexican representative to IOC, 1961–1991; honorary member, IOC, 1991–present. Mexico City. 17 November 2001.

Hegstrom, Ray. Member of Mexican baseball league, 1963–1968. Asheville, North Carolina. 17 August 2001.

Hernandez Schafler, Carlos. Member of Mexican Olympic Committee, 1968. Mexico City. 15 November 2001.
Isaenko, Anatoly. Former Soviet wrestler. Columbus, GA. 18 Oct. 2002.
Martinez, Juan. Student in Mexico City, 1968. Mexico City. 11 November 2001.
Ugalde, Ana Mary. Translator for MOC, 1968. Mexico City. 10 November 2001.

Newspapers and Periodicals

America (1968)
The Black Liberator (1968)
Black Politics (1968–1969)
Bulletin du Comité International Olympique (1950–1972)
Business Week (1962–1970)
The Crisis (1968)
Detroit News (1963, 1967–1968)
Ebony (1967–1969)
Esquire (1967–1968)
Excelsior (1963, 1967–1969)
Guardian, London (1968)
Harper's Bazaar (1968)
Holiday (1967–1968)
Intercontinental Press, New York (1968)
Life (1966–1969)
Look (1968)
Los Angeles Times (1962–1963)
El Nacional (1963, 1967–1969)
The Nation (1968)
National Review (1968)
New Left Review (1968)
Newsweek (1963–1972)
New York Times (1962–1972)
Official Boletin (Mexican Olympic Committee) (1967–1968)
The Olympian (1962–1972)
Olympic Review (1966–1975)
Parks and Recreation (1966)
Ramparts (1968–1970)
Reader's Digest (1968)
Runner's World (1991)
San Francisco Express Times (1967–1968)
Saturday Evening Post (1965)
Senior Scholastic (1968)
Sports Illustrated (1962–2004)
Sunset (1968)
Time (1963–1968)
El Universal (1963, 1967–1969)
US News (1968)
Yessis Translation Review (1965–1968)

Secondary Sources

Books and Essays

Ali, Tariq, and Susan Watkins. *1968: Marching in the Streets*. New York: The Free Press, 1998.

———. *Street Fighting Years: An Autobiography of the Sixties*. London: Collins, 1987.

Allison, Lincoln, ed. *The Global Politics of Sport: The Role of Global Institutions in Sport*. New York: Routledge, 2005.

Allison, Lincoln, and Terry Monnington. "Sport, Prestige, and International Relations." In Allison, *The Global Politics of Sport*. 2005.

Anderson, Terry G. *The Sixties*. New York: Pearson-Longman, 2004.

Appy, Christian G. "Eisenhower's Guatemalan Doodle, or: How to Draw, Deny, and Take Credit for a Third World Coup." In Christian G. Appy, ed., *Cold War Constructions: The Political Culture of United States Imperialism, 1945–1966*. Amherst: University of Massachusetts Press, 2000, 183–213.

Arbena, Joseph L. *Annotated Bibliography of Latin-American Sport: Pre-Conquest to the Present*. New York: Greenwood Press, 1989.

———. *Latin American Sport: An Annotated Bibliography, 1988–1998*. Westport, CT: Greenwood Press, 1999.

———. "Nationalism and Sport in Latin America, 1850–1990: The Paradox of Promoting and Performing 'European' Sports." *The International Journal of the History of Sport* 12:2 (Aug. 1995): 220–38.

———. "Sport, Development, and Mexican Nationalism, 1920–1970." *Journal of Sport History* 18:3 (Winter 1991): 350–64.

Arbena, Joseph L., ed. *Sport and Society in Latin America: Diffusion, Dependency and the Rise of Mass Culture*. Westport, CT: Greenwood Press, 1988.

Arndt, Richard T. *The First Resort of Kings: American Cultural Diplomacy in the Twentieth Century*. Washington: Potomac Books, 2005.

Arnoud, Pierre, and James Riordan, eds. *Sport and International Politics*. New York: Taylor and Francis, 1998.

Ashe, Arthur R. *A Hard Road to Glory: Baseball*. New York: Amistad Press, 1988.

———. *A Hard Road to Glory: Basketball*. New York: Amistad Press, 1988.

———. *A Hard Road to Glory: Boxing*. New York: Amistad Press, 1988.

———. *A Hard Road to Glory: Football*. New York: Amistad Press, 1988.

———. *A Hard Road to Glory: Track and Field*. New York: Amistad Press, 1988.

Bailey, John, and Leopoldo Gomez. "The PRI and Political Liberalization." *Journal of International Affairs* 43:2 (Winter 1990): 291–312.

Baker, Bill. *Jesse Owens: An American Life*. New York: Free Press, 1986.

Barney, Robert K., Stephen R. Wenn, and Scott G. Martyn. *Selling the Five Rings: The International Olympic Committee and the Rise of Olympic Commercialism*. Salt Lake City: University of Utah Press, 2002.

Bass, Amy. *Not the Triumph but the Struggle: The 1968 Olympics and the Making of the Black Athlete*. Minneapolis: University of Minnesota Press, 2002.

Beamon, Bob, and Milana Walter Beamon. *The Man Who Could Fly: The Bob Beamon Story*. Columbus, MS: Genesis Press, 1999.

Beezley, William H. *Judas at the Jockey Club and Other Episodes of Porfirian Mexico*. Lincoln: University of Nebraska Press, 1987.

Benjamin, Thomas. "The Leviathan on the Zocalo: Recent Historiography of the Postrevolutionary Mexican State." *Latin American Research Review* 20:3 (1985): 195–217.

Bloom, Alexander, and Wini Breines, eds. *"Takin' It to the Streets": A Sixties Reader.* New York: Oxford University Press, 2003.

Blum, John Morton. *Years of Discord: American Politics and Society, 1961–1974.* New York: W.W. Norton, 1992.

Blundell, Nigel, and Duncan Mackay. *The History of the Olympics.* London: PRC Publishing, 1999.

Braun, Herbert. "Protests of Engagement: Dignity, False Love, and Self-Love in Mexico during 1968." *Comparative Studies in Society and History* 39:3 (July 1997): 511–49.

Brichford, Maynard. "Avery Brundage and Racism." *Fourth International Symposium for Olympic Research.* International Centre for Olympic Studies, University of Western Ontario, Oct. 1998.

Brooks, David. "Mexico: Whose Crisis, Whose Future." *NACLA Report on the Americas* 21:5–6 (Sept.–Dec. 1987): 14–29.

Brown, Elaine. *A Taste of Power: A Black Woman's Story.* New York: Pantheon Books, 1992.

Buchanan, Ian. *Historical Dictionary of the Olympic Movement.* Lanham, MD: Scarecrow Press, 1995.

Cable, Carole. *Architecture of the Olympics, 1960–1980.* Monticello, IL: Vance Bibliographies, 1982.

Cabrera Parra, José. *Díaz Ordaz y el '68.* Mexico D.F.: Editorial Grijalbo, 1982.

Camp, Roderic Ai. *Generals in the Palacio: The Military in Modern Mexico.* New York: Oxford University Press, 1992.

Camp, Roderic Ai, ed. *Mexico's Political Stability: The Next Five Years.* Boulder: Westview Press, 1986.

Carey, Elaine. *Plaza of Sacrifices: Gender, Power, and Terror in 1968 Mexico.* Albuquerque: University of New Mexico, 2005.

Carmona, Roberto B. "Biography of Jose de Jesus Clark Flores: 'Man of Honor.'" Ph.D. diss., Brigham Young University, 1981.

Carr, Barry. *Marxism and Communism in Twentieth-Century Mexico.* Lincoln: University of Nebraska Press, 1992.

———. *Mexican Communism 1968–1983: Eurocommunism in the Americas?* San Diego: Center for U.S.-Mexican Studies, 1985.

Castañeda, Jorge. *Perpetuating Power: How Mexican Presidents Were Chosen.* New York: The New Press, 2000.

Caute, David. *The Dancer Defects: The Struggle for Cultural Supremacy during the Cold War.* New York: Oxford University Press, 2003.

Chester, David. *The Olympic Games Handbook.* New York: Charles Scribner's Sons, 1971.

Churchill, James E., Jeff Hacker, and Edward Humphrey, eds. *Pursuit of Excellence: The Olympic Story.* New York: Franklin Watts, 1979.

Coakley, Jay J. *Sport in Society: Issues and Controversies.* St. Louis: Times Mirror/Mosby, 1990.

Collins, Douglas. *Olympic Dreams: 100 Years of Excellence.* New York: Universe Publishing, 1996.

Coupat, Alain. "Grenoble and the Xth Winter Games." *Olympic Review* 56–57 (May–June 1972): 225–38.

Daley, Arthur, and John Kiernan. *The Story of the Olympic Games, 776 B.C. to 1968.* New York: J.B. Lippincott Co., 1969.

Davis, Diane. "Social Movements in Mexico's Crisis." *Journal of International Affairs* 43:2 (Winter 1990): 343–67.

Davis, Lenwood G. *Black Athletes.* Westport, CT: Greenwood Press, 1986.

Davis, Michael D. *Black American Women in Olympic Track and Field*. Jefferson, NC: Mc-Farland & Co., 1992.

De Groot, Gerard, ed. *Student Protest: The Sixties and After*. New York: Addison Wesley Publishing Co., 1998.

De Mora, Juan Miguel. *Tlatelolco 1968: Por Fin Toda la Verdad*. Mexico D.F.: Edamex, 1979.

Denbeck, Debbie J. "A Comparison of the United States Olympic Athletes Concerning Political Involvement in the Olympic Games." In Gerald Redmond, ed., *Sport and Politics*. Champaign, IL: Human Kinetics Publishers, Inc., 1986, 179–84.

Edwards, Harry. "Crisis in the Modern Olympic Movement." In Chu and Segrave, *Olympism*. 1981.

———. "The Olympic Project for Human Rights: An Assessment Ten Years Later." *The Black Scholar* 10 (1979): 2–8.

———. *Revolt of the Black Athlete*. New York: Free Press, 1969.

———. "The Sources of Black Athletic Superiority." *The Black Scholar* 3 (Nov. 1971): 32–41.

Eimon, Pan Dodd. "The City Tells Its Story." *The American City* 83:8 (Aug. 1968): 133–34.

Encinas, Rosario. "José Vasconcelos." *Prospects* 24:3–4 (1994): 719–29.

Entine, Jon. *Taboo*. New York: Public Affairs, 2000.

Espy, Richard. *The Politics of the Olympic Games*. Berkeley: University of California Press, 1979.

Evans, Sara. *Personal Politics: The Roots of Women's Liberation in the Civil Rights Movement and the New Left*. New York: Vintage, 1979.

Farber, Daniel, ed. *The Sixties: From Memory to History*. Chapel Hill: University of North Carolina Press, 1994.

Fein, Seth. "Myths of Cultural Imperialism and Nationalism in Golden Age Mexican Cinema." In Joseph et al., eds., *Fragments*, 159–98.

Findling, John E., and Kimberly D. Pelle, eds. *Encyclopedia of the Modern Olympic Movement*. Westport, CT: Greenwood Press, 2004.

Fliegner, Frederick, ed. *1968 United States Olympic Book*. New York: United States Olympic Committee, 1969.

Foster, Lynn V. *A Brief History of Mexico*. New York: Facts on File, Inc., 1997.

Franco Ramos, Luis, ed. *Pensar el 68*. Mexico: Cal y Arena, 1988.

Fraser, Ronald. *1968: A Student Generation in Revolt*. New York: Pantheon Books, 1988.

Garrido, Luis J. "The Crisis of Presidencialismo." In Wayne E. Cornelius, Judith Gentleman, and Peter H. Smith, eds., *Mexico's Alternative Political Futures*. San Diego: University of California Press, 1989, 417–34.

Gentleman, Judith. "Prospects for Stability and Change in Mexico." *Latin American Research Review* 23:3 (1988): 188–98.

George, Nelson. *Elevating the Game: Black Men and Basketball*. New York: HarperCollins Publishers, 1992.

Gil, Carlos B., ed. *Hope and Frustration: Interviews with Leaders of Mexico's Political Opposition*. Wilmington, DE: Scholarly Resources, Inc., 1992.

Gitlin, Todd. *The Sixties: Years of Hope, Days of Rage*. New York: Bantam, 1987.

Goodsell, James N. "Mexico: Why the Students Rioted." *Current History* 58:329 (Jan. 1969).

Gorn, Elliott J., ed. *Muhammad Ali: The People's Champ*. Urbana: University of Illinois Press, 1995.

Guinness Book of Olympic Records. New York: Sterling Publishing Co., 1975.

Gutiérrez, Ivonne, ed. *Entre el Silencio y la Estridencia: La Protesta Literaria del 68*. Aldus, 1998.

Guttmann, Allen. *Games and Empires: Modern Sports and Cultural Imperialism.* New York: Columbia University Press, 1994.

———. *The Games Must Go On: Avery Brundage and the Olympic Movement.* New York: Columbia University Press, 1984.

———. *The Olympics: A History of the Modern Games.* Champaign: University of Illinois Press, 1992.

———. *Women's Sports: A History.* New York: Columbia University Press, 1991.

Hansen, Roger D. *Mexican Economic Development: The Roots of Rapid Growth.* Washington: National Planning Association, 1971.

———. *The Politics of Mexican Development.* Baltimore: Johns Hopkins University Press, 1974.

Hart-Davis, Duff. *Hitler's Games.* London: Century, 1986.

Hartmann, Douglas. *Race, Culture, and the Revolt of the Black Athlete: The 1968 Olympic Protests and Their Aftermath.* Chicago: University of Chicago Press, 2003.

Heath, Jonathan. *Mexico and the Sexenio Curse: Presidential Successions and Economic Crises in Modern Mexico.* Washington: Center for Strategic and International Studies, 1999.

Hellman, Judith Adler. *Mexico in Crisis.* New York: Holmes and Meier, 1978.

Henry, Bill. *An Approved History of the Olympic Games.* New York: G.P. Putnam's Sons, 1976.

Hill, Christopher R. *Olympic Politics.* Manchester: Manchester University Press, 1992.

Hixson, Walter L. *Parting the Curtain: Propaganda, Culture, and the Cold War, 1945–61.* New York: St. Martin's Press, 1997.

Hoberman, John M. *Darwin's Athletes.* New York: Houghton Mifflin Co., 1997.

———. *The Olympic Crisis: Sport, Politics and the Moral Order.* New Rochele, NY: Aristide D. Caratzas, 1986.

———. *Sport and Political Ideology.* Austin: University of Texas Press, 1984.

Hodges, Donald, and Ross Gandy. *Mexico under Siege: Popular Resistance to Presidential Despotism.* New York: Zed Books, 2002.

Holman, Steve. "Significance of '68 Salute Is Still Right on Time." *USA Today.* Section C, p. 1, Oct. 1998. <http://www.johncarlos.com/1998_article_Holman.htm>

Hoose, Phillip. *Necessities.* New York: Random House, 1989.

Houlihan, Barrie. *Sport, Policy, and Politics: A Comparative Analysis.* London: Routledge, 1997.

Howell, Colin D. "Baseball and Borders: The Diffusion of Baseball and Other Sports into Mexican and Canadian-American Borderlands Regions, 1885–1911." Presentation at the 116th AHA Annual Meeting in San Francisco, 5 Jan. 2002.

Ignacio Taibo II, Paco. *'68.* Translated by Donald Nicholson-Smith. New York: Seven Stories Press, 2004.

Isaacs, Neil D. *All the Moves: A History of College Basketball.* New York: J.B. Lippincott Co., 1975.

Jackson, C.D. *Why? The Biography of John Carlos.* Los Angeles: Milligan Books, 2000.

James, C.L.R. *Beyond a Boundary.* Durham: Duke University Press, 1993.

Jarvie, Grant. *Class, Race and Sport in South Africa's Political Economy.* London: Routledge & Kegan Paul, 1985.

Jennings, Andrew. *The New Lords of the Rings: Olympic Corruption and How to Buy Gold Medals.* London: Simon & Schuster, 1996.

Jennings, Andrew, and Clare Sambrook. *The Great Olympic Swindle: When the World Wanted Its Games Back.* London: Simon & Schuster, 2000.

Jennings, Andrew, and Vyv Simson. *The Lords of the Rings, Dishonored Games: Corruption, Money and Greed at the Olympics.* New York: Spi Books Trade, 1992.

Johnson, John J. *Political Change in Latin America.* Stanford: Stanford University Press, 1958.

Johnson, William O. *All that Glitters Is Not Gold.* New York: Putnam, 1972.

Joseph, Gilbert M., and Timothy J. Henderson, eds. *The Mexico Reader: History, Culture, Politics.* Durham: Duke University Press, 2002.

Joseph, Gilbert M., Anne Rubenstein, and Eric Zolov, eds. *Fragments of a Golden Age: The Politics and Culture in Mexico since 1940.* Durham: Duke University Press, 2001.

Kaiser, Charles. *1968 in America: Music, Politics, Chaos, Counterculture, and the Shaping of a Generation.* New York: Weidenfeld and Nicolson, 1988.

Kiernan, John, and Arthur Daley. *The Story of the Olympic Games, 776 B.C. to 1968.* New York: J.B. Lippincott Co., 1969.

Knight, Alan. "Cardenismo: Juggernaut or Jalopy?" *Journal of Latin American Studies* 26:1 (Feb. 1994): 73–107.

———. "The Peculiarities of Mexican History: Mexico Compared to Latin America, 1821–1992." *Journal of Latin American Studies* 24 (Quincentenary Supplement, 1992): 99–144.

Krauze, Enrique. *Mexico, Biography of Power: A History of Modern Mexico, 1810–1996.* New York: HarperCollins, 1997.

Kruger, Arnd, and James Riordan, eds. *The Story of Worker Sport.* Champaign, IL: Human Kinetics, 1996.

Kurlansky, Mark. *1968: The Year that Rocked the World.* New York: Ballantine Books, 2004.

Lapchick, Richard. *Broken Promises: Racism in American Sports.* New York: St. Martin's, 1984.

———. *The Politics of Race and International Sport.* Westport, CT: Greenwood Press, 1975.

Large, David Clay. *Nazi Games: The Olympics of 1936.* New York: W.W. Norton & Co., 2007.

Leiper, J.M. "Political Problems in the Olympic Games." In Segrave and Chu, *Olympism.* 1981.

Lenskyj, Helen Jefferson. *Inside the Olympic Industry.* Albany: State University of New York Press, 2000.

Levy, Daniel, and Gabriel Szekely. *Mexico: Paradoxes of Stability and Change.* Boulder: Westview Press, 1987.

Lozoya, Veronica Guttierrez. "Olympism in Mexico." *Olympic Review* 26 (Oct.–Nov. 1996).

MacAloon, John J. "Steroids and the State: Dubin, Melodrama and the Accomplishment of Innocence." *Public Culture* 2:2 (1990): 41–64.

Maclachlan, Colin M., and William H. Beezley, *El Gran Pueblo: A History of Greater Mexico.* Upper Saddle River, NJ: Prentice Hall, 1999.

Major, Patrick, and Rana Mitter, eds. *Across the Blocs: Cold War Cultural and Social History.* London: Frank Cass, 2004.

Mallon, Bill. *The Olympics: A Bibliography.* New York: Garland Publishers, 1984.

Mandell, Richard. *The Nazi Olympics.* New York: Macmillan, 1971.

Martin, Charles H. "Jim Crow in the Gymnasium: The Integration of College Basketball in the American South." *The International Journal of the History of Sport* 10:1 (April 1993): 68–86.

Marwick, Arthur. *The Sixties: Cultural Revolution in Britain, France, Italy, and the United States, c. 1958–1974.* New York: Oxford University Press, 1998.

McGehee, Richard V. "The Origins of Olympism in Mexico: The Central American Games of 1926." *International Journal of the History of Sport* 10:3 (Dec. 1993).

Medina Valdés, Gerardo. *El 68, Tlatelolco y el Pan.* Mexico D.F.: Epessa, 1990.

Menéndez, Oscar. *Códica Tlatlelolco 1968–1988.* Plaza and Valdes Publishers, 1988.

Mexico XIX Olympic Games. Mexican Olympic Committee (1968). Mexican Olympic Committee archives, Mexico D.F., #796.48 J44.

Mexico '68, vol. 1–4. Mexican Olympic Committee (1969).

Meyer, Michael C., ed. *Essays on the Mexican Revolution: Revisionist Views of the Leaders.* Austin: University of Texas Press, 1979.

Miller, Patrick B., and David K. Wiggins, eds. *Sport and the Color Line: Black Athletes and Race Relations in Twentieth-Century America.* New York: Routledge, 2004.

Monsiváis, Carlos. "From '68 to Cardenismo: Toward a Chronicle of Social Movements." *Journal of International Affairs* 43:2 (Winter 1990).

Morgan, Robin. *Going too Far.* New York: Random House, 1977.

Morris, Stephen D. *Gringolandia: Mexican Identity and Perceptions of the United States.* New York: Rowman and Littlefield, 2005.

Murphy, Frank. *The Last Protest: Lee Evans in Mexico City.* Kansas City: Windsprint Press, 2006.

Newton, Huey P. *Revolutionary Suicide.* New York: Writers and Readers Publishing, 1995.

Ninkovich, Frank. "The Currents of Cultural Diplomacy: Art and the State Department, 1938–1947." *Diplomatic History* (Summer 1977): 215–37.

Oleksak, Michael M., and Mary Adams Oleksak. *Béisbol: Latin Americans and the Grand Old Game.* Grand Rapids, MI: Masters Press, 1991.

Olsen, Jack. *The Black Athlete, A Shameful Story: The Myth of Integration in American Sport.* New York: Time-Life Books, 1968.

O'Mahony, Mike. *Sport in the U.S.S.R.: Physical Culture—Visual Culture.* London: Reaktion Books, 2006.

Orr, Jack. *The Black Athlete: His Story in America.* New York: Lion Press, 1969.

Padilha, Major Sylvio de Magalhaes. "The Olympic Movement in the Americas." *Olympic Review* 78:78 (1974).

Page, James. *Black Olympian Medalists.* Englewood, CO: Libraries Unlimited, 1991.

Paul, C. Robert, Jr. "Setting the 1968 Record Straight." *International Journal of Olympic History* 5:1 (Spring 1997).

Paz, Octavio. *The Labyrinth of Solitude.* New York: Grove Press, 1985.

———. *The Other Mexico: Critique of the Pyramid.* New York: Grove Press, 1985.

Pepe, Phil. *Stand Tall: The Lew Alcindor Story.* New York: Grosset & Dunlap, 1970.

Peppard, Victor, and James Riordan. *Playing Politics: Soviet Sport Diplomacy to 1992.* Greenwich, CT: JAI Press, 1993.

Plowden, Martha Ward. *Olympic Black Women.* Gretna, LA: Pelican, 1996.

Poniatowska, Elena. *La Noche de Tlatelolco.* Mexico: Biblioteca ERA, 1993.

Pope, S.W. *Patriotic Games: Sporting Traditions in the American Imagination, 1876–1926.* New York: Oxford University Press, 1997.

Preston, Julia, and Samuel Dillon. *Opening Mexico: The Making of a Democracy.* New York: Farrar, Straus and Giroux, 2004.

Raat, W. Dirk. *Mexico and the United States: Ambivalent Vistas.* Athens, GA: University of Georgia Press, 1992.

Raat, W. Dirk, and William H. Beezley, eds. *Twentieth Century Mexico.* Lincoln, NE: University of Nebraska Press, 1986.

Rampersad, Arnold. *Jackie Robinson.* New York: Ballantine Books, 1997.

Reeve, Simon. *One Day in September: The Full Story of the 1972 Munich Olympics Massacre and the Israeli Revenge "Operation Wrath of God."* New York: Arcade Publishing, 2000.

Revueltas, Jose. *México '68: Juventud y Revolucion.* Mexico: Ediciones Era, 1978.

Rhoden, William C. *Forty Million Dollar Slaves: The Rise, Fall, and Redemption of the Black Athlete.* New York: Crown Publishers, 2006.

Ribowsky, Mark. *A Complete History of the Negro Leagues.* New York: Carol Publishing Group, 1995.

Richmond, Douglas W. *The Mexican Nation: Historical Continuity and Modern Change.* Upper Saddle River, NJ: Prentice Hall, 2002.

Richmond, Yale. *Cultural Exchange and the Cold War: Raising the Iron Curtain.* University Park, PA: Pennsylvania State University Press, 2003.

Rinehart, Robert E. "'Fists Flew and Blood Flowed': Symbolic Resistance and International Response in Hungarian Water Polo at the Melbourne Olympics, 1956." *Journal of Sport History* 23:2 (Summer 1996): 120–39.

Riordan, James, ed. *Sport and International Politics.* New York: E & FN Spon, 1998.

———. *Sport, Politics, and Communism.* Manchester: Manchester University Press, 1991.

Rippon, Anton. *Hitler's Olympics: The Story of the 1936 Nazi Games.* South Yorkshire: Pen & Sword Books Limited, 2006.

Robertson, Ian, and Phillip Whitten. "The Olympics: Keep South Africa Out." *The New Republic* 158:15 (13 Apr. 1968).

Roche, Maurice. *Mega-events and Modernity: Olympics and Expos in the Growth of Global Culture.* New York: Taylor & Francis Group, 2000.

Rodríguez Kuri, Ariel. "Hacia México 68: Pedro Ramírez Vázquez y el proyecto olímpico." *Secuencia* 56 (May–Aug. 2003): 37–73.

———. "El otro 68: Política y estilo en la organización de los juegos olímpicos de la ciudad de México." *Relaciones* 19 (Fall 1998): 109–29.

Rodriguez O., Jaime E., ed. *The Evolution of the Mexican Political System.* Wilmington, DE: Scholarly Resources, Inc., 1993.

Rodriguez O., Jaime E. *The Revolutionary Process in Mexico.* Los Angeles: UCLA Latin American Center Publications, 1990.

Rosenthal, Harold. "The War with Mexico." *Baseball Digest* 22 (Dec. 1963–Jan. 1964): 53–56.

Russell, Bill. *Go Up for Glory.* Berkeley: Berkeley Publishing Group, 1980.

Sammons, Jeffrey T. "'Race' and Sport: A Critical, Historical Examination." *Journal of Sport History* 21:3 (1994): 203–78.

Saragoza, Alex. "The Selling of Mexico: Tourism and the State, 1929–1952." In Joseph et al., eds., *Fragments,* 91–115.

Saunders, Frances Stonor. *The Cultural Cold War: The CIA and the World of Arts and Letters.* New York: The New Press, 1999.

Schaap, Dick. "The Revolt of the Black Athletes." *Look* 32 (6 Aug. 1968): 72–77.

Schaap, Jeremy. *Triumph: The Untold Story of Jesse Owens and Hitler's Olympics.* New York: Houghton Mifflin, 2007.

Scherer García, Julio, and Carlos Monsiváis. *Parte de Guerra, Tlatelolco 1968: Documentos de General Marcelino García Barragán, los hechos y la historia.* Nuevo Siglo Aguilar, 1999.

Schmidt, Arthur. "Making It Real Compared to What? Reconceptualizing Mexican History since 1940." In Joseph et al., eds., *Fragments,* 23–68.

Schmidt, Samuel. *The Deterioration of the Mexican Presidency: The Years of Luis Echeverria.* Translated by Dan A. Cothran. Tucson: University of Arizona Press, 1991.

Schollander, Don, and Duke Savage. *Deep Water.* New York: Crown Publishers, Inc., 1971.

Segrave, Jeffrey, and Donald Chu, eds. *Olympism.* Champaign, IL: Human Kinetics, 1981.

Senn, Alfred E. *Power, Politics, and the Olympic Games: A History of the Power Brokers, Events, and Controversies that Shaped the Games.* Champaign, IL: Human Kinetics, 1999.

Sevilla, Renata. *Tlatelolco: Ocho Años Despues.* (University of Florida, Latin America Collection, LA 428.7 .S4x.)

Slater, John. "Changing Partners: The Relationship between the Mass Media and the Olympic Games." *Fourth International Symposium for Olympic Research.* London, Ontario, Canada: University of Western Ontario (Oct. 1998): 49–68.

Smith, Ronald A. *Sports and Freedom: The Rise of Big-time College Athletics.* New York: Oxford University Press, 1990.

Smith, Tommie, with David Steele. *Silent Gesture.* Philadelphia: Temple University, 2007.

Spivey, Donald. "The Black Athlete in Big-Time Intercollegiate Sport, 1941–1968." *Phylon* 44 (June 1983): 116–25.

———. "Black Consciousness and Olympic Protest Movement." In Donald Spivey, ed., *Sport in America: New Historical Perspectives*. Westpoint, CT: Greenwood Press, 1984, 239–62.

Steinberg, David A. "The Workers' Sport International, 1920–28." *Journal of Contemporary History* 13 (April 1978): 228–51.

Stevens, Evelyn P. *Protest and Response in Mexico*. Cambridge, MA: The MIT Press, 1974.

Strathmore, William. *Muhammad Ali: The Unseen Archives*. Bath, UK: Parragon Publishing, 2001.

Strenk, Andrew. "Amateurism: Myth and Reality." In Segrave and Chu, *Olympism*. 1981.

Sullivan, Robert, ed. *The Olympics from Athens to Athens*. New York: Time, Inc., 2004.

Suri, Jeremi. *The Global Revolutions of 1968*. New York: W.W. Norton & Co., 2007.

———. *Power and Protest: Global Revolution and the Rise of Détente*. Cambridge, MA: Harvard University Press, 2003.

Taylor, Clyde. *Vietnam and Black America: An Anthology of Protest and Resistance*. Garden City, NY: Anchor Press, 1973.

Tenorio-Trillo, Mauricio. *Mexico at the World's Fairs: Crafting a Modern Nation*. Berkeley: University of California Press, 1996.

Tricard, Louise. *American Women's Track and Field: A History, 1895 through 1980*. Jefferson, NC: McFarland and Co., 1996.

Tygiel, Jules. *Baseball's Great Experiment: Jackie Robinson and His Legacy*. New York: Vintage, 1983.

Van Deburg, William L. *New Day in Babylon*. Chicago: University of Chicago Press, 1992.

Vaughn, Mary Kay. "Cultural Approaches to Peasant Politics in the Mexican Revolution." *Hispanic American Historical Review* 79:2 (1999): 269–305.

Vertinsky, Patricia, and Gwendolyn Captain. "More Myth than History: American Culture and Representations of the Black Female's Athletic Ability." *Journal of Sport History* 25 (Fall 1998): 532–61.

Vinokur, Martin B. *More than a Game: Sports and Politics*. New York: Greenwood Press, 1988.

Von Eschen, Penny M. *Satchmo Blows Up the World: Jazz Ambassadors Play the Cold War*. Cambridge, MA: Harvard University Press, 2004.

Walters, Guy. *Berlin Games: How the Nazis Stole the Olympic Dream*. New York: HarperCollins, 2006.

Wells, Allen. "Oaxtepec Revisited: The Politics of Mexican Historiography, 1968–1988." *Mexican Studies* 7:2 (Summer, 1991): 331–45.

Wendl, Karel. "The Route of Friendship: A Cultural/Artistic Event of the Games of the XIX Olympiad in Mexico City—1968." *Olympika: The International Journal of Olympic Studies* 7 (1998): 113–34.

Wenn, Stephen R. "Growing Pains: The Olympic Movement and Television, 1966–1972. *Olympika: The International Journal of Olympic Studies* 4 (1995): 1–22.

———. "An Olympian Squabble: The Distribution of Olympic Television Revenue, 1960–1966." *Olympika: The International Journal of Olympic Studies* 3 (1994).

Wenn, Stephen R., and Jeffrey P. Wenn. "Muhammad Ali and the Convergence of Olympic Sport and U.S. Diplomacy in the 1980s: A Reassessment from Behind the Scenes at the U.S. State Department." *Olympika: The International Journal of Olympic Studies* 2 (1993): 45–66.

Wheeler, Robert F. "Organized Sport and Organized Labour: The Workers' Sports Movement." *Journal of Contemporary History* 13 (April 1978): 188–210.

Wiggins, David K. "'The Future of College Athletics Is at Stake': Black Athletes and Racial Turmoil on Three Predominantly White University Campuses, 1968–1972." *Journal of Sport History* 15:3 (Winter 1988): 304–33.

————. *Glory Bound: Black Athletes in a White America*. Syracuse: Syracuse University Press, 1997.

————. "Prized Performers, but Frequently Overlooked Students: The Involvement of Black Athletes in Intercollegiate Sports on Predominately White University Campuses, 1890–1972." *Research Quarterly for Exercise and Sport* 62 (June 1991): 164–77.

————. "'The Year of Awakening': Black Athletes, Racial Unrest and the Civil Rights Movement of 1968." *The International Journal of the History of Sport* 9:2 (Aug. 1992).

Wiggins, David K., and Patrick B. Miller. *The Unlevel Playing Field: A Documentary History of the African American Experience in Sport*. Urbana: University of Illinois Press, 2003.

Wilkie, James W. *The Mexican Revolution: Federal Expenditure and Social Change since 1910*. Berkeley: University of California Press, 1970.

Young, Dolly J. "Mexican Literary Reactions to Tlatelolco 1968." *Latin American Research Review* 20:2 (1985): 71–85.

Zirin, Dave. *What's My Name, Fool? Sports and Resistance in the United States*. Chicago: Haymarket Books, 2005.

Zolov, Eric. "Discovering a Land 'Mysterious and Obvious': The Renarrativizing of Postrevolutionary Mexico." In Joseph et al., eds., *Fragments*, 234–72.

————. "Popular Perceptions and Official Concerns Toward Mexico, 1966–1968." Unpublished, Conference of Mexican and North American Historians, Ft. Worth, Texas, November 19–21, 1999.

————. "Showcasing the 'Land of Tomorrow': Mexico and the 1968 Olympics." *The Americas* 61:2 (October 2004): 159–88.

Film/video

Fields of Fire: Sports in the 60s. HBO Films, 1995.
Fists of Freedom. HBO Films, 1998.
Olympiada en Mexico. Mexican Olympic Committee, Mexico City.
Tlatelolco, las claves de la massacre. Jose Galan and Jorge Caballero, Demos Desarrollo de Medios, SA, 2002.

Websites

<http://aolsvc.news.aol.com>
<http://en.wikipedia.org>
<http://english/people.com.cn>
<http://english/pravda/ru>
<http://flag.blackened/net>
<http://sportsillustrated.cnn.com>
<http://olympic-museum.de/torches/torch1968.htm>
<http://washingtonpost.com>
<http://www.aafla.org>
<http://www.cbc.ca>
<http://www.johncarlos.com>
<http://www.kiat.net/olympics/history>
<http://www.museum.tv>
<http://www.olympic.org>
<http://www.rose-hulman.edu>
<http://www.tommiesmith.com>
<http://www.usatoday.com>
<http://www.worldpress.org>

Index